# CRITICAL GEOGRA
# CHILDHOOD AND YOUTH

## Policy and practice

*Edited by Peter Kraftl, John Horton and Faith Tucker*

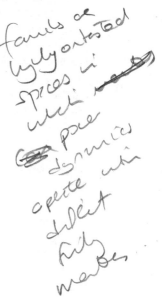

First published in Great Britain in 2012 by

The Policy Press
University of Bristol
Fourth Floor
Beacon House
Queen's Road
Bristol BS8 1QU
UK

Tel +44 (0)117 331 4054
Fax +44 (0)117 331 4093
e-mail tpp-info@bristol.ac.uk
www.policypress.co.uk

North American office:

The Policy Press
c/o The University of Chicago Press
1427 East 60th Street
Chicago, IL 60637, USA
t: +1 773 702 7700
f: +1 773-702-9756
e:sales@press.uchicago.edu
www.press.uchicago.edu

British Library Cataloguing in Publication Data
A catalogue record for this book is available from the British Library.

Library of Congress Cataloging-in-Publication Data
A catalog record for this book has been requested.

ISBN 978 1 84742 845 5 paperback
ISBN 978 1 84742 846 2 hardcover

Cover design by Qube Design Associates, Bristol
Front cover: Children of the Thar Desert – Rajasthan, India. Kindly supplied by Dr Sophie Hadfield-Hill
Printed and bound in Great Britain by Hobbs, Southampton
The Policy Press uses environmentally responsible print partners

# Dedication

For Professor Hugh Matthews

# Contents

Contents

# List of tables, figures and boxes

## List of tables

## List of figures

## List of boxes

# Notes on contributors

**Nicola Ansell** is a Reader in Human Geography at Brunel University. Her research interests focus on social and cultural change in the lives of young people in southern Africa, and particularly the impacts of AIDS and education on young people's lives. She is the author of *Children, youth and development* (Routledge, 2005) and nearly 50 book chapters and journal articles. She directs an MA programme in Children, Youth and International Development at Brunel, and sits on the editorial boards of *Children's Geographies* and the *Journal of Geography in Higher Education*.

**Laura Novo de Azevedo** has a background in architecture, planning and urban design. Since 2002 she has been a Lecturer at the Joint Centre for Urban Design at Oxford Brookes University. Before working in the UK she worked in Brazil teaching and consulting in architecture and urbanism, mostly through community participation. Her main research interests focus on understanding people's perceptions and behaviour for the design and management of places, with a particular interest in children and young people. Laura is also interested in pedagogic research using mobile technologies and daily experiences of built environments to enhance people's understanding of urban design qualities (see www.urbandesignexperience.com).

**John Barker** is a geographer based at Brunel University. His teaching and research interests focus on the lives of children and young people. In particular, John has expertise in relation to mobility, play and care, and methodological issues. John works with a variety of organisations and has successfully been awarded grants from government departments, local authorities and the voluntary sector. John has published widely in a variety of internationally renowned journals. He is also the secretary of the Royal Geographical Society's Geographies of Children, Youth and Families Research Group.

**Lorraine van Blerk** is a Senior Lecturer in Human Geography at the University of Dundee. Her research interests focus on the lives of children, youth and families in East and Southern Africa; particularly young people living in street situations and the impacts of AIDS, poverty and mobility on children and their families over the lifecourse. Lorraine has published over 40 book chapters and journal articles, and is co-editor (with Mike Kesby) of *Doing children's geographies: methodological issues in research with young people* (Routledge, 2009). She also sits on the editorial boards of *Children's Geographies* and the *Open Area Studies Journal*.

**Gavin Brown** has been a Lecturer in Human Geography at the University of Leicester since 2007. Prior to that, he ran a large widening participation project in inner London for many years. His academic work on widening participation and young people's aspirations is, in part, the result of critical reflections on his experiences in that role. He recently edited a special issue of *Children's Geographies* (with Sarah Holloway and Helena Pimlott-Wilson) on the theme of 'education and aspiration'. Gavin has also published widely on sexuality and social movement activism, and co-edited *Geographies of sexualities: theory, practices and politics* (Ashgate, 2007).

**Isabel Cartwright** is a Senior Lecturer in the Youth and Community Division at De Montfort University. Her teaching and research interests include informal education (particularly in formal and contested spaces), work with young women, and exploring notions of identity in relation to young people's development. She is a professionally qualified youth worker and has been involved in managing a range of global youth projects for international non-governmental organisations, focusing on peace education and work with young people from conflict areas. Isabel has also managed youth projects in secondary schools in the London Boroughs of Newham and Hackney, specialising in initiatives to engage those young people at risk of exclusion.

**Derek Colquhoun** was the first Professor of Urban Learning in the UK. He is also Director of Research for the Faculty of Education, University of Hull. Before joining the University of Hull, Derek was an Associate Professor of Health Promotion in Australia. His main research interest is in healthy school communities including policy, curriculum, professional practice and the health of children and adults in these school communities. Derek has published widely and has also managed major research and evaluation projects in school communities in Australia and the UK. His current research interests centre on Health Promoting Schools, social capital, resilience and connectedness.

**Alexandra Cox** is a doctoral student in Criminology at the University of Cambridge, where she is also a Gates Cambridge Scholar. Prior to attending Cambridge, she worked as a social worker in the criminal justice system in New York City and as a policy analyst and researcher about America's 'war on drugs'. She is currently a Soros Justice Fellow conducting research about the dynamics of resistance to juvenile justice reform in an American state.

**Richard Davies** is a Senior Lecturer in Youth Work at De Montfort University, Leicester. He was previously a youth worker and school teacher. He gained his doctorate from Lady Margaret Hall, Oxford and his research interests are in the application of neo-Aristotelian moral and political theory to youth work policy and practice. He is an Executive Officer of the Philosophy of Education Society of Great Britain, a member of the Secretariat of the Professional Association of Lecturers in Youth and Community Work, and a co-convenor of the Philosophy of Education Special Interest Group, British Educational Research Association.

**Bethan Evans** is a Lecturer in the Department of Geography and Centre for Medical Humanities at Durham University. She has previously worked as a Lecturer in Human Geography at Manchester Metropolitan University and the University of Liverpool. Her research interests are in the role of childhood and youth in contemporary policy and critical geographies of obesity. She is currently co-ordinating an ESRC seminar series on *Fat studies and health at every size*, working on projects on the role of urban designers in anti-obesity policy and on intergenerational embodiment, and is writing a book *Fat bodies, fat spaces: critical geographies of obesity*.

**Flora Hajdu** is a Researcher at the Uppsala Centre for Sustainable Development, funded by Uppsala University and the Swedish University for Agricultural Sciences. Her research interests have centred on various perspectives on rural livelihoods in Southern Africa, from local as well as policy perspectives. After receiving her PhD in 2006 from Linköping University, Sweden, she was employed as a researcher by Brunel University and carried out the main fieldwork for the 'Averting new variant famine in Southern Africa' research project.

**Emma-Jay Honeyford** is an independent researcher who has completed an MSc in Environmental Management and Sustainable Development, following a BSc in Human Geography, both at Manchester Metropolitan University. Her research interests focus on understanding the social drivers of sustainability, social consumption and production, sustainable economic wellbeing and environmental education, along with the determinants of pro-environmental behaviour and humans' interrelationships with nature via culture (looking at class, ethnicity and religion).

**John Horton** is a Senior Lecturer based in the Centre for Children and Youth at The University of Northampton. He has worked on around 40 academic and policy-oriented research projects exploring the everyday issues and experiences of children and young people in the UK. With Pia Christensen and Peter Kraftl, he is currently working on an ESRC-funded investigation of young people's lives in new urban communities in the UK. John is on the editorial board of the *Children's Geographies* journal.

**Eleanor Jupp** is a Research Associate in the Department of Geography at The Open University and is interested in issues of neighbourhood governance, community organising, and families and young people. She holds a PhD from the Department of Geography, The Open University, on community groups and neighbourhood governance in the UK. She has lectured in urban policy and social and cultural geography at Oxford Brookes University and the University of Reading. Before starting her PhD she worked as a policy advisor and consultant on issues of social inclusion, neighbourhood renewal and the built environment, for the voluntary sector and UK government.

**Peter Kraftl** is a Senior Lecturer in Human Geography at Leicester University. He is the author of more than 30 journal articles and book chapters on young people, education and built spaces. He holds a PhD from the Geography Department at Swansea University. Before moving to Leicester, he worked at the Centre for Children and Youth at The University of Northampton. With Pia Christensen and John Horton, he is currently working on an ESRC-funded project on young people living in new urban communities in the UK. He currently preparing two other books: a textbook on *Cultural geographies* (with John Horton, for Pearson) and a monograph on *Alternative geographies of education* (for The Policy Press).

**Peter K. Mackie** is a Lecturer in Housing at Cardiff University. A geographer by training, Peter has a particular research interest in the housing experiences and pathways of vulnerable people, in which he seeks to combine theoretical and practical insights. His recent studies have explored the hidden housing experiences of A8 migrant workers in Wales and the transitions of disabled young people to independent living. Peter has particularly focused his research on youth housing and homelessness, a field in which he has sought to understand the experiences of young people from their perspectives via participatory research methods, including the peer approach. Peter is currently the convenor of the Wales Institute of Social and Economic Research, Data and Methods (WISERD) Housing Research Network and a trustee of Llamau, a charity working with homeless young people in Wales. He previously held the post of Senior Research Officer at Shelter Cymru.

**Elodie Marandet** is a doctoral student with the Centre for Human Geography at Brunel University. Her PhD research focuses on the governmentalisation of international aid through the 'new aid effectiveness' agenda, as articulated in Malawi in the area of funding for AIDS. Elodie previously worked at Brunel University as a researcher and took part in a number of projects related to gender, parental responsibilities, lifelong learning and leisure. She also worked on a participatory project appraising children's play provision in the London Borough of Redbridge.

**Amy Norman** is a doctoral student at the Department of Geography, Queen Mary, University of London. She has been researching social aspects of the HIV/AIDS epidemic in southern Africa since 2004, exploring diverse issues such as food security, HIV disclosure, and 'AIDS orphan tourism'. She has collaborated with the International Food Policy Research Institute in Washington, DC, the Regional Network on HIV/AIDS, Rural Livelihoods and Food Security (RENEWAL), and the Human Sciences Research Council, South Africa.

**Jo Pike** is a Research Project Manager at the University of Hull. Her research interests include children's geographies, learning environments and children's health. Her published work explores the spatiality of school dining rooms and her current research focuses upon boys' gun play in the early years.

**Jessica Pykett** is a Lecturer in Human Geography at Aberystwyth University. Prior to this she was an ESRC Research Fellow at The Open University, and she has also worked for Bristol University and Futurelab Education. Her research interests are concerned with how citizens are made, and she has explored this question through analysis of citizenship education, personalisation, ethical consumption and pedagogical tactics, including publications in *Critical Social Policy*, the *Journal of Education Policy* and *Citizenship Studies*. Since 2008 she has been researching the ethics and politics of 'behaviour change' policies and the use of the behavioural and neuro-sciences in public policy-making, published in *Progress in Human Geography* and *Antipode*.

**Elsbeth Robson** is an Associate Lecturer, Brunel University, based in Malawi. Her research interests encompass young people's lives in sub-Saharan Africa, focusing on children's work, education, mobility and impacts of AIDS. Elsbeth is a founding associate editor of *Children's Geographies* and editorial board member of *Journal of Geography in Higher Education*. She has published more than 20 research articles and book chapters about youth and children in Europe, Nigeria, Kenya, Zimbabwe, Malawi and Lesotho. With Ruth Panelli and Samantha Punch, Elsbeth is co-editor of *Global perspectives on rural childhood and youth: young rural lives* (Routledge, 2007).

**Faith Tucker** is a Senior Lecturer in Geography, based in the Centre for Children and Youth at The University of Northampton. Her research, which has stemmed from her doctoral work on the lifestyles of rural teenage girls in Northamptonshire, UK, focuses upon younger people's use of outdoor spaces. Faith is on the editorial board of *Children's Geographies* journal, and is a Committee Member of the Royal Geographical Society's Geographies of Children, Youth and Families Research Group.

**Susie Weller** is a Senior Research Fellow in the Families & Social Capital Research Group at London South Bank University. Her research interests include: geographies of childhood and youth; citizenship and participation; family relationships; and social networks. Susie is author of *Teenagers' citizenship: experiences and education* (Routledge, 2007), as well as numerous book chapters and articles on teenagers' participation, children's social capital, sibling relationships and friendships, and creative, participatory and longitudinal research methods. Forming part of the ESRC *Timescapes* programme her current research tracks change and continuity in children's lateral relationships over time.

# Acknowledgements

The editors would like to thank the chapter authors without whom this diverse and thought-provoking volume would have been impossible.

We also extend our thanks to our editors at The Policy Press – and especially Karen Bowler, Laura Vickers and David Simmons – for their help and guidance through the process of producing this book.

Peter Kraftl would like to thank Juliet and Emily, his parents, brother, Great Aunt and Lyn for their love and support. Thanks also to the University of Leicester for providing a research sabbatical during which some of the manuscript was prepared. Finally, thanks to his colleagues, especially Jenny Pickerill, Gavin Brown and Martin Phillips, for their encouragement.

John Horton would like to thank his parents for their support. He would also like to thank three former colleagues – Beth Greenhough, Emma J. Roe and Sergei Shubin – who helped to make the University of Bristol's School of Geographical Sciences an inspiring and supportive place to be.

Faith Tucker would like to thank her family, and Geography colleagues at the University of Northampton, for their support, advice and encouragement.

Thanks also to Professor Hugh Matthews for his inspiration and constant support.

one

# Editors' introduction: critical geographies of childhood and youth

*Peter Kraftl, John Horton and Faith Tucker*

## Why critical *geographies* of childhood and youth?

In May 2010, a General Election resulted in a change of government in the United Kingdom. A Conservative-Liberal Democrat Coalition replaced the New Labour party that had ruled since 1997. Between 1997 and 2010, New Labour had launched a succession of 'landmark' policy programmes targeted at young people. Policies like *Every child matters* (DfES, 2004), *Youth matters* (DfES, 2005) and the *National service framework for children, young people and maternity services* (DH, 2004) sought to improve safeguarding of, and service provision for, children and young people. Furthermore, the inclusion of the word 'children' in the name of the government department charged with policy for young people (what was then the Department for Children, Schools and Families; formerly the Department for Education and Skills) was viewed as a positive step in the UK's relatively slow implementation of the United Nations *Convention on the rights of the child* (UN, 1989), ratified by the UK in 1990.

The change of government in 2010 has been followed by a series of 'austerity measures': ostensibly swingeing cuts in public service provision, initiated in an attempt to reverse the country's economic fortunes after the financial crisis of 2007. Many of these cuts will directly affect children and young people: from the removal of a cap on university tuition fees to the scrapping of one of the largest school-building programmes in the UK for decades; from the withdrawal of funding for local youth work programmes to the reorientation and rationalisation of policy programmes relating to early years provision, widening participation in education, and young people not in education, employment or training. Moreover, for many practitioners, the swift renaming of the department responsible for education and children's services, with the removal of the word 'children' from what is now simply the 'Department for Education', has been viewed as a retrograde step in youth policy.

To some extent, these post-election changes mirror the waxing and waning of (youth) policy in other geographical and historical contexts. However, we

1

chose to begin our introduction to this volume with this recent UK context because it highlights why *geography* matters, profoundly, to any analysis of youth policies and professional practices. If nothing else, it should be clear that geographical and historical context are central to understanding the state of contemporary childhood and youth, and policies relating to them: so, for example, the preceding paragraph suggests a range of ways in which being a young person in the UK, at the time of writing, in the wake of particular, complex, geographically-specific political, economic and social circumstances, is likely to be characterised by some particular experiences and issues. Moreover, though, the contributions in this book highlight how key geographical themes – like space, place, scale and network – are central to the ways in which policies are created, talked about and put into practice. Many of these themes are apparent if one examines changing youth policy in the UK and elsewhere, as do the chapters in this book. As an entry point, this introductory chapter will highlight a few *geographical* implications of these kinds of change, in respect of a selection of youth policies from the UK and around the world.

First, in the UK and elsewhere, the past decade has witnessed an increased emphasis upon child and youth policy-making at the *national* scale. By this, we mean that state governments have explicitly promoted the advantages of national frameworks for youth policy-making, in some cases following international guidance to do just that (ICNYP, 2002; UNESCO, 2004). In the UK's *Every child matters* White Paper (DfES, 2004) and Germany's *Child and youth plan of the Federation* (BFSFJ, 2009), for example, it was expressly argued that local authorities alone were not able to effectively deliver or sponsor services for young people. In the case of the latter, for instance, *national* youth policy was required because particular concerns – gender equality, disability and citizenship – had significance for the whole German State. Similar justifications have driven youth policy in the US in the recent past: notably in the controversial *No child left behind* programme inaugurated in 2001 (USDE, 2001), where it was claimed that local testing of children's learning was failing and that a universal, national system was required instead. In a number of African nations, meanwhile, young people have been progressively positioned as a 'concern' for *national* governments as they represent increasing proportions of the population (as in the Republic of Malawi's (2011) *National Youth Policy*). However, returning to the UK, a significant 'spatial shift' since the election has been the privileging of *localism* as a way to save money and afford local decision-makers greater autonomy. The implications of this spatial shift for young people have yet to be charted but are likely to be profound.

Second, the notion of 'the nation' reminds us that the geographies of youth policy-making are inextricably entwined with *histories* of state intervention. As Massey (2005) has argued, space and time (geography and history) can never be disentangled – both in consideration of the past and the future (Anderson, 2010). For instance, notions of 'crises' in or the 'disappearance' of childhood (Postman, 1994) have persisted for centuries, taking shape in slightly different ways in different historical and geographical contexts. Those notions draw both on popular forms of nostalgia for childhoods that (probably) never existed, and upon projections that imagine children as 'the future'. On this theme, Gagen's (2004) work critically analyses how US national identity was instilled into immigrant populations in New York City through the urban playground movements of the early twentieth century, in direct response to concerns for the 'future health of the nation'. These are both longstanding *and* dynamic concerns that are 'spatialised': they connect children's micro-scale spatial practices – their play, their mobility, their use of urban environments – with the futures of whole nation states. This kind of 'scale-jumping' is also apparent in recent UK policy on children's health, which links children's reduced opportunities for outdoor play with an apparent obesity 'time bomb' that may detonate among the future adult population of 2030 if nothing is done (Evans, 2010). Developing earlier work by childhood studies and subcultures scholars (James and James, 2004; Gelder, 2005), several chapters in this volume critique how particular, limiting notions of space, scale *and* time are (re)produced in policy-making relating to childhood and youth people (see Chapter Fifteen by Norman and Chapter Three by Ansell et al). In particular, they note that notions of 'crisis' and 'futurity' are becoming equally apparent in non-Western youth policies: for instance the Government of Lesotho's (2002) *National Youth Policy for Lesotho* positions young people as both a future 'resource' and as a social group characterised by deviance, substance misuse and criminality.

Third, in combination with the 'national' scale, many policies emphasise the *local* as a key scale at which to intervene with young people, because they are often 'tied' into communities and social relations in their home neighbourhoods. This is perhaps most apparent where disadvantaged young people live in particular places affected by policies designed to combat social exclusion. In France, where the term 'social exclusion' originated, the *Politique de la Ville* public policy of the mid-1980s implied that *general* social issues in France could not be addressed without first overcoming the problems of around 500 identified urban neighbourhoods, including education and employment opportunities for the young (Tissot, 2007). A danger of the current UK government's 'localism' agenda is that it will simply reinforce a particular spatial logic already at play under the previous New Labour regime: to effectively blame local places (especially disadvantaged neighbourhoods) for nationwide problems, like antisocial behaviour or social exclusion (Cobb, 2007). As Angus Cameron (2006) argues, this approach renders social exclusion a form of *spatial exclusion* and – as authors in this volume also point out – ignores how the causes of social exclusion may originate far away from and at scales out of the control of those local places (see, for instance, Brown, this volume, Chapter Six). Thus, a critical-geographical approach – which highlights in particular the problems of relying on the 'local' as a scale for policy intervention for young people – is arguably key in undertaking critical policy analyses and *any* research with young people (Ansell, 2009).

Finally, the role of *built spaces* – in projects designed to literally re-make places – has, like the significance of 'the nation', waxed and waned with successive governmental regimes. During the late nineteenth century, several countries undertook large-scale school building programmes designed to improve literacy and lift disadvantaged children out of poverty. Burke and Grosvenor (2008) document how successive 'waves' of school design have foregrounded the importance of 'good' and modern school buildings to education for children – from the philanthropic schools of late-nineteenth century Spain and the US to the 'schools of tomorrow' planned in 1930s Britain. More recently, more-or-less nationwide programmes of school-building have sought to transform children's education – and the nation's fortunes – by relying on the symbolic promise and durability of bricks and mortar (Kraftl, 2011). Examples include Portugal's *Secondary school modernisation programme* (OECD, 2009) and Australia's *Building the education revolution* (DEEWR, 2010), the latter a scheme to rebuild 8,000 primary schools and help stimulate the nation's economic growth. In the UK, the *Building schools for the future* (BSF) programme (DfES, 2003), which was to see the rebuilding of every secondary school in England, held similar ambitions for the transformative promise of a nationwide policy of school building (den Besten et al, 2011). Yet, soon after taking power, the UK Coalition government quickly axed this overtly 'concrete' and spatial strategy. In his speech announcing the cancellation of BSF, the Secretary of State for Education, Michael Gove, dismissed the importance of the school environment to improving children's learning. Instead, emphasis has been placed on a far less costly and ostensibly more subtle spatial strategy: *Free schools* (DfE, 2011), which are to be created and run by *local* alliances of teachers, parents, councils and private interests but which are, ideally, to be located in an existing building. And, thus, with the changing imperatives of political ideology and economic circumstance, the significance of built spaces in policy discourses continues to wax and wane over time.

One of the key themes running through this book is that policy discourses often – if not always – involve *spatial* discourses. Similarly, any change in youth policy has geographical implications. Those implications may be felt at various scales. In the UK, for instance, BSF was meant not only to transform educational provision nationally, but to help regenerate the local communities and, particularly, the aspirations of young people living in disadvantaged communities (DCSF/4ps/PFS, 2008). Spatial discourses can also be symbolic: built spaces *signified* first the very best and then the very worst of education policy in the UK, as the changing fortunes of BSF demonstrated the very centrality of the geographical imagination to rhetoric around youth policy-making.

The chapters in this collection touch on these and many other geographical themes. Some chapters are written by academic geographers. Others are by academics who draw on geographical concepts (like space and scale) or who seek to understand how youth policies might have uneven outcomes on different groups of young people in different places. Others still (for example Chapter Nine by Cartwright and Chapter Five by Davies) are by authors who reflect on their experiences as professional practitioners who have worked with young people, and for whom space and place have become key ways to critically analyse that work. The aims of this book are fourfold:

• to analyse how geographical processes matter within youth policy formulation;
• to consider how policies 'take place' through professional practice and young people's own agency;
• to explore the theoretical and applied contributions of a geographical approach to youth policy and professional practice;
• to constitute a resource for students, academics and practitioners who study or work with young people.

Taken together, the chapters in this volume represent an intervention in a number of different sub-disciplinary areas, for which we provide an overview in the following sections of this introduction. They also constitute a collective statement about how cognate sub-disciplines – especially social studies of childhood in sociology and anthropology – might usefully engage with geographical concepts and research. Significantly, the chapters in this book do not simply 'read critically' this or that youth policy; rather, they draw out and develop broader conceptual issues, often beyond the specific geographical context in which they are situated. To name but a few of these, the chapters contribute to theorisations of youth around aspiration, governmentality, heritage and sustainability. As we suggest in the following overviews, while social scientists working with children and young people continue to debate the merits and pitfalls of 'policy-relevant' versus 'theoretical' research, this book demonstrates that it is possible – and indeed important – to do both together. Indeed, we hope that this book will be of interest to researchers in diverse disciplines, as well as to policy-makers, practitioners and students seeking examples of how social and spatial theories can enrich 'real-world' work with young people and that it will afford new understandings and critical thinking about that work.

## Academic context: studying children and young people in an era of 'relevance'

The remainder of this introductory chapter provides a threefold orientation to the chapters that follow. First, we provide an overview of the context of research and enquiry from which the chapters have emerged, and which the authors seek to extend. We foreground the broadly interdisciplinary 'New Social Studies of Childhood' and the more specifically-focused sub-discipline of 'Children's Geographies'. We note how each of these bodies of work has contributed to understandings of children and young people's everyday lives and spaces, and have both latterly demanded heightened attention to ways in which policy contexts intersect with these lives and spaces. Second, developing this latter point, we situate the book's chapters in relation to ongoing debates about 'relevance' and 'usefulness' within the 'New Social Studies of Childhood' and 'Children's Geographies'. Specifically, we outline recent calls for theoretically-informed critical policy discourse analyses in these contexts. Then, third, we introduce and unpack the notion of 'critical policy discourse analysis' which is fundamental to each of this book's chapters. Finally, we provide a brief introduction to the book's sections, and each chapter in turn.

### New Social Studies of Childhood and Children's Geographies: principles and new directions

The chapters in this collection are rooted in, and seek to extend, two profuse fields of research and enquiry: (i) the interdisciplinary 'New Social Studies of Childhood' (NSSC); (ii) the more specifically-oriented sub-discipline of 'Children's Geographies'.

The first of these terms – the NSSC – denotes an extensive field of sociological, anthropological and interdisciplinary research and scholarship regarding childhood and youth in diverse contexts. There have been several excellent overviews of the burgeoning development of the NSSC during the 1980s and 1990s (James et al, 1998; Jenks, 2005), so we will not repeat this story. Rather, we seek to contextualise this book's chapters by identifying how some of the NSSC's founding principles have increasingly directed attention to complex intersections between policy contexts and the everyday practices of children and young people. Four foundational concerns of researchers working in the NSSC were as follows (after Prout and James, 1990):

- To explore the *social construction* of 'childhood' and 'youth': that is, how 'childhood, as distinct from biological immaturity, is neither a natural nor universal feature of human groups, but appears as a specific structural and cultural component of many societies' (Prout and James, 1990, p 8).

• To critique the assumption that 'childhood' is universally experienced and understood. For example NSSC researchers explored intersections between childhood and variables including gender, ethnicity and social class, and conducted comparative, cross-cultural analyses of different *childhoods*.

• To foreground children's and young people's *own* issues, experiences, concerns, practices and perspectives. That is, to approach children's everyday lives as worthy of study in their own right, and to value children as experts in this context.

• To recognise and explore children's and young people's *agency* in the constitution of their lives, and contemporary social structures more broadly.

As a number of commentators on the NSSC have noted (Miles, 2000), in practice these concerns tended to pull researchers in two directions. For on one hand the NSSC has constituted an important body of work exploring the ways in which childhood and childhoods are constructed, shaped and determined by societal structural factors. These determinants include 'such social factors as family structure, the nature of kin and gender relations, the structure of the school system; conceptions of the educational process and of the child's health and welfare; secular and religious discourses about what children are or should be; and the economic and political conditions which underpin such discourses' (James and James, 2004, p 7). In so doing, NSSC researchers have drawn attention to the fundamental importance of legal and policy contexts in shaping these social structures and therefore structuring contemporary childhoods. Note here, the importance of 'discourse' signalled in the preceding quotation: this concept will be discussed later.

On the other hand, the NSSC has contributed substantially to understandings of children's and young people's agency: being 'active in the construction and determination of their own social lives, the lives of those around them, and societies in which they live' (Prout and James, 1990, p 8). In a broad sense, this acknowledgement of children's and young people's agency has demanded a methodological reorientation in social scientific research: 'repositioning children as the subjects, rather than objects of research' and taking seriously their everyday practices, experiences and perspectives (Christensen and James, 2008, p 5). More specifically, too, many NSSC researchers have explored specific situations where children and young people exercise tangible forms of politicised agency through diverse encounters with, and participation in, formal or informal P/politics.

Through both of these foci, the NSSC has proved tremendously fruitful and important in conceptualising and understanding children's and young people's lives. Certainly, the motive concerns of the NSSC course through the chapters in this book. However, the chapters in this book can also be read as somewhat critical responses to the NSSC in two senses. First, the chapters can be understood as a set of responses to claims that NSSC research has tended to focus upon *either* the structuring of childhood and youth *or* children and young people's agency (see Miles, 2000, p 35). Thus the chapters explore specific points of intersection between powerful policy discourses/processes and the everyday lives of children and young people. As the chapters illustrate across diverse contexts, these policies and childhoods must be understood as always, and complexly, interrelated. Second, moreover, the chapters can be read as responses to recent calls for NSSC researchers – as well as policy-makers and practitioners working with children and young people – to develop more careful understandings of the importance of *spaces* and *geographies* for their work (Foley and Leverett, 2011; Horton et al, 2011). The work of Children's Geographers is of especial importance here.

'Children's Geographies' is the second field of research and scholarship which contextualises this book's chapters. This term describes a sub-discipline of human geography which has rapidly expanded since the mid-1990s. Here, many human geographers have sought to understand the complex *spaces* of childhood and youth in diverse contexts (for overviews of the development of this sub-discipline, see Holloway and Valentine, 2000; Holloway and Pimlott-Wilson, 2011). Children's Geographies may be understood as both an offshoot and a spatially-focused critique of the NSSC. We focus upon this critical edge here, as we suggest that Children's Geographies demand more nuanced and spatially aware research regarding children and young people, and that this demand is perhaps especially keen when considering intersections between policy contexts and childhood/youth. Some key challenges emerging from Children's Geographies have been as follows:

- That researchers, policy-makers and practitioners working with children and young people should be more aware of how *spaces* are important in/for their work.
- That multiple, interconnected spaces are important for children's and young people's lives: children's everyday lives, experiences and issues are thus distributed across multifarious spaces.
- That the characteristics of particular spaces – perhaps classrooms, homes, streets, parks, institutions – can be profoundly important in shaping the lives of individual children and young people.
- That the construction of spaces can be instrumental in the social construction of childhood (and indeed in the staging and reproduction of discourses which powerfully shape childhoods, as we discuss later).

- That relationships, rules and conflicts relating to spaces can reveal contemporary social norms and structures.
- That spaces are complex: they have 'unutterably' complex details and features; they are shaped by countless interactions between people, objects, technologies, textures, utilities, atmospheres, the built, natural and social environments; they are dynamic and always subject to change; they are experienced differently by different people.
- That engaging with social theory relating to spatiality (for example on place, space, scale, events, processual complexity) is an important way of understanding how spaces matter in/for children's and young people's lives.

In some respects, many of these challenges may seem commonsensical. However, we suggest that they are important when thinking about intersections between policy contexts and childhood/youth. They prompt an array of questions intended to hone the broad, important concerns of the NSSC in this context. For example: how are particular spaces important for policy agendas? How are policy contexts constituted in, and distributed across, spaces in practice? How do policy contexts create and shape spaces, how are these spaces instrumental in the construction of childhoods, and how are these spaces experienced? How are policies received, understood, lived-through, or perhaps resisted, by children and young people in diverse spaces? The chapters in this book represent a series of different takes on these *spatial* concerns: in all kinds of ways, they demonstrate the importance of a keen spatial attentiveness when seeking to understand childhood, youth and policy contexts.

As we note in the following section, there have been recent calls for research in Children's Geographies to engage more with policy-makers and practitioners, and to foster more mutually constructively-critical interactions with other areas and disciplines of research and practice. Moreover, as we note in the penultimate section of this introduction, there have been recent calls for researchers in NSSC and Children's Geographies to undertake theoretically-informed critical policy discourse analyses. The chapters in this collection are diverse responses to these calls: as such they can be approached as a kind of barometer of the state of play in research regarding childhood, youth and policy within the NSSC and Children's Geographies.

## Children's Geographies, public geographies and the 'relevance' debate

Much child- and youth-focused research is empirical and applied. Many significant papers in Children's Geographies and elsewhere are, indeed, based upon consultancy and research funded by policy-makers. Given an emphasis upon giving children 'voice' – and upon fostering their participation in society – this is hardly surprising. The fact that youth research could and should be 'useful' in some sense seems, at face value, rather tricky to discount. Yet, of late, in sub-disciplinary Children's Geographies alone, there have been competing calls for research to be both *more* policy-relevant and to be *more* theoretically progressive (and, consequently, to worry *less* about being 'useful'). In the first instance, several commentators have (rightly) argued that Children's Geographers could better-intervene in more purposeful ways, contributing both evidence and critical analyses that will direct policy and public opinion (for example, Cunningham, 2003; Cahill, 2004; Pain, 2004). In particular, Vanderbeck (2008) has argued that although contributing evidence to (often local) policies around health, play or participation, Children's Geographers have been remarkably silent in debates around statutory education or the rights and responsibilities that children *should* or *should not* be afforded. In the second instance, others (including two of us) have argued for greater theoretical innovation in Children's Geographies (for example Jones, 2003; Philo, 2003; Horton and Kraftl, 2005; 2006; Katz, 2008).

Questions of 'usefulness' in Children's Geographies mirror debates in human geography more broadly, and elsewhere (on 'public sociology', see Burawoy (2005); on 'public anthropology', see Eriksen (2006)). A steady stream of papers has characterised theoretically-innovative research as somehow geared towards '"sexy" philosophical, linguistic and theoretical issues' (Martin, 2001, p 189) or 'detached from [the] real world' (Hamnett, 1997, p 127) or even 'without discipline' (Dorling and Shaw, 2002, p 638). Rather, geographers – like sociologists – have been compelled to consider the ways in which their work might work 'in the pursuit of the betterment of society' (Martin, 2001, p 190): how they might gain the ear of decision-makers, provide evidence for public policy, or contribute to better and/or more equitable distributions of service provision (Peck, 1999). These 'policy geographies' involve the work of geographers in policy formulation – 'from inputting into its formation to tendering for its evaluation' (Ward, 2007, p 699). In response to changes in public service financing and provision in the UK and other contexts, these policy geographies need not of necessity be limited to influence on 'public' organisations: as Ward (2007) highlights, several geographers have worked with private and voluntary organisations, non-governmental organisations and community groups, all of whom create 'policy' of different kinds.

If you read this as a policy-maker or professional who works with young people, you may well be wondering what all the fuss is about! Indeed, you may well be wondering why and how one could contest the pursuit of 'useful' research that might lead to better service provision for young people. And, to be clear, we are not arguing against applied youth research; and nor are any of the authors in this volume. However, we do contend that this binary formula – 'applied *versus* theoretical' – is inherently problematic.

As two of us have argued elsewhere, there are multiple forms and styles in which youth research could be useful; and there are multiple, creative ways in which 'useful' research may *also* be theoretically invigorating (Horton and Kraftl, 2005; 2009a; 2009b; Kraftl and Horton, 2007; Kraftl, 2008; also Pain, 2006; Ward, 2007). Rather than provide individual examples from our research, however, we want to 'step back' into broader research in geography which has really pushed the boundaries of how research can be both 'useful' and 'exciting'. Increasingly, these kinds of research have been labelled 'public geographies'; *but* it is in their creative ways of defining and working with 'publics' that this work cuts across the applied/theoretical divide. In a review paper – which draws upon work in Children's Geographies – Kevin Ward (2007) outlines three kinds of 'public geography' (see also Fuller, 2008; Fuller and Askins, 2010). One kind – 'policy geographies' – has already been discussed; but in contextualising the chapters in this book it is useful to briefly outline the other two, 'activist' and 'participatory' geographies:

- *Activist geographies*. Academics have always had lives 'outside' of the academy. Many have been involved in protest, direct political action, or the creation of alternative spaces like eco-communities, squats, social centres and the like. But, increasingly, many academics have become frustrated at a seeming divide between the 'academic' spheres and the 'everyday', politicised activities in which they are engaged (Fuller and Kitchin, 2004). Rather, they seek to employ their academic skills (especially critical thinking) to *work and live* with oppressed social groups and challenge existing power structures. 'Real-world' action is central to this approach because the distinction between 'the academy' and 'everything else' is blurred through an academic researcher also being part of this or that 'real' social group (Chatterton, 2006). Crucially, as well as involvement in these kinds of action, much of this work has been theoretically innovative: from Brown and Pickerill's (2009) theorisation of the emotions involved in becoming- and being-activist; to Routledge et al's (2007) development of Actor-Network Theory through study of Global Justice Networks; to Pickerill and Chatterton's (2006) detailed conceptualisation of 'autonomous geographies' in social centres and communities with which they are affiliated. Despite an association of young people with protest in subcultures work (for example Hebdidge, 1975), little geographical work has explored the academy/activist link in respect of youth – perhaps, in part, because of the typical age difference between academics and young people.
- *Participatory geographies*. The notion of participation will probably need little introduction to youth researchers from within and beyond geography; nor will it be a foreign term for policy-makers and practitioners who have worked with children, enshrined as it is in the United Nations *Convention*

*on the rights of the child* (UN, 1989) and, to varying degrees, subsequent local and national legislation (Skelton, 2008; *Children's Geographies*, 2009). As Ward (2007) suggests, there are several approaches to participatory research, which we do not have space to document here (see Pain and Francis, 2003; Kindon et al, 2007). The core principle in participatory research is that 'research is carried out by community or group members on issues decided and defined *by them* as relevant *to them*' (Ward, 2007, p 699). Participatory geographies can range from the use of 'participatory geographic information systems (GIS)' to foster people's participation in community planning and research (Elwood, 2006; Mikkelsen and Christensen, 2009); to collaborative research with young women in New York City (Cahill, 2006); to the use of participatory methods to foster intergenerational dialogue between the young and the elderly (Hopkins and Pain, 2007). While discussions of participation are well-trodden, several chapters in this book use empirical material gained through participatory research as part of their critical analyses.

None of the chapters in this book falls neatly into one or other of these categories. Several of the authors writing for this volume *have* influenced policy through evaluations and the provision of evidence bases; others are activist-academics; others have worked with young people in a professional capacity; and others draw on participatory research with young people as part of their contributions to this book. Thus, the central premise of this book is that each author draws on one or more of these kinds of 'public geography' in order to construct what we would consider a further kind of public geography, which *also* cuts across the 'policy/theory' divide. That is to say, they each provide a *theoretically informed, critical policy discourse analysis*. While policy-makers and the public may not necessarily be the immediate audience for this kind of scholarship, it does have a place as a kind of public geography. For – as 'public intellectuals' – a key component of academic endeavour is to offer critical reflections and comparative analyses that expose both the successes and shortcomings of any policy. The next section of this introduction explores in more detail what 'critical policy discourse analyses' entail, and what contribution a *geographical* approach might make here.

## Critical policy discourse analysis: definitions and approaches

As noted previously, each chapter in this book can be read as a kind of critical policy discourse analysis. To better understand this term, let us consider its component elements.

## Critical

The term 'critical' – prominent in this book's title, and also in many individual chapters – has two specific meanings here. First, the term signals how many chapters are linked by some degree of commitment to a *critical geographical* sensibility. Four characteristics of this approach are as follows (after Blomley, 2009):

- Work is often underpinned by a commitment to politicised areas of social theory such as Marxian political economy, feminism, postcolonialism, queer theory, or poststructuralism. This commitment is often manifest via engagement with the kinds of 'useful', 'activist', 'participatory' or 'policy' geographies sketched in the preceding section.
- Following from these conceptual and political commitments, criticality takes diverse forms of 'self-consciously oppositional enquiry; scholarship that seeks to unmask power, demonstrate inequality, uncover resistance and foster emancipator politics' (Blomley, 2009, p 123).
- There is often a substantive focus upon representations and discourses, particularly the ways in which discourses sustain and legitimise power relations and social injustices in diverse geographical contexts.
- There is an underlying concern with the mutually constitutive role of space and place in power relations, discourses and social injustices. That is: how particular spaces and geographical contexts can effectively (re)produce particular power relations and inequalities; how particular social and political practices produce certain spatialities and are lived-out in everyday spaces; and how discourses are central to all of this.

Second, and relatedly, the term 'critical' suggests how many chapters are explicitly or implicitly aligned with the aims and principles of *critical discourse analysis*.

## Discourse

'Discourse' is a complex, contested term with multiple, overlapping meanings in everyday and academic parlance. The work of the French post-structuralist philosopher Michel Foucault has been important for many social scientists seeking to understand discourse(s): indeed, Foucault's work is explicitly a touchstone for several chapters in this book. Foucault (1972, p 80) defines discourse by suggesting that the term is used:

> sometimes as the general domain of all statements, sometimes as an individualizable group of statements, and sometimes as a regulated practice that accounts for a number of statements.

Consider each of these three meanings in turn. First, Foucault suggests that discourse is often used as a loose, general, catch-all term for 'all statements'. It can be used, perhaps particularly in everyday language, to describe any form of written, verbal and representational communication: 'all utterances and texts which have meaning and which have some effects in the real world' (Mills, 1997, p 7). Second, and more importantly here, Foucault argues that it is possible to identify particular, coherent, interconnected 'groups of statements' in any given time and place. As Foucault explored throughout much of his work, influential norms, representations, rhetorics and assumptions are (re)produced and circulated by powerful contemporary institutions and organisations. In this sense, discourses are 'groups of related statements which govern the variety of ways in which it is possible to talk about something and which thus make it difficult, if not impossible, to think and act outside them' (Allen, 2003, p 18). As such, discourses are always already central to the pursuit and maintenance of power and the practices of politics. Indeed, for Foucault:

> power and knowledge directly imply one another ... There is no power relation without the correlative constitution of a field of knowledge, nor any knowledge that does not presuppose and constitute ... power relations. (1975, p 22)

Moreover, Foucault's work illustrates how certain discourses are more obdurate, longstanding, powerful and efficacious than others, noting:

> a kind of gradation among discourses [between]: those which are said in the ordinary course of days and exchanges and which vanish as soon as they have been pronounced; and those which give rise to ... new speech acts which take them up, transform them or speak of them, in short those discourses which, over and above their formulation, are said indefinitely, remain said, and are to be said again. (1981, p 56)

Third, and again importantly here, Foucault directs attention to the *practices* that produce discourses: particularly those discourses which, as per the preceding quotation, 'remain said, and are to be said again'. At first glance, this may seem a pretty straightforward task. However, in our understanding, this attentiveness to practices is profoundly challenging, demanding analysis of the complex ways in which discourses – and forms of power predicated upon them – are produced and actually *done*. Social scientists have taken diverse approaches to this challenge, for example focusing upon: verbal and textual techniques of discourse production (for example rhetoric, metaphors, grammar, imagery); nonverbal and performative tactics which produce powerful discourses (for example gestures, staging, presentational skills); the materials, tools, texts and technologies which constitute discourses in practice; the organisations, institutions and networks which work to produce, disseminate and control discourses; or emotional/affective components of, and responses to, discourses. A net result of this work is a realisation of the complexly *distributed* nature of discourse(s): that is, any 'discourse' comprises a complex array of texts, statements, practices, processes, events and interactions.

Foucault's work on discourse thus challenges social scientists to critically reflect upon powerful discourses within contemporary societies and the ways in which they are (re)produced and encountered in practice. Each chapter in this book has attempted to do precisely this, in relation to a specific facet of contemporary 'policy discourse'. The research methods that chapter authors have deployed to this end are discussed later. We note there that this book's chapters should be understood as exemplifying a much broader social scientific field of critical policy discourse analysis: though we also note that the chapters should be understood as distinctive and challenging in this context because of their focus upon *geographies* of policies, policy-formation and childhood and youth.

## Policy discourse

Following the 'Foucauldian' conceptualisation of discourse sketched in the preceding subsection, we understand the term 'policy discourse' to denote: (i) the particular, interconnected groups of texts, statements and representations which emerge from geographically- and historically-specific policy contexts or agendas; (ii) the entire array of practices through which such contexts and agendas are constituted, sustained and experienced. The chapters in this book illustrate just some of the multiple ways in which policy discourses circulate and take place: as documents, agendas, statistics, press releases; via meetings, presentations, briefings, media reportage. In so doing, they glimpse something of the radical *distributedness* of policy discourses: comprising multiple formal mechanisms and informal processes across all manner of interlinked spaces and events. Indeed, the complex geographies of policy discourses are evident throughout this book: as you read, note how specific chapters about particular policy agendas demonstrate how local, regional, national and international spaces and politics are constantly interconnected. The chapters also appear to suggest that policy discourses have become increasingly *geographically complex* and increasingly distributed over the last decade: an expanded and apparently proliferating field of actors – encompassing public/private partnerships, non-governmental agencies, supranational decision-making fora, transnational agencies, globalised interests, norms and practices – is part-and-parcel of all of the policy discourses discussed in this book. The chapters reveal numerous ways in which particular policy discourses intersect with everyday spaces and practices in diverse local, regional, national and international contexts.

## Discourse analysis

Diverse researchers in the social sciences and humanities have sought to analyse and understand discourses in diverse contexts. Multiple methods of 'discourse analysis' have developed in the disciplines of literary studies, history, media studies, political science, psychology. Indeed, Titscher et al (2000, p 51) identify at least 12 well-established and widely used techniques of discourse analysis, and at least 27 distinctive methodological traditions underlying the application of these techniques. The authors of chapters in this book use diverse methods and approaches in their respective chapters. However, we suggest that the chapters cohere around a set of aims and principles which are broadly aligned with the approach known as 'critical discourse analysis' (CDA).

Four key principles of CDA are as follows (after Wodak, 1996; Titscher et al, 2000):

- CDA seeks to critically reflect upon 'truths' which are taken-for-granted, and forms of knowledge which seem 'natural', 'official' and 'authoritative', in particular social-historical contexts. Here the notion of 'critical' analysis is both a statement of method (that is 'daring' to critique powerful discourses, or using the techniques of literary and cultural criticism) and frequently closely linked to the politicised forms of criticality outlined earlier.
- CDA seeks – often explicitly after Foucault – to uncover relationships between discourse and power relations, ideologies, hierarchies and inequalities. These relationships are understood to be complex, deeply embedded, and often concealed: CDA thus requires rigorous, detailed and quite laborious research.
- CDA focuses upon individual, or a limited number of, key texts or 'communicative events' as a way of unveiling the broader contemporary 'order of discourse' (Fairclough, 1995). That is, individual instances of discourse are understood to be potentially revealing about much broader contemporary power relations, social structures and politics. Moreover, this approach can reveal the cultural/historical specificity of apparently taken-for-granted knowledges, social structures and ideologies.
- In practice, CDA calls for in-depth research analysing the content of key groups of texts or statements, and/or exploring their production, reception and consequences. Key methods can include content analysis of key documents (for example exemplifying the textual and rhetorical

strategies through which particular worldviews are naturalised/ legitimated) or (slightly more unusually) qualitative research to e: the reception or outcomes of a particular text.

We suggest that the chapters collated in this book share the spirit of this approach, although they are richly diverse and distinctive in their choice of topic and methodology. Moreover, the chapters are linked by the authors' *geographical* sensibility, and specifically by their focus upon intersections between policy agendas and everyday spaces. Indeed, the chapters in this book exemplify both a turn to conduct critical discourse analyses among geographers interested in childhood/youth (see Evans, 2010; Kraftl, 2011) and a gathering tendency for many social scientists, educational researchers and policy-oriented practitioners to explicitly consider the importance of spatiality in/for their work (Foley and Leverett, 2011). What emerges from these chapters, individually and collectively, is a sense of how spaces matter in, and can be constituted by, policy discourses, and how policy discourses are distributed and encountered – and have tangible consequences – across all manner of everyday spaces. Across the chapters, this attentiveness to spatial detail affords numerous insights into the everyday workings of some contemporary policy contexts.

## Structure of the book

The remainder of this book is divided into four parts. The themes and concerns of each of these parts are now described and each chapter briefly outlined.

### Part I: (Inter)national youth policies: politics and practices of spatial translation

The first part of the book explores how geographical processes matter within the formulation and implementation of policy at a national level. The examples presented show the focus in much contemporary policy-making is on young people as 'adults in the making' (Holloway and Valentine, 2000).  This tendency to 'futurity' is explored through both inter-departmental policies (such as the *National Youth Policy* for Lesotho) and intra-departmental policies (such as Citizenship Education in English schools). The chapters present critical readings of specific policies, but draw out issues of relevance to both our understanding of childhood and youth and policies which impact upon young people's everyday lives.

In Chapter Two Jessica Pykett explores cultural politics in the English school curriculum, examining the value of a Foucauldian spatial analytic. Pykett provides a critical analysis of Citizenship Education and considers the performative role of cultural practices within schools spaces in the constitution of 'youth publics' and 'neuro-citizens'. Nicola Ansell, Flora Hajdu, Elsbeth Robson, Lorraine van Blerk and Elodie Marandet (Chapter Three) examine whether youth policies represent a form of transnational governmentality, contributing to the production of neoliberal subjects for a globalising market. The chapter contains an analysis of an UNESCO guidance document and the recently formulated youth policies of Malawi and Lesotho. In contrast, Bethan Evans and Emma-Jay Honeyford (Chapter Four) discuss pre-emptive and anticipatory politics and policies in relation to Sustainable Development. Using the UK's *Brighter futures, greener lives* policy and the notion of 'Education for Sustainable Development' as an example, they consider the place of young people in such future-oriented policies. In Chapter Five Richard Davies provides a practitioner's perspective on youth work policies in England. He presents a critical reading of changing youth work discourses.

### Part II: Education and employment policies: learning beyond schools and schools beyond learning

The second part of the book explores the impacts of policies on everyday experiences. The chapters in this section critically consider spaces of education and employment, which are central to many policies relating to children's and young people's lives. In contrast to the discussions in the previous section, these chapters focus on the impacts of policies for the future on children and young people in the here-and-now.

Gavin Brown (Chapter Six) outlines three distinct phases in British widening participation policy (1997–2010). He shows how widening participation policy and practice has sought to work on young people's aspirations for the future in different ways. In Chapter Seven Susie Weller considers the British education system and how policies promoting parental choice in relation to which school their child attends are differentially experienced. Concepts of social capital are used to uncover inequalities in parents' agency and children's everyday experiences. Jo Pike and Derek Colquhoun use the concept of territorialisation as a tool to examine the spatial implications of a UK school meals policy (Chapter Eight). They draw attention to the ways in which national-level policies shape the practices of individuals and groups. Reflecting upon her experiences as a practitioner, Isabel Cartwright considers how informal education may be constrained by the policies embedded in formal education settings (Chapter Nine). Her work shows how different interpretations of informal education by individual schools can lead to diverse experiences for children and young people.

## Part III: Intervening in 'everyday life': scales, practices and the 'spatial imagination' in youth policy and professional practice

The third part of the book presents examples from a range of geographical contexts to demonstrate how policies impact upon and intervene in children's and young people's everyday lives. Focusing on how policies are implemented and experienced at a local level, these chapters explore children's participation in planning and policy-making (Chapters Ten and Eleven), the implementation of policy in community spaces (Chapters Twelve and Thirteen), and how the terminology used in policies may be problematic (Chapters Fourteen and Fifteen).

In Chapter Ten John Barker uses three examples from the UK of young people's participation in transport planning and policy development. Barker shows the importance of scale in understanding these youth-led campaigns. The Brazilian city of Pelotas is the focus of Laura Novo de Azevedo's work (Chapter Eleven). She shows how a lack of consideration of the value of young people as active participants in heritage conservation policy-making may lead to outcomes which exclude the views of a key sector of the population. In Chapter Twelve Alexandra Cox looks at how 'responsibility' is both embedded within US youth justice policies and differentially conceived and experienced by individuals. Case study evidence from interviews with young offenders is used to illustrate the points raised. Eleanor Jupp examines how parenting policies are implemented within the 'caringscape' of a Sure Start Children's Centre in Oxford, UK (Chapter Thirteen). Jupp explores the relationships between central government policies and everyday community spaces. Chapter Fourteen considers the impacts of homelessness policies on young people in Wales. Peter K. Mackie suggests that these policies display an arbitrary use of age and prioritise individuals according to a set of criteria which is interpreted differently in different places and at different times, resulting in unequal treatment of young homeless people. Terminology used in relation to children affected by the HIV/AIDS epidemic in South Africa is explored by Amy Norman in Chapter Fifteen. She argues that terms such as 'AIDS orphan' and 'vulnerable children' overlook complexities and nuances of experience. Norman shows how the labels used in policy documents can be problematic and can conceal everyday issues and geographies.

## Part IV: Concluding reflections

The final chapter (Chapter Sixteen) reflects on the policies, geographies and lifecourses explored in Parts I, II and III. Peter Kraftl, John Horton and Faith Tucker draw together key themes and issues discussed in the preceding chapters, and suggest future directions for critical geographies of youth policy and practice.

## References

Allen, J. (2003) 'A question of language', in M. Pryke, G. Rose and S. Whatmore (eds) *Using social theory: thinking through research*, Buckingham: Open University Press, pp 11-27.

Anderson, B. (2010) 'Preemption, precaution, preparedness: anticipatory action and future geographies', *Progress in Human Geography*, vol 34, pp 777-98.

Ansell, N. (2009) 'Childhood and the politics of scale: descaling children's geographies?', *Progress in Human Geography*, vol 32, pp 190-209.

Blomley, N. (2009) 'Critical human geography', in D. Gregory, R. Johnston, G. Pratt, M.J. Watts and S. Whatmore (eds) *The dictionary of human geography*, (5th edn), Oxford: Wiley-Blackwell, pp 123-24.

Brown, G. and Pickerill, J. (2009) 'Space for emotion in the spaces of activism', *Emotion, Space and Society*, vol 2, pp 24-35.

Bundesministerium fuer Familie, Senioren, Frauen und Jugend (BSFSJ) (2009) *Richtlinien über die gewährung von zuschüssen und leistungen zur förderung der kinder- und jugendhilfe durch den kinder- und jugendplan des bundes* (Officially translated as *Child and Youth Plan of the Federation*), Berlin: Ministry of the Interior.

Burawoy, M. (2005) 'The critical turn to public sociology', *Critical Sociology*, vol 31, pp 313-26.

Burke, C. and Grosvenor, I. (2008) *School*, London: Reaktion.

Cahill, C. (2004) 'Defying gravity? Raising consciousness through collective research', *Children's Geographies*, vol 2, pp 273-86.

Cahill, C. (2006) '"At risk?" The fed-up honeys represent the gentrification of the Lower East Side', *Women's Studies Quarterly*, vol 34, pp 334-63.

Cameron, A. (2006) 'Geographies of welfare and exclusion: social inclusion and exception', *Progress in Human Geography*, vol 30, pp 396-404.

Chatterton, P. (2006) '"Give up activism" and change the world in unknown ways: or, learning to walk with others on uncommon ground', *Antipode*, vol 38, pp 259-81.

*Children's Geographies* (2009) 'Special issue: UN Convention on the Rights of the Child 20 years on: the right to be properly researched', *Children's Geographies*, vol 7, pp 365-486.

Christensen, P. and James, A. (2008) 'Introduction: researching children and childhood cultures of communication', in P. Christensen and A. James (eds) *Research with children: perspectives and practices*, (2nd edn), London: Routledge, pp 1-9.

Cobb, N. (2007) 'Governance through publicity: anti-social behaviour orders, young people, and the problematization of the right to anonymity', *Journal of Law and Society*, vol 34, pp 342-73.

Cunningham, C. (2003) 'A fruitful direction for research in children's geography: fat chance?' *Children's Geographies*, vol 1, pp 125-8.

DCSF/4ps/PfS (Department for Children, Schools and Families/Public Private Partnerships Programme/Partnerships for Schools) (2008) *An introduction to building schools for the future*, London: 4ps.

DEEWR (Australian Department of Education, Employment and Workplace Relations) (2010) *Building the education revolution: overview*, http://www. deewr.gov.au/Schooling/BuildingTheEducationRevolution/Pages/ default.aspx.

den Besten, O., Horton, J., Adey, P. and Kraftl, P. (2011) 'Claiming events of school (re)design: materialising the promise of *Building schools for the future*', *Social and Cultural Geography*, vol 12, no 1, pp 9-26.

DfE (Department for Education) (2011) *Free schools*, http://www.education. gov.uk/freeschools.

DfES (Department for Education and Skills) (2003) *Building schools for the future: consultation on a new approach to capital investment*, London: DfES.

DfES (Department for Education and Skills) (2004) *Every child matters* White Paper, London: HMSO.

DfES (Department for Education and Skills) (2005) *Youth matters* White Paper, London: HMSO.

DH (Department of Health) (2004) *National service framework for children, young people and maternity services*, London: HMSO.

Dorling, D. and Shaw, M. (2002) 'Geographies of the agenda: public policy, the discipline and its (re)turns', *Progress in Human Geography*, vol 26, pp 629-46.

Elwood, S. (2006) 'Critical issues in participatory GIS: deconstructions, reconstructions, and new research directions', *Transactions in GIS*, vol 10, pp 693–708.

Eriksen, T. (2006) *Engaging anthropology: the case for a public presence*, Oxford: Berg.

Evans, B. (2010) 'Anticipating fatness: childhood, affect and the pre-emptive "war on obesity"', *Transactions of the Institute of British Geographers*, vol 35, pp 21-38.

Fairclough, N. (1995) *Media discourse*, London: Edward Arnold.

Foley, P. and Leverett, S. (2011) 'Introduction', in P. Foley and S. Leverett (eds) *Children and young people's spaces: developing practice*, Buckingham: Open University Press, pp 9-24.

Foucault, M. (1972) *The archaeology of knowledge*, London: Tavistock.

Foucault, M. (1975) *Discipline and punish: the birth of the prison*, London: Allen Lane.

Foucault, M. (1981) 'The order of discourse', in R. Young (ed) *Untying the text: a post-structural reader*, London: Routledge, pp 48-78.

Fuller, D. (2008) 'Public geographies: taking stock', *Progress in Human Geography*, vol 32, pp 834-44.

Fuller, D. and Askins, K. (2010) 'Public geographies II: being organic', *Progress in Human Geography*, vol 34, pp 654-67.

Fuller, D. and Kitchen, R. (2004) 'Radical theory/critical praxis: academic geography beyond the academy?', in D. Fuller and R. Kitchen (eds) *Radical theory/critical praxis: making a difference beyond the academy*, E-press: Praxis, pp 1-20.

Gagen, E. (2004) 'Making America flesh: physicality and nationhood in early-twentieth century physical education reform', *Cultural Geographies*, vol 11, pp 417-42.

Gelder, K. (2005) *The subcultures reader*, London: Routledge.

Government of Lesotho (2002) *National youth policy for Lesotho*, Maseru: Ministry of Gender and Youth, Sport and Recreation.

Hamnett, C. (1997) 'The sleep of reason?' *Environment and Planning D: Society and Space*, vol 15, pp 127-8.

Hebdidge, D. (1975) 'The meaning of mod', in S. Hall and T. Jefferson (eds) *Resistance through rituals*, London: Routledge, pp 87-98.

Holloway, S. and Pimlott-Wilson, H. (2011) 'Geographies of children, youth and families', in L. Holt (ed) *Geographies of children, youth and families: an international perspective*, London: Routledge, pp 9-24.

Holloway, S. and Valentine, G. (2000) 'Children's geographies and the new social studies of childhood', in S. Holloway and G. Valentine (eds) *Children's geographies: playing, living, learning*, London: Routledge, pp 1-26.

Hopkins, P. and Pain, R. (2007) 'Geographies of age: thinking relationally', *Area*, vol 39, pp 287-94.

Horton, J. and Kraftl, P. (2005) 'For more-than-usefulness: six overlapping points about Children's Geographies', *Children's Geographies*, vol 3, pp 131-43.

Horton, J. and Kraftl, P. (2006) 'What else? Some more ways of thinking about and doing children's geographies', *Children's Geographies*, vol 4, pp 69-95.

Horton, J. and Kraftl, P. (2009a) 'Small acts, kind words and "not too much fuss": implicit activisms', *Emotion, Space and Society*, vol 2, pp 14-23.

Horton, J. and Kraftl, P. (2009b) 'What (else) matters? Policy contexts, emotional geographies', *Environment and Planning A*, vol 41, pp 2984-3002.

Horton, J., Kraftl, P. and Tucker, F. (2011) 'Spaces-in-the-making, childhoods-on-the-move', in P. Foley and S. Leverett (eds) *Children and young people's spaces: developing practice*, Buckingham: Open University Press, pp 40-57.

ICNYP (International Council on National Youth Policy) (2002) *Training manual on the fundamentals of a national youth policy*, ICNYP.

James, A. and James, A.L. (2004) *Constructing childhood: theory, policy and practice*, Basingstoke: Palgrave Macmillan.

James, A., Jenks, C. and Prout, A. (1998) *Theorizing childhood*, Oxford: Blackwell.

Jenks, C. (2005) *Childhood* (2nd edn), London: Routledge.

Jones, O. (2003) '"Endlessly revisited and forever gone": on memory, reverie and emotional imagination in doing children's geographies', *Children's Geographies*, vol 1, pp 25-36.

Katz, C. (2008) 'Childhood as spectacle: relays of anxiety and the reconfiguration of the child', *Cultural Geographies*, vol 15, pp 5-17.

Kindon, S., Pain, R. and Kesby, M. (2007) *Participatory action research approaches and methods: connecting people, participation and place*, London: Routledge.

Kraftl, P. (2008) 'Young people, hope and childhood-hope', *Space and Culture*, vol 11, pp 81-92.

Kraftl, P. (2011) 'Utopian promise or burdensome responsibility? A critical analysis of the UK Government's Building Schools for the Future Policy', *Antipode,* doi: 10.1111/j.1467-8330.2011.00921.x

Kraftl, P. and Horton, J. (2007) '"The health event": everyday, affective politics of participation', *Geoforum*, vol 38, pp 1012-27.

Martin, R. (2001) 'Geography and public policy: the case of the missing agenda', *Progress in Human Geography* , vol 25, pp 189-210.

Massey, D. (2005) *For space,* London: Sage.

Mikkelsen, M. and Christensen, P. (2009) 'Is children's independent mobility really independent? A study of children's mobility combining ethnography and GPS/mobile phone technologies', *Mobilities*, vol 4, pp 37-58.

Mills, S. (1997) *Discourse*, London: Routledge.

Miles, S. (2000) *Youth lifestyles in a changing world*, Buckingham: Open University Press.

OECD (Organisation for Economic Co-operation and Development) (2009) Portugal's secondary school modernization programme, *CELE Exchange*, vol 66, pp 1-9.

Pain, R. (2004) 'Introduction: children at risk?' *Children's Geographies*, vol 2, pp 65-8.

Pain, R. (2006) 'Social geography: seven deadly myths in policy research', *Progress in Human Geography*, vol 30, pp 250-9.

Pain, R. and Francis, P. (2003) 'Reflections on participatory research', *Area*, vol 35, pp 56-64.

Peck, J. (1999) 'Editorial: grey geography', *Transactions of the Institute of British Geographers*, vol 24, pp 131-5.

Philo, C. (2003) '"To go back up the side hill": memories, imaginations and reveries of childhood', *Children's Geographies*, vol 1, pp 3-24.

Pickerill, J. and Chatterton, P. (2006) 'Notes towards autonomous geographies: creation, resistance and self management as survival tactics', *Progress in Human Geography*, vol 30, pp 1-17.

Postman, N. (1994) *The disappearance of childhood*, London: Vintage.

Prout. A. and James, A. (1990) 'A new paradigm for the sociology of childhood? Provenance, promise and problems', in A. James and A. Prout (eds) *Constructing and reconstructing childhood*, London: Falmer Press, pp 7-33.

Republic of Malawi (2011) *National youth policy,* Lilongwe: Ministry of Youth Development and Sports.

Routledge, P., Cumbers, A. and Nativel, C. (2007) 'Grassrooting network imaginaries: relationality, power, and mutual solidarity in global justice networks', *Environment and Planning A*, vol 39, pp 2575-92.

Skelton, T. (2008) 'Research with children and young people: exploring the tensions between ethics, competence and participation', *Children's Geographies*, vol 6, pp 21-36.

Tissot, S. (2007) *L'Etat et les quartiers: genèse d'une catégorie d'action publique,* Paris: Le Seuil.

Titscher, S., Meyer, M., Wodak, R. and Vetter, E. (2000) *Methods of text and discourse analysis,* London: Sage.

UN (United Nations) (1989) *Convention on the rights of the child*, New York: United Nations.

UNESCO (United Nations Educational, Scientific and Cultural Organisation) (2004) *Empowering youth through national policies,* Paris: Section for Youth of the Bureau of Strategic Planning.

USDE (United States Department of Education) (2001) *No child left behind*, Washington, DC: USDE.

Vanderbeck, R. (2008), 'Reaching critical mass? Theory, politics, and the culture of debate in children's geographies', *Area*, vol 40, pp 393–400.

Ward, K. (2007) 'Geography and public policy: activist, participatory, and policy geographies', *Progress in Human Geography*, vol 31, pp 695-705.

Wodak, R. (1996) *Disorders of discourse*, London: Longman.

# Part I
## (Inter)national youth policies: politics and practices of spatial translation

two

# Making 'youth publics' and 'neuro-citizens': critical geographies of contemporary educational practice in the UK

*Jessica Pykett*

## Introduction

School life arguably dominates the everyday worlds of young people in countries such as the UK. In recognition of this, geographies of education constitute an increasingly varied and vibrant area of concern for geographers and educational theorists alike – incorporating the distinctive worlds of children and young people, the spatial division of opportunities, the global political economy of knowledge production and consumption, and issues of place-based identity and subject-formation. The aims of this chapter are two-fold. Firstly, it considers some of the ways in which recent progress in this field has been characterised in relation to the analytics of space, spatiality and geography. Secondly, it explores the implications of these spatial approaches for interrogating contemporary educational policy and professional practice. What is the difference between different spatial concepts, and what is at stake in slipping between them? By introducing alternative accounts of the notion of 'space' as it is employed by geographers, the chapter examines lessons that can be taken from state schools in the UK as sites with a distinctive cultural politics (lessons which may equally apply in educational contexts outside of the UK). It explores how we might go about pursuing an ambitious, contextualised analysis of education which takes into account the wider significance of educational practices (including beyond the space of the school), without losing site of the specific nature of schools as spaces, and the specifically pedagogic modes of power characterising schools as institutions. After identifying key insights taken from both critical geographies of education and geographies of children and young people, the chapter explores the importance of a 'sense of space' for better understanding two contemporary trends in educational (and broader youth) policy and practice: the making of 'youth publics' and the shaping of 'neuro-citizens'. The chapter provides critical analysis of

'Citizenship Education', introduced in England as a new compulsory school subject in 2002 after the recommendations of a parliamentary committee (QCA, 1998) soon after New Labour's election to UK government. This is considered alongside developments in the neurosciences as applied within the educational sphere, and currently attracting both political (Goswami, 2008) and popular attention, through so-called 'brain-training' computer games and exercises. What is at stake politically in imagining children and young people simultaneously as political subjects (citizens) and brain-driven personas?

## Educational geographies – space, spatiality and geography

Education researchers are increasingly interested in the significance of spatial theory for understanding contemporary schooling and education policy. Gulson and Symes (2007, p 1), for instance, call on educationalists to address the spatial turn in geography and social theory. Robertson (2010, p 16) argues for the application of a 'critical spatial lens' to the sociology of education – comprising of the 'difference that space, along with time and sociality' makes to knowledge, social reproduction and subjectivities. Such authors draw their visions of space primarily from the Lefebvre-inspired work of human geographers David Harvey, Doreen Massey and Edward Soja, for whom space is constitutive of and constituted by social relations. As such, a critical theory of space based on a neo-Marxist account of spatial and social reproduction – albeit an account which has become sensitive to the contingency and relationality of spatial formations – has arguably become the predominant account within critical educational research. Space is considered as the conduit and locus of power which is strategically manipulated in the interests of the powerful (usually the nation-state or transnational capital) through spatial architectures and changes in the built environment. This work argues that critical geographies of education must focus on the spatial drivers of global economic restructuring which lie behind educational policy, the form of schooling and the very 'pedagogic identities' (Robertson, 2010, p 16) which are produced through schooling. Conversely, as has been widely argued, approaching educational spaces in light of their underlying political-economic structure may obscure the multiplicity of responses, ambiguities and reflexive pedagogic subjectivities which are constituted through educational spaces (Kraftl, 2011). So while the spatiality of education draws attention to the concept of space not as an entity but as an active process, additional theoretical perspectives are required in order to closely examine the modes of power, cultural politics and notions of subject-formation implicated in critical spatial theories of education.

   Meanwhile, and with surprisingly little cross-referencing to emergent geographies of education (as noted by Holloway et al, 2010), a sub-field of 'geographies of children and young people' (often referred to as 'Children's Geographies') has established itself as a response to the apparent blindness of 'mainstream' geography to the distinctive worlds of children and young people (Aitken, 2001; Matthews, 2003), including work on young people's use of public space (Tucker and Matthews, 2001), and the spaces of the school (Valentine, 1999). The focus of this work is on the particularities of young people's geographical experiences, and there is a strong sense of advocacy for the hidden voices of young people as they are (mis)represented in or excluded from an 'adultist' world (Weller, 2007, p 161). However, it has been argued that critical geographies of children and young people tend to be too particular, underplaying the *dynamics of power at play in constituting children and young people as subjects*, and in addition failing to state the relevance of children and young people's geographies to more general concerns. Overcoming this conceptual (and disciplinary) split between the local particularism of childhood and the apparent universalism of social structures underpinning accounts of the critical geographies of education is an ambition forwarded by Holloway and Valentine (2000), and provides the starting point for this chapter.

The notion of 'educational geographies' here draws attention to the potential of research on education and young people to develop geographers' theorisations of space, rather than to seek to transplant spatial theory into the realm of education. But both geographers and educationalists could be more sensitive to the multiple readings and conceptualisations of space which make up geography's diverse theoretical repertoires. Critical geographies of youth policy and education could benefit from a more dialogical relationship between theories of space and theories of education. And this dialogue could be helpfully centred on the distinctive nature of the educational sphere as a reflexive space of learning, and on schools as institutions concerned *both* with disciplining subjects and developing capabilities. An academic geography which learns from educational experience could thus help us to better understand the geographies of educational policy-making, the wider significance of policies aimed at youth and the importance of space in shaping the way in which youth policies are performed 'on the ground'. This approach shows a sensitivity to the educational realm as a distinctive sphere of social reproduction, cultural and economic change, political struggle, and community and citizen-formation. Furthermore, it provides useful insights into the significance of education practices beyond the realm of formal schooling and the life-worlds of young people. Thiem (2009, p 155) has described such a perspective as a more 'outward-looking geography of education', concerned not simply with the difference that space makes, but with 'how education "makes space"' (Thiem, 2009, p 157). To fully attend to this appeal, it is necessary to consider a wider range of concepts of space than has hitherto been the case, and to call on perspectives both from geographies of education and from children's and young people's geographies.

## Schools as spaces with distinctive cultural politics

Human geographers are by no means limited in their accounts of space and spatiality. Indeed, these concepts continue to sustain a wealth of debate in the academic discipline. In summary, Derek Gregory (2000, pp 780–2) notes at least four such trajectories: phenomenological accounts of spatial experience; Marxist notions of spatial structures in alignment with particular modes of production; the Lefebvrian (Lefebvre, 1991) concept of the social production of space, or the mutual constitution of space and society; and poststructuralist definitions of space as the confluence of power and knowledge, whereby space plays an active part in producing subject-positions. To this schema could be added actor-network and non-representational notions of space, which emphasise the confluence of material and semiotic phenomena in networks of relations which 'perform' the space of the school. This highlights the need for continual work (by human and non-human actors) to ensure that what we conceive of as the school 'hangs together' and is sustained over time (Latour, 2005; Thrift, 2007). But the spatial turn in educational theory has arguably relied on a Lefebvrian conception of space.

An alternative starting point is a Foucauldian analysis of schools and schooling. This strand of poststructural thought has implications for the way in which we might conceptualise space and thus develop a critical geography of education. A useful summary of Foucault's influence in geographical research on children and education is provided by Philo (2010). Research in education has also developed Foucauldian theoretical perspectives on topics ranging from the micropolitics of the school (Ball, 1991; Mac An Ghaill, 1994), restructuring of the knowledge economy (Peters, 2001; Olssen, 2004) and education policy analysis (Ball, 2003; Tickly, 2003). But what does a Foucauldian interpretation of *space* tell us about the distinctive nature of schools, and what are the implications for youth policy and practice in the sphere of formal schooling?

Geographers have now paid considerable attention to Foucault's contribution to theorising space (Hannah, 1997; Barnett, 1999; Allen, 2003; Huxley, 2006; Crampton and Elden, 2007). What these contributions share is a commitment to understanding the intersections of space, power and knowledge, which are arguably also central to young people's experiences of schooling. But as Peta Mitchell (2003, p 49) has argued, Foucault did not offer a theory of space, offering instead a 'spatial praxis' for understanding power and knowledge. His recognition of space, she argues, opens up historical processes to considerations of power – whether in accounts of the body as a site of inscripted power, or of architecture as a technique of disciplinary power. As Crampton and Elden (2007, p 9) have noted, spatiality for Foucault is a 'tool of analysis' rather than an object of concern. We are prompted to consider power in schools through a spatial lens, but equally, we must consider the specificity of the school as a rather peculiar kind of space (Barnett, 1999). In this way, the rich empirical research of school spaces and school-based practices carried out by educational sociologists and children's geographers alike can help geographers to think differently about space. Having a 'sense of space' in this way (drawing on Massey's multiple, open and processual account of a *sense of place*), does not, as demonstrated below, detract from the critical vigour of neo-Marxist visions of spatiality as a way to approach educational research and youth policy. What it adds is a more refined account of subjectivity and of subject-formation than has been offered thus far by the spatial turn in education.

It is commonplace to think of schools as mirroring social relations. But in fact, they are in many ways strange institutions characterised by hierarchical, disciplinary and ritualised relations in enclosed sites. Intended to govern social norms, build nations, and acculturate young people, schools rely on a conception of children as future, incomplete adults in need of development, as various chapters in this volume attest. As such, schools have been heavily criticised by children's geographers as hypocritical, controlling institutions acting contrary to young people's human rights. In accounts of the geography of education and critical education theory, there is also a tendency to presume that 'hegemonic' power as it is exercised within schools is extendable to wider society to serve a neoliberal political agenda and the production of a particular 'brand' of entrepreneurial, self-managing, skilled future workers and consumers, particularly by critics based in a North American context (Giroux, 2004; K. Mitchell, 2006). In contrast, if we consider for a moment the nature of power within the formal educational sphere as distinctly *pedagogical*, we can begin to appreciate how cultural politics within schools may be concerned with developing the capacities of students to act autonomously in the future. This inciting form of power cannot be understood in the narrow terms of domination and resistance offered in approaches focused on the apparent neoliberalisation of education.

Rather than regarding space as a conduit of power, as in a Lefebvrian theorisation of spatiality, space can be used as an analytical frame to understand how particular forms of power are *exercised*. So we need not rely on just one account of spatiality in our analysis of educational policy and practice. To illustrate the utility of a more plural spatial analytic, the next two sections examine the performative role of cultural practices within school spaces in the constitution of 'youth publics' and 'neuro-citizens'. Although counter-posing two contemporary educational trends as they play out in the UK – Citizenship Education and neuroeducation – the conceptual approach may be equally appropriate in relating to educational policy and professional practice in other contexts (with research into neuroeducation and/or lessons on citizenship or civics already being pursued in Australia, Argentina, France, Germany, Italy and the US).

## The spatial imagination of 'youth publics' at school

It is rare for 'critical' geographers of education to complement government initiatives and policies of whichever governing party. But it is important to distinguish between what the much maligned education policies under New Labour attempted to achieve for children and young people, and the policies of the Conservative-Liberal Democrat Coalition government since May 2010. That is not to say that New Labour's education policies were beyond reproach – the personalisation agenda was criticised as an individualising and responsibilising programme (Pykett, 2009), for instance. However, at the risk of going against the grain of critical education policy analysis, this section examines a recent facet of the former New Labour government's education policy: the introduction of Citizenship Education, which – in a qualified way - might be considered to take youth policy in the formal education sphere in a positive direction. This is a direction which is currently under threat, bearing in mind the Coalition government's lukewarm attitude to Citizenship Education, its traditionalist approach to a 'facts'-based curriculum, and proposals to take teacher training further away from the hands of universities and straight into classrooms (DfE, 2010). The more generous account of Citizenship Education posited here has implications for how we might understand the relationship between space and power from a broadly Foucauldian perspective, where it is education itself, not just space, which makes a difference – both theoretically and practically.

Citizenship Education was described as a response to a perceived apathy and increasingly anti-social behaviour of young people, and to apparent cultural and ethnic divisions emerging in the UK in the 1990s (QCA, 1998, p 15). Critics in the popular press condemned Citizenship Education as a form of state indoctrination (O'Hear, 1999, p 12) and as 'soggy Leftwing propaganda' (Phillips, 2006, p 14). A number of academic critics also took issue with the new subject as signifying a cover-up for institutional racism within schools (Gillborn, 2006), and as a hypocritical subject (given the lack of meaningful opportunities for young people to claim real citizenship rights within the formal setting of the school (Weller, 2007, p 82)). However, Citizenship Education is the only subject which is aimed explicitly at equipping 'young people with the knowledge, skills and understanding to play an effective role in *public life*' (QCA, 2007, p 41, my emphasis).

In the face of much criticism, teachers and teacher-trainers got on with the task. And both within and (uncharacteristically for schools) beyond the classroom, young people were given the opportunity to take part in activities such as visits to local council offices, off-timetable days in celebration of diverse cultures, and UK youth parliament meetings. They also debated contemporary political issues such as migration and diversity, local and parliamentary decision-making processes, human rights, freedom of speech and the role of the voluntary sector. Perhaps most crucially, Citizenship Education prompted students to consider the question of *how they as citizens are made governable*. It is arguably this question, and the performative space of the school (that is, the sense in which education policies generate meanings, subjects and social relations through everyday material and semiotic practices) in which the question becomes pedagogically powerful, marking the significance of Citizenship Education to the lives of children and young people.

The Citizenship Education policy, as brought to life by its policy texts, curricular documents, text books and classroom practice, imagines the ideal citizen as active, empathetic, responsible and publicly-minded. It is through the cultural practices of the school that a 'youth public' can be seen to be constituted. The public to be educated is constituted through that very same education (see Newman and Clarke, 2009, p 2). But the youth public is also mediated by space – as in the contexts or geographies of schooling in UK towns and cities. *Where* you live and go to school still has an impact on your educational achievement and future prospects (HEFCE, 2010, p 2). Young people learn to be citizens in an uneven educational landscape. A modest conception of space, as a recognition of the spatial quality of educational inequalities can help us to critically interrogate the apparently 'local' geographies of education which have an important impact on the lives of young people, and research in this area could helpfully inform policies relating to inequalities in educational provision across cities and in rural areas; teachers' and students' perceptions of their own capabilities; the reputation of schools; local authority admissions policies and procedures; and so on.

But a critical geography of education need not be either inward or outward-looking – it can be both. A detailed, 'inward' interrogation of curriculum content, classroom practice and reflexive, sceptical citizen-formation, can indeed change the way in which we think about the relationship between power and space *outside* of formal education. Education itself as a formative cultural sphere shapes and is shaped by active spatial processes. This can be witnessed in the way in which teachers, parents and pupils deploy geographical metaphors for 'good schools' and 'good pupils' – often equating the potential 'teachability' of certain students with which estate or neighbourhood they come from – constituting an urban politics which is derived from the educational realm. This can be seen, for example, in situations where schools have been labelled as 'failing' or in 'special measures' – when students can internalise this sense of failure. Or where a school or academy in a particular neighbourhood specialises in performing arts/

literature or sports or business. Students quickly learn how the school, local authority or educational establishment perceive, pigeonhole and arguably limit their localised 'aptitudes' or 'aspirations'.

Education policies are thus mediated through the local settings of the school, and images of spatial disadvantage often inform classroom practices and attitudes. citizenship education may play an important role in making these governing practices visible, and as such, common dismissals of this new agenda may be misplaced. At the same time, however, such optimism may seem equally misguided in light of a second educational agenda growing in influence; the use of neuroscientific approaches in education provides a new area of concern for which a more theoretically pluralist geography of education can offer a critical perspective.

## The psychological imagination of neuro-citizens

> Linda presents a 'brain-gym' exercise to her fellow PGCE students, demonstrating how she has been using it as a literacy strategy for her class. She writes the alphabet on the board, and we all act out her instructions: raise your left arm and then your right arm, following her lead, whilst reading the alphabet. Someone mentions this is particularly good for 'EBD kids' [pupils designated as having emotional and behavioural difficulties], since they are 'visual learners', and 'just can't sit down'. (Research diary, PGCE [Post-Graduate Certificate in Education/teaching qualification] course, 8 December 2003)

The potential contribution of novel developments in the neurosciences is, like the introduction of Citizenship Education, a matter of great debate in education. This section considers the political implications of a neuroscientific approach to education, particularly in terms of the production of particular imaginaries of the neurological subject which may be seen to be at odds with the constitution of youth publics outlined in the previous section. In employing the alternative spatial analytics provided by Foucauldian geographers already outlined, critical geographies of contemporary education practices need not be limited to a Lefebvrian notion of spatiality, and indeed that the force of our critiques may benefit from a more eclectic model of the relations between space, power and subjectivity.

Several recent 'future-thinking' commentaries have taken up the challenge of describing the potential contribution of neuroscientific advances to changing educational practices (Goswami, 2008; Howard-Jones, no date). Many have been interested in shaping the foundations for new interdisciplinary or transdisciplinary dialogues between neuroscientists and educationalists (Geake and Cooper, 2003; Samuels, 2009; Dommett et al, 2010), identifying practical and conceptual issues faced by teachers in translating such neuroscientific insights into classroom practice. Others have been concerned with ensuring the development of an accurate, scientifically rigorous and 'educationally relevant' (Howard-Jones, no date, p 23) 'evidence-based neuroeducation' (Goswami, 2008, p 2). They caution against the use of 'brain-based programmes' such as the widely-used ideas of the 'brain-gym', as in the research observation cited above, and the pseudo-science behind notions of 'visual, auditory and kinaesthetic' learning styles and 'multiple intelligences' – dispelling these approaches as 'neuromyths' (Goswami, 2008, p 5). In debunking these myths, such authors are careful to point out intricately debated facets of neuroscience which are all too superficially brushed over in the popular enthusiasm for neuroscientific approaches to education. Moreover, they highlight an important misperception in current thinking: that although we can 'see' the brain through functional Magnetic Resonance Imaging (fMRI) scans, '[t]hey do not allow us to "see" thinking or learning directly'; in between the image and our understanding there must be a psychological or cognitive model (Howard-Jones, no date, p 17). Here it is necessary to add the caveat that all cognitive models must necessarily be contestable approximations of reality.

But what remains intact in these critical commentaries is the powerful re-imagination of the young person to be educated specifically as an individuated neurological subject, and the re-imagination of education as a set of functional competencies such as numeracy, literacy and (latterly) creativity. As others have noted, this is an education arguably devoid of content (Morgan and Lambert, 2005, p 40). In this scenario, the teacher becomes a mere conduit of information; a mechanic of the brain, and their expertise in any subject-matter is displaced by the superior expertise of the neuroscientist. Perhaps even more worryingly, a neuroscientific approach locates education and learning internally within the brain, dislocating the person from their constitutive outside. This problem pertains as much to critical commentaries on neuroscience and education as it does to the promotion of commercial brain-based programmes: 'The brain is the major organ of learning, and neuroscience is the study of the brain' (Goswami, 2008, p 2). In seeking scientific scrutiny of the visible brain, this apparently common-sense assertion, as Purdy and Morrison (2009, p 105) have noted, maintains a 'Cartesian separation of the inner and outer'. Furthermore, such an account also obscures the role of the body in learning, and decouples the brain from its actual context – that is, as an integral part of *embodied subjectivity*, its very materiality (dendrites, synapses and all), processes, interactions with hormonal systems, food intake, physical activity and so on, re-shaped and re-configured through a person's experience of being alive in a particular time and place, living among others (a point already central to specific approaches to social and cultural neuroscience but not thus far considered in detail in educational research, see Cacioppo et al, 2000; Chiao, 2009). In rendering the brain visible, neuroeducation also has the potential to render the *social consciousness* of the person invisible (H. Rose, 2004, p 61). This psychologised notion of selfhood can divert attention from the spatial inequalities which shape the conditions in which people learn and which shape, through the education system, how people are formed as 'neuro-citizens'.

This is the point at which a sensitivity to space – a geographical approach – can become critical to the investigation of such forward-thinking educational trends. It is not Lefebvre's concepts which prove most fruitful here, but those of Foucault. For this opens up an analytical frame which identifies schools as spaces which render visible the relations between power and knowledge in a particular context. Such an approach can lead to an explosion of new avenues for critical analysis. Two such avenues for critical neuroeducational research are outlined briefly here.

Primarily, a Foucauldian approach to educational practice prompts geographers to consider the school as a space through which particular knowledges become powerful, and through which people are made up as subjects. This allows us to see the bigger picture surrounding the emergence of a neuroscientific approach to education. New ventures in 'Critical Neuroscience' (Choudhury et al, 2009), also inspired by the work of Foucault, can help us to ask different questions about neurosciences – not in terms of the effectiveness, accurateness and scientific rigour of their adoption by teachers and schools, but in terms of the political dynamics at work in rendering neurosciences as a legitimate form of knowledge for educational policy and professional practice. This work, with its roots in critical psychology, is well-versed in understanding the growth, institutionalisation and wide-spread adoption of the psychological sciences – not just in education but in managing populations (N. Rose, 1998). So instead of asking how we can foster dialogue between neuroscientists and educationalists, we must also ask what are the driving forces behind the uses of neurosciences in education? As Choudhury et al (2009, p 66) put it, 'how do particular problems become questions for the neurosciences'? One might venture that the search for neurological explanations and pharmacological solutions to 'behavioural problems' in schools has more to do with competitive pressures on attainment and standards and changing notions of the *purpose* of childhood and appropriate classroom behaviours, than with new ways of diagnosing brain-'deficits'. Widespread concern about the over-diagnosis of ADHD and the prescription of Ritalin to children is a salient example (N. Rose, 2007, p 95). As such, networks of agents, from policy-makers, doctors, pharmacists, drug companies, neuroscientists, teachers, parents and pupils are always going to 'get in the way' of applied neuroeducation, bringing with them a complex web of political, social and cultural relations which together make up our experiences of *learning how to become ourselves* – confirming the philosophical contention that we are not merely defined by our synapses (Malabou, 2008).

The second critical avenue for a critical geography of neuroeducation concerns the notion of subjectivity. This notion draws attention to the formation of personhood, rather than assuming that this is something rooted internally in the brain. Foucault's concept of *subjectivation* is crucial here (Milchman and Rosenburg, 2007, p 55) – whereby people are both subjectified and yet autonomously constitute themselves through social (and spatial) relations. This links back with the making up of youth publics outlined in the previous section. Representations of particular youth behaviours were used in the justification of Citizenship Education, and are spatially located outside of the brain, but integral to the making up of 'neuro-citizens' through educational practice. They serve to normalise acceptable citizenly behaviours and idealisations of the good citizen, doing so by telling stories, construing meanings and offering interpretations which are in turn interpreted and acted up by those subjects they subjectify. Neuroscientists are not without models to try to understand this process of what they might call 'feedback', but certainly lack the conceptual apparatus of social scientists to identify:

> cultural shifts in advance capitalist and highly medicalized societies through which citizenship and personhood are increasingly constituted by notions of individual choice and autonomy. (Choudhury et al, 2009, p 62)

What a geographical 'sense of space' can add here is a way to understand the spatial networks of relations which make up the subject – whether that be global processes of competitive pupils in a 'world class' education, national agendas for the cultivation of a sense of 'Britishness' among pupils, or more local imperatives for community and publicly-minded citizens. Each of these identities are actively performed in the coming together of political agendas, social, economic cultural and material contexts – through specific spatial arrangements, policy documentation, educational philosophies and dominant forms of knowledge and expertise, teacher-training practices, classroom activities, and cultural representations of behavioural norms. The key question here is to identify how such arrangements converge in the making of a particular imagination of the neuro-citizen, and to consider the political consequences of so doing.

For some, developments in neuroscience pose significant challenges to our conceptions of selfhood. For Maasen and Sutter (2007, p 3), brain-based explanations of voluntary action and self-reflection threaten the very notion of free will on which our ethical and political sensibilities are founded. They argue that neurosciences are part-and-parcel of a neoliberal imperative which seeks to produce self-governing and entrepreneurial subjects and the marketisation of all life. For Nikolas Rose (2007, p 82), the subordination of the (philosophy of) mind to the (sciences of the) brain achieved through neurochemical explanation renders behaviours outside of the norm as matters of biological defect; calculable, curable and correctable. This gives rise to a situation in which voluntary action, or free will itself, becomes an object of governmental intervention – through behavioural programmes, gene therapies and psychopharmacologies. In the world of education, this means so-called 'smart drugs' as well as treatment for all kinds of behavioural and attitudinal disorders which threaten the tranquillity of the classroom. In this scenario, anxiety is the norm; the neurotic subject is expected to manage their anxieties, and others (for example, parents, teachers, experts) are enrolled in supporting their management. This suggests a new form of what Engin Isin terms 'neuropolitics', which is 'marked by an increasing appeal to neurogenetic science and its associated neurochemical industries, drug production and the pharmaceutical–governmental–industrial complex that is concerned with production of tranquillity' (Isin, 2004, p 228).

## Conclusions

In a much lauded 'twenty-first-century learning environment', the school remains an enduring part of the lives of children and young people. Critical geographies of youth offer important insights on the life-worlds of children and young people as particular to that age group. In contrast, emerging critical geographies of education have taken a macro-level lens through which to examine the spatial politics of schooling. This chapter has outlined an inter-disciplinary approach which embraces both the particular specificities of constituting 'youth publics' via Citizenship Education, and the wider significance of pedagogical forms of power in contemporary practices of governing, illustrated through an account of the influence of neurosciences in education.

In exploring a range of spatial concepts available to critical geographers of education, the chapter has outlined the contribution of a Foucauldian spatial analytic to understanding contemporary educational policies and practices. This adds to the critical perspectives from which to approach the geographies of schooling, offering an appreciation of the complex political rationalities of educational practice and, in particular, the formation of identities and subject-positions of those young people to be educated. The chapter has explored how such rationalities push and pull in different directions – imagining the ideal, outward-looking and collectivised 'youth public' simultaneously with the ideal, individualised and internalised 'neuro-citizen'. Focusing on the school as a specific space in which certain confluences of power, knowledge and subjectivity become embedded, it is possible to demonstrate the wider significance of school-based practices such as Citizenship Education and neuroeducation for the setting of behavioural norms, the shaping of governable subjects and the re-articulation of political forms themselves.

## References

Aitken, S. (2001) *Geographies of young people: the morally contested spaces of identity,* London: Routledge.

Allen, J. (2003) *Lost geographies of power,* Oxford: Blackwell.

Ball, S.J. (1991) 'Power, conflict, micropolitics and all that!', in G. Walford (ed) *Doing educational research,* London: Routledge, pp 166-92.

Ball, S.J. (2003) 'The teacher's soul and the terrors of performativity', *Journal of Education Policy,* vol 18, no 2, pp 215-28.

Barnett, C. (1999) 'Culture, government and spatiality: reassessing the "foucault effect" in cultural-policy studies', *International Journal of Cultural Studies,* vol 2, pp 369–97.

Cacioppo, J.T., Berntson, G.G., Sheridan, J.F., and McClintock, M.K. (2000) 'Multilevel integrative analyses of human behavior: social neuroscience and the complementing nature of social and biological approaches', *Psychological Bulletin,* vol 126, pp 829-43.

Chiao, J.Y. (ed) (2009) *Cultural neuroscience: cultural influences on brain function,* Oxford: Elsevier.

Choudhury, S., Nagel, S.K. and Slaby, J. (2009) 'Critical neuroscience: linking neuroscience and society through critical practice', *BioSocieties,* vol 4, no 1, pp 61-77.

Crampton, J.W. and Elden, S. (eds) (2007) *Space, knowledge and power: Foucault and geography,* Aldershot: Ashgate Publishing Ltd.

DfE (Department for Education) (2010) *The importance of teaching: the Schools White Paper 2010,* Norwich: TSO.

Dommett, E.J., Devonshire, I.M., Plateau, C.R., Westwell, M.S. and Greenfield, S.A. (2010) 'From scientific theory to classroom practice', *The Neuroscientist OnlineFirst,* DOI 10.1177/1073858409356111, http://nro.sagepub.com/content/early/2010/04/29/1073858409356111.full.pdf+html.

Geake, J. and Cooper, P. (2003) 'Cognitive Neuroscience: implications for education?' *International Journal of Research & Method in Education,* vol 26, no 1, pp 7-20.

Gillborn, D. (2006) 'Citizenship education as placebo: 'standards', institutional racism and education policy', *Education, Citizenship and Social Justice,* vol 1, no 1, pp 83-104.

Giroux, H.A. (2004) 'Cultural studies and the politics of public pedagogy: making the political more pedagogical', *Parallax,* vol 10, no 2, pp 73–89.

Goswami, U. (2008) *State-of-science review: SR-E1, neuroscience in education*, The Government Office for Science, http://www.bis.gov.uk/assets/bispartners/foresight/docs/mental-capital/sr-e1_mcw.pdf

Gregory, D. (2000) 'Spatiality', in R.J. Johnson, D. Gregory, G. Pratt and M. Watts (eds) *The dictionary of human geography,* 4th edn, Oxford: Blackwell Publishers Ltd.

Gulson, K. and Symes, C. (2007) *Spatial theories of education: policy and geography matters,* London: Routledge.

Hannah, M. (1997) 'Space and the structuring of disciplinary power: an interpretive review', *Geografiska Annaler: Series B, Human Geography,* vol 79, no 3, pp 171–80.

HEFCE (Higher Education Funding Council for England) (2010) *Trends in young participation in higher education: core results for England,* http://www.hefce.ac.uk/pubs/hefce/2010/10_03/10_03.pdf.

Holloway, S. L. and Valentine, G. (2000) 'Spatiality and the new social studies of childhood', *Sociology,* vol 34, no 4, pp 763-83.

Holloway, S.L., Hubbard, P., Jöns, H. and Pimlott-Wilson, H. (2010) 'Geographies of education and the significance of children, youth and families', *Progress in Human Geography,* vol 34, no 5, pp 583-600.

Howard-Jones, P. (no date) *Neuroscience and education: issues and opportunities. A commentary by the teaching and learning research programme,* London: TLRP.

Huxley, M. (2006) 'Spatial rationalities: order, environment, evolution and government', *Social and Cultural Geography,* vol 7, no 5, pp 771-87.

Isin, E.F. (2004) 'The Neurotic Citizen', *Citizenship Studies,* vol 8, no 3, pp 217-35.

Kraftl, P. (2011) 'Utopian promise or burdensome responsibility? A critical analysis of the UK Government's Building Schools for the Future Policy', *Antipode,* doi: 10.1111/j.1467-8330.2011.00921.x

Latour, B. (2005) *Reassembling the social: an introduction to actor-network-theory,* Oxford: Oxford University Press.

Lefebvre, H. (1991) *The production of space,* Oxford: Blackwell.

Maasen, S. and Suttter, B. (eds) (2007) *On willing selves: neoliberal politics vis-à-vis the neuroscientific challenge,* Basingstoke: Palgrave Macmillan.

Mac An Ghaill, M. (1994) *The making of men: masculinities, sexualities and schooling,* Buckingham: Open University Press.

Malabou, C. (2008) *What should we do with our brain,* New York: Fordham University Press.

Matthews, H. (2003) 'Coming of age for children's geographies: inaugural editorial', *Children's Geographies,* vol 1, no 1, pp 3-5.

Milchman, A. and Rosenberg, A. (2007) 'The aesthetic and ascetic dimensions of an ethics of self-fashioning: Nietzsche and Foucault', *Parrhesia,* vol 2, pp 44-65.

Mitchell, K. (2006) 'Neoliberal governmentality in the European Union: education, training and technologies of citizenship', *Environment and Planning D: Society and Space,* vol 24, no 3, pp 389-407.

Mitchell, P.R. (2003) 'Spatial metaphor as spatial technique in the work of Michel Foucault', in L. Pinnell (ed) *Interruptions: essays in the poetics/politics of space,* North Cyprus, Turkey: Eastern Mediterranean University Press, pp 49-55.

Morgan, J. and Lambert, D. (2005) *Geography: teaching school subjects 11–19,* Abingdon: Routledge.

Newman, J. and Clarke, J. (2009) *Publics, politics and power: remaking the public in public services,* London: Sage.

O'Hear, A. (1999) 'Enter the new robot citizens', *Daily Mail,* 14 May 1999, p 12.

Olssen, M. (2004) 'Neoliberalism, globalization, democracy: challenges for education', *Globalization, Societies, and Education,* vol 2, no 2, pp 231-75.

Peters, M. (2001) 'National education policy constructions of the 'knowledge economy': towards a critique', *Journal of Educational Enquiry,* vol 2, no 1, pp 1-22.

Phillips, M. (2006) 'Lessons in being good citizens? No, propaganda that undermines British values', *Daily Mail,* 29 September 2006, p 14.

Philo, C. (2010) 'Foucault's Children', in L. Holt (ed) *Geographies of children, youth and families: an international perspective,* London: Routledge, pp 27-54.

Purdy, N. and Morrison, H. (2009) 'Cognitive neuroscience and education: unravelling the confusion', *Oxford Review of Education,* vol 35, no 1, pp 99-109.

Pykett, J. (2009) 'Personalization and de-schooling: uncommon trajectories in contemporary education policy', *Critical Social Policy,* vol 29, no 3, pp 374–97.

QCA (Qualifications and Curriculum Authority) (1998) *Education for citizenship and the teaching of democracy in schools: final report of the advisory group on citizenship,* London: QCA.

QCA (Qualifications and Curriculum Authority) (2007) *Citizenship. Programme of study for key stage 4,* London: QCA.

Robertson, S. (2010) '"Spatialising" the sociology of education: stand-points, entry-points, vantage-points', in M. Apple, S. Ball and L. Gandin (eds) *The Routledge international handbook of sociology of education,* Abingdon: Routledge, pp 15-26.

Rose, H. (2004) 'Consciousness and the limits of neurobiology', in D. Rees and S. Rose (eds) *The new brain sciences: perils and prospects,* Cambridge: Cambridge University Press, pp 59-70.

Rose, N. (1998) *Inventing our selves: psychology, power and personhood,* Cambridge: Cambridge University Press.

Rose, N. (2007) 'Governing the will in a neurochemical age', in S. Maasen and B. Suttter (eds) *On willing selves: neoliberal politics vis-à-vis the neuroscientific challenge,* Basingstoke: Palgrave Macmillan, pp 81-99.

Samuels, B.M. (2009) 'Can the differences between education and neuroscience be overcome by mind, brain, and education?', *Mind, Brain and Education,* vol 3, no 1, pp 45-55.

Thiem, C.H. (2009) 'Thinking through education: the geographies of contemporary educational restructuring', *Progress in Human Geography,* vol 33, no 3, pp 154-73.

Thrift, N. (2007) *Non-representational theory,* London: Routledge.

Tickly, L. (2003) 'Governmentality and the study of education policy in South Africa', *Journal of Education Policy,* vol 18, no 2, pp 109-33.

Tucker, F. and Matthews, M. (2001) '"They don't like girls hanging around there": conflicts over recreational space in rural Northamptonshire', *Area,* vol 33, no 2, pp 161-8.

Valentine, G. (1999) 'Being seen and heard? The ethical complexities of working with children and young people at home and at school', *Philosophy & Geography*, vol 2, no 2, pp 141–55.

Weller, S. (2007) *Teenagers' citizenship: experiences and education,* London: Routledge.

three

# Youth policy, neoliberalism and transnational governmentality: a case study of Lesotho and Malawi

*Nicola Ansell, Flora Hajdu, Elsbeth Robson, Lorraine van Blerk and Elodie Marandet*

## Introduction

Over the past few decades governments worldwide have developed youth policies, encompassing diverse measures to address the problems and potentials of their younger populations. Hitherto, studies of these policies have focused on differentiating the goals and target groups inscribed in different national policies and on the relationship between youth policies and national political agendas. However, youth policies have not emerged independently in diverse countries; inter-governmental organisations and international discourses are involved. In this chapter we explore the value of Foucault's concept of governmentality for understanding youth policies in this wider context. Notions of governmentality and biopower shed light on how policies perform as technologies of power, enabling states to exercise control over populations; and on the ways such technologies produce individual subjects that are valuable to neoliberal economies. It is increasingly recognised that in a neoliberal global order, governmentality is exercised not only by nation states but also transnationally, via networks of corporations, agencies and organisations. Through analysis of a UNESCO (2004) publication designed to guide youth policy development, and the recently-formulated youth policies of Malawi and Lesotho, we explore whether youth policies represent a form of transnational, neoliberal governmentality.

The chapter begins with an outline of the approaches adopted in previous research on youth policy, followed by an argument for adopting a lens of governmentality. The chapter then analyses the three documents, investigating whether and how they operate as technologies of power, produce neoliberal subjects, and their transnational construction. This exercise of power is far from all-encompassing, however, and the chapter concludes by emphasising the unevenness and incompleteness of the exercise of neoliberalising power through youth policies.

## Analysing youth policy

There exist relatively few transnational and comparative studies of youth policy, but certain aspects have been examined. Wallace and Bendit (2009) suggest policies differ in their philosophies of intervention (conception of youth; aim of intervention; problems associated with young people) and target groups (age groups; sub-groups of youth). (They also identify the organisation of the youth sector, but that is not a focus of this chapter.) We briefly outline these dimensions below.

Youth policies are strongly influenced by policy-makers' conceptualisations of youth. Where youth are characterised as a problem, policy focuses on unemployment, homelessness, AIDS, drug abuse and delinquency; where youth are viewed as a resource, education, training, participation and empowerment are emphasised (Zeldin, 2004; Wallace and Bendit, 2009). Even in the latter case, however, youth are generally seen as future leaders rather than current contributors to communities (Roger, 2008). In China, youth have historically been regarded in political and ideological terms (Ngai et al, 2001). Concepts of youth are also reflected in the age ranges targeted: some European youth policies apply to all from birth to 25 or 30; others exclude pre-teenagers (Wallace and Bendit, 2009). While some policies encompass youth broadly defined, others focus on 'at risk' youth (Bogenschneider and Gross, 2004).

Youth policies differ in their aims. Herrera (2006, p 1426) points out that policies 'intervene into the realm of young people's morals, behaviour and dispositions', besides social and economic arenas. Wallace and Bendit (2009) suggest that some policies aim primarily to enable young people to live independently, others emphasise political and social participation, while others seek to integrate young people into adult society. These emphases change over time, as exemplified in Timmerman's (2009) study of Dutch youth policy where a post-war focus on assimilation (to the existing social order) gave way in the 1960s to an emancipatory approach, focused on developing self-confident, self-controlled individuals. The ultimate purpose of participation-focused policies (pedagogic, that is advancing civic education, or allowing young people real influence) is often ambiguous (Laine and Gretschel, 2009).

While most youth policies focus ostensibly on young people's current or future needs, they also have wider objectives. Labour market requirements are often a driving force (Ngai et al, 2001). In post-apartheid South Africa, concern quickly shifted from the needs of marginalised youth to the needs of business and organised labour (Chisholm et al, 1997). The UK's New Labour government emphasised 'progressive competitiveness' through providing education, training and qualifications to attract inward investment, as well as minimising 'social exclusion' (Mizen, 2003).

While current analyses of youth policy identify dimensions of difference, they are less effective in explaining these differences. Some analysts recognise that youth policy is an exercise of power, serving social, economic and political purposes (Ngai et al, 2001; Mizen, 2003). Young people are tethered to political interests through inculcation of values and by using, for instance, youth participation as an outlet for grievances (Ngai et al, 2001). Youth policy that directs intense activity at young workers can divert attention from deeper questions about young people's claims on the resources that could transform their lives, and shift responsibility for poor educational outcomes, unemployment or low wages onto young people themselves (Mizen, 2003). Attention to the power relations underlying the production of youth policy is also needed, including financing and implementation (Karger and Stoesz, 2006). The next section of this chapter proposes an alternative approach to examining how power operates through youth policy.

## Governmentality and biopower as alternative lenses

The concepts of governmentality and biopower relate to ways in which diverse states (and other institutions) assert control through technologies of power based on different rationalities (Foucault, 2007). Sovereign power – highly centralised and exercised through violence by early European rulers – diminished in significance with the emergence of modern states exercising disciplinary power, a more dispersed form of power exercised through institutions and social practices via normalising discourses and the constant ordering, classification and minute supervision of individual bodies (Foucault, 1991). In the late twentieth century, a new technology of power gained prominence in the West. Governmentality is associated with the emergence of neoliberalism, the political doctrine that society should be organised around self-regulating markets with minimal political interference. Neoliberalism's espousal of freedom from direct political intervention encourages governmentality as an alternative exercise of power: a tool for the 'conduct of conduct' (Foucault, 1980, p 119) involving government of the self by the self.

Both disciplinary power and governmentality have operated in part through 'biopower', which refers to power over life. Whereas sovereign power was exercised over territories, biopower refers to states regulating and managing both individual bodies and entire populations (Foucault, 2008). Biopower is today the characteristic form of power of the neoliberal state, and functional to market capitalism through promoting agendas of choice, individual autonomy and a shift of risk from governments and corporations onto individuals. Through biopower, neoliberal subjects are produced as entrepreneurs of the self, in charge of optimising their use of human capital. Social risks are recoded as problems of self-care, as responsibility is shifted from society to the individual (Lemke, 2001). For Dean (2010), governmentality concerns the 'administration' of the collective body of society, and how society is regulated through the self-control of populations on a daily basis. State policies and practices, including moves toward localised and participatory decision-making (see Raco and Imrie, 2000), promote the production of self-governing subjects by fostering suitable behaviours.

Although in conceptualising governmentality and biopower Foucault did not explore geographical differences, space 'has always, in one sense or another, been right at the heart of his concerns' (Driver, 1985, p 425). Geographers have taken up Foucault's ideas to draw attention to variations not only over time in how states govern, but also 'the role of space in disciplining, fostering, managing and monitoring the conducts of individuals and the qualities of populations' (Huxley, 2007, p 185; see also Philo, 1992; Hannah, 2000; Eldon, 2007; Pykett, this volume, Chapter Two). Geographical applications extend to examining differences between contemporary states. Alatout (2006), for instance, distinguishes between Palestinian environmental narratives, built on sovereign-territorial view of power and Israeli narratives based on biopower which is focused more on population than territory. While Foucault's work has been accused of ethnocentrism (McNay, 1994), depicting a progression toward ever more sophisticated forms of power originating in the West (Li, 2009), geographers have applied the concept to non-Western spaces (for example, Corbridge et al, 2005). Moreover, increasingly governmentality has been used to explore relations between, as well as within, states.

In the analysis that follows, we use the concept of governmentality to explore the production of youth policies, focusing on the following three elements.

### (a) Youth policy as a technology of power

Governmentality is conceived as enabling a state to 'govern at a distance' (Murdoch and Ward, 1997, p 307). Despite (and enabling) an ostensible diminution of the state under neoliberalism, state power extends to regulate society beyond its direct control, through collecting and monitoring statistics (Murdoch and Ward, 1997) and other forms of surveillance (Brooks, 2008). Such techniques shape conduct and produce 'governable subjects' (Cupers, 2008). Youth policy might well be envisaged as a tool for monitoring and surveillance, and youth as a prime target to render 'governable'. Indeed, the concept of governmentality has been used to explore practices employed to shape youth. Schee and Baez (2001, p 33), for instance, investigate

'HIV/AIDS education as a method of neoliberal governmentality concerned with regulating the categories of health, risk, and disease in relation to youthful identities'.

## (b) The production of neoliberal subjects

A key objective of technologies of power exercised in relation to youth is the production of subjectivities that are amenable to a neoliberal politics and economy. In neoliberal states, training policies and programmes are oriented toward producing mobile, flexible and self-governing labourers rather than personal development (Mitchell, 2006). Numerous youth-focused policies and practices promote individualisation, personal responsibility and freedom of choice (Share and Strain, 2008). These practices are used to 'foster appropriate subjectivities and regulate troublesome behaviours' (Huxley, 2006, p 771) with 'technologies of the self', including socio-psychological interventions, deployed to control youth 'at risk' (Besley, 2010). The production of a neoliberal ethic of self also works to obscure the significance of structural inequalities by shifting the responsibility for success to individuals regardless of life-chances.

## (c) Transnational governmentality

Youth policies in Africa are not simply tools of sovereign states. Non-state actors, which also deploy technologies of power, are involved (Rose-Redwood, 2006; Garmany, 2010), employing discourses and practices similar to states in promoting their own agendas and contesting policy frameworks (Raco, 2003). Indeed, biopower is exercised at a spectrum of levels from the global through to individual self-management in interrelated and interdependent ways (Foucault, 2008).

Ferguson and Gupta (2002) suggest the sovereignty of many African states is severely impaired by transnational modes of government operating through agencies (such as the IMF), international corporations, and the outsourcing of state functions to NGOs. Fraser's (2009, p 169) concept of 'globalising governmentality' describes the dispersed, flexible and autonomous networks through which power circulates internationally. Without formal control over territories, and avoiding the stigma associated with violence, international development organisations are said to exercise influence by shaping the desires of their target populations (Li, 2009). By offering technical knowledge and techniques for measuring progress, development organisations depoliticise problems (Li, 2009) and render populations amenable to the ingress of capitalist production and consumption.

## Transnational governmentality? An analysis of three documents

Youth policy in Africa is partly a response to the growing political and demographic salience of youth. Africa has a youthful population with 20 per cent aged 15–24 years and a further 40 per cent under 15 years (United Nations, 2009). As Herrera (2006, p 1426) notes, there is 'mounting awareness of the potential roles of young people in forging more stable, democratic and economically prosperous societies. Conversely, when development goes awry, they can also represent forces of instability, radicalism and impoverishment.' African youth policies also reflect transnational influences. The UN has been encouraging the development of national youth policies for decades (United Nations, 1985) and numerous international organisations have produced guidelines (including AYCEOs, 2000; ICNYP, 2002; GTZ, 2005; USAID, 2010). Moreover, policy-making takes place in a neoliberal international environment; youth policy is arguably part of the way in which international organisations are contributing to the neoliberalisation of African countries, a more subtle successor of the structural adjustment programmes and aid conditionality that have for decades been deployed to persuade the governments of Lesotho and Malawi and other African countries to liberalise their economies in exchange for debt rescheduling and international aid.

Below we examine one international guidance document and two national policies. We refer to various versions and drafts of the policies, and interviews undertaken in Malawi and Lesotho in 2007 and 2008 with individuals from youth ministries and other organisations. The documents and interview transcripts were subjected to critical discourse analysis (Kress, 1990; see also this volume, Chapter One), being read first in relation to themes identified in youth policy research and subsequently in relation to governmentality.

### (a) UNESCO (2004) Empowering youth through national policies

UNESCO has been one of the key bodies supporting the development of youth policies globally, and *Empowering youth through national policies* (2004) is addressed to national decision-makers wishing to formulate or to evaluate national youth policies. Youth are defined as 'a specific social category' (p 6) that is problematic and vulnerable, rather than a mere resource. Youth policy is advocated as a response to the challenges of youth, focusing on their felt needs and concerns, their mobilisation and empowerment, both in the present and the future. On occasion the publication suggests wider benefits, noting for instance that 'improvements in the quality of life of youth will most certainly translate into improvements in the quality of life of society as a whole' (p 13). In terms of target groups, countries are recommended to adopt the UN definitions of youth (aged 15–24 years) and young people (aged 10–19 years), and focus particularly on vulnerable groups.

The advocacy of a universal definition of youth highlights a tension in the guidelines. Governmentality is understood to secure control through technologies of self-government: UNESCO's (2004) guidance to governments in some ways exemplifies this. The publication claims not to be a rigid template for youth policy; it advocates policy formulation that is consultative and involves youth participation. The message is that governments need to act responsibly and take charge of their own policies. Yet phrases like 'must' and 'it is essential to' pepper the report, advising for instance that 'all national youth policies must address the gender/rural-urban/minority-majority divide' (p 22). While the publication suggests flexibility, it tightly prescribes the policy process and much of the content. Lacking direct control over governments, authority is generated through repeated reference to reports and declarations from intergovernmental agencies (for example, *World programme of action for youth to the year 2000 and beyond* (UN, 1997); *World youth report* (UN, 2003)) and international alliances of civil society organisations (for example, AYCEOs, 2000).

Governmentality operates at multiple levels. The same technologies of power that UNESCO employs in relation to governments, it advises governments to deploy in relation to their youthful populations. While not explicitly advocating producing economic agents, the publication represents youth policy as a means of producing particular kinds of subjects. It quotes AYCEOs (2000, p 3): 'Any long-term national youth policy should have a clear, consensus-based vision of the kind of men and women for tomorrow's world needs'. Although the suggestion is that this vision should be nationally-determined, the AYCEOs publication's subtitle, 'Towards an autonomous, supportive, responsible and committed youth' proclaims its advocacy of neoliberal subjecthood. Autonomy and responsibility are also highlighted in the UNESCO report. Moreover, in keeping with governmentality operating through self-management, policy-makers are advised of the need for 'effective strategies able to help young people to make the right choices' (p 6).

The publication strongly advocates youth participation, arguing for working *with* young people, not *for* them and that they should participate in all stages of youth policy formulation, implementation, monitoring and evaluation (although not the delineation of strategic goals). Participation is recommended on the basis that giving young people responsibility makes them responsible at a younger age and that participation increases self-reliance, reiterating hallmark governmentality themes of responsibility for the self and self-reliance.

Apart from advocating the production of autonomous, responsible subjects, the document supports a neoliberal agenda in other ways. It advises consultation with civil society and NGOs, and for NGOs, the private sector and local agencies to be involved in implementation. Furthermore, it recommends governments choose a non-partisan person to lead the development and consultation process, reinforcing the view of youth policy as apolitical, and supportive of a neoliberal approach based on technical rather than transparently political intervention. This publication may thus be understood to enact transnational governmentality, aiming at producing particular self-regulated performances by governments and in turn producing policies and subjects oriented to a neoliberal global order. The outcomes are explored further below through analysis of two national youth policies.

### (b) Republic of Malawi (2011) National youth policy

Malawi's *National youth policy* represents young people as vulnerable and as objects of concern, but emphatically also as a resource. The focus is on their future lives and opportunities, rather than the present. The policy's 'mission' is 'to create an enabling environment for all young people to develop to their full potential in order to contribute significantly to personal and national development' (p 3). Youth is defined as 'a definitive social entity' (echoing UNESCO, 2004), comprising persons aged 10–29 years (broadened from 14–25 in the 1996 policy) and priority target groups identified include orphans, youth with disabilities, youth living with HIV, young people on the street, youth in conflict with the law, unemployed youth and teenage mothers.

Policy development involved transnational influences. The first national youth policy, adopted in 1996, was supported by UNICEF, UNFPS, DANIDA, the Commonwealth Youth Programme and UNESCO. After a false start in 2001, a review process began in 2004, funded by UNFPA and UNICEF. A consultant (a Malawian UNESCO employee) produced the first revised draft in 2007. Interestingly, the current (2011) version is considerably more conservative than the 2007 draft. The policy is contextualised in relation to national and international benchmarks and the revision (now awaiting final approval from Malawi's Office of the President and Cabinet) introduces language from the UNESCO publication ('definitive social entity', 'youth profile', 'mainstreaming'). The Principal Youth Officer at the Ministry of Youth Development and Sports conceded that the funding organisations played a role in shaping the policy "because they are professionals in the areas of young people ... They had quite an influence on the policy, but not negatively".[1]

The policy is explicit about its ambition to produce individuals useful to the economy. The foreword emphasises youth as 'a vast human resource potential' (p iii) and the 'vision' is of 'an educated, healthy, well trained, vibrant and productive young people' (p 3). Tapping this resource will be achieved by 'promot[ing] a sense of individual responsibility' (p 3) and through self-development and participation. The policy lists at length young people's responsibilities (paired with a shorter list of their rights) and outlines in detail adults' roles towards youth. The onus is thus on individual young people (and adults in their lives) to ensure they become appropriate subjects.

The policy's orientation to neoliberal 'human resource development' (p 8) is apparent in strategies for education ('an important ingredient towards economic growth and development' (p 8)) and health ('to enjoy a health status that enables them to lead an economically and socially productive life' (p 10)). Even the goal for 'youth participation and leadership' is '[t]o ensure that youth meaningfully participate in the social, economic and political life of the nation and contribute to growth and development of the country' (p 13). Biopower is also apparent, particularly in relation to health, where statements focus on changing behaviour: promoting abstinence and faithfulness, life skills, later marriage and childbearing. The previous policy's concern about population growth is replaced by a commitment to providing information to enable choice regarding childbearing, again emphasising individual choice and responsibility, although this is greatly diminished between the 2007 and 2010 drafts.

Beyond shaping subjectivities, like the UNESCO guidelines, Malawi's youth policy promotes a neoliberal agenda in other ways. It aims to influence both public and private sectors and the 2007 draft indicated a commitment to liberalising the education system to allow more private sector participation. It incorporates an extensive table outlining targets for monitoring and evaluating implementation. Interestingly, the impetus for this came from Malawi's Office of the President and Cabinet, not from the funders. The indicators, baselines and targets might be thought to manifest governmentality, but they are often incoherent, they no longer relate directly to statements in the main policy document, much baseline data is missing, targets are unrealistic and timeframes are poorly specified. The table thus seems more a tokenistic representation of neoliberal governance than a mechanism of control.

The policy does not wholeheartedly serve the agenda advanced in UNESCO (2004) or unequivocally inscribe governmentality. The Principal Youth Officer asserted that the policy was not entirely determined by the review's funders:

> "… at the end of the day I don't think those development partners who assisted us shaped the policy because … we were able to make changes as we saw fit. As we knew issues that are coming from the people and if we don't address those issues our people, especially young people, will not own the policy."

He gave the example of the age definition of youth used in the policy to illustrate:

> "Our partners insisted that the age limit should be that of 25 … But when we consulted the youth they were talking about 30 some 35 … by the age of 25 most of the youth are still dependent on their parents and guardians; very few are employed by someone else. So why should we say that one is no longer youth when he/she still needs the support of services from government and the parents? We extended the age from 25 to 29 so most of these partners do not know that the age is 29. They still think the age is 25 because the last time we discussed with them it was 25."

Many internal inconsistencies, probably reflecting the involvement of diverse actors in the policy process, limit the policy's expression of (transnational) governmentality. Some sections contain long lists – greatly augmenting the previous version – which suggest incorporation of diverse ideas generated through the consultation process. These are embedded in often contradictory moral frameworks and not all align with a neoliberal agenda. Thus the 'Principles and Values' section includes involvement in decision-making, self-development, youth participation and pursuit of assertiveness, but also respect for elders and cultural values, promotion of national unity, obedience, loyalty and patriotism. Another anomaly is that while the policy generally emphasises empowerment, participation and involvement in development rather than provision for youth, the 'rights of the youth' section has been revised to replace mainly civil rights with socioeconomic rights, emphasising access to good health, quality education, social and economic services and gainful employment (derived from the United Nations *Convention on the rights of the child* (1989)).

Irrespective of inconsistencies, the policy's likely influence on young people's lives is limited. The 'responsibilities of the youth' or 'role of adults towards the youth' (the areas where Malawian voices are most evident) are clearly unenforceable. Moreover, the implementation plan reads as a wish list, with no mechanism to secure compliance. The Ministry of Youth and Sports Development is not powerful, and the aim to 'guide the allocation of resources' (p 4) for young people, rather than actually to mobilise resources is telling.

### (c) Government of Lesotho (2002) The national youth policy for Lesotho

Like the Malawian policy, Lesotho's National Youth Policy describes youth as a 'definitive social group', but it expresses more concern with young people's current (and future) wellbeing. The policy begins by describing youth as 'an essential human resource' but quickly moves on to the problems they confront. The tone of the policy is inconsistent: in places very positive about youth, in others portraying them as deviant, with a tendency 'to become delinquents, alcoholics and drug abusers, who engage in criminal activities' (p 7). Youth are also represented as a burden (population growth having increased their numbers). The explicit goal is to promote dignity and self-esteem among youth (ironic, given how it describes them elsewhere), ensure their well-being and accelerate their participation in society as 'healthy, active and productive citizens' (p 11). Youth are defined as persons between 15 and 35 (expanded from 15–25 in the 1998 draft) and divided into overlapping categories which encompass all youth.

The policy is represented as domestically-produced rather than an outcome of transnational processes. The current policy (Lesotho's first) arose from a 1995 National Youth Conference and also reflects consultation from youth policies from Commonwealth countries and beyond. Representatives of youth organisations also contributed. As in Malawi, a consultant was hired – in this case a local. Following consultations and revisions, the policy was approved in 2002. Unlike the Malawian document, there are no references to external conventions or declarations.

In contrast to Malawi's policy, the aspirations for youth are not confined to productivity, economic growth and individualisation. Human development is emphasised, which includes moral, spiritual, intellectual and social aspects. Rather than individualisation, the policy aims to develop a sense of belonging. Other elements of neoliberal subjectivity are, however, highlighted. Youth are understood to 'strive to be independent in a society which treats them as dependents' (p 7). The policy aims for 'development of a sense of self-esteem and self-reliance' (p 14). Strategies are geared to 'enhancing the integration of the youth into the socio-political development of the country' (p 14), mainly by encouraging youth to participate and providing opportunities. The policy declares that it is 'incumbent on youth, that they take advantage of all these opportunities' (p 1), again making them responsible for their own futures.

Economic productivity occasionally features, as in the vision of producing 'healthy, active and productive citizens' (p 11). However, despite some emphasis on the supply of suitable labour to the market, and enabling youth to compete through, for instance, the 'prioritisation of business training' (p 12), the policy acknowledges the challenge of creating employment and speaks of young people's 'right to work' (p 12). While youth 'problems' are primarily associated with technological changes and shifting values, some attention is given to structural contexts. Lesotho's youth policy, then, does not express unequivocally global neoliberal interests. Like Malawi's policy, it is inconsistent, in this case between constructive assessments of youth matched with measured policy strategies, and assessments of the 'problem' of youth which resort to tabloid-style hyperbole. The section on health, for instance, declares that with 'adolescent pregnancies, the end results are illegal, unplanned families and child abuse. All these results always lead to suicides, stress and trauma' (p 8). The statement that 'the youth feel more comfortable and at home with the wrong social groups and friends' (p 8) suggests a classification of youth into 'good' and 'bad' categories, and implies the latter fall outside the policy's ambit.

The policy is highly critical of 'foreign negative influences' (p 9). Child rights discourse is often invoked as foreign interference in African child-rearing traditions. The policy complains: 'in cases where disciplining a child is regarded as child abuse, parents can no longer discipline their children because of the fear of being prosecuted' (p 9). Directly critiquing neoliberal subjectification, the policy bemoans how foreign influence results in 'too much freedom' (p 9) for children, and highlights the problem of 'moving away from communal responsibility' (p 9). This section, framed very differently from the Malawi policy, suggests minimal direct international influence over at least parts of the policy. Indeed, the Lesotho policy arguably draws more heavily on a disciplining economy of power rather than governmentality through, for instance, the labelling of youth as certain 'types' associated with behaviours constructed as problematic.

## Conclusions

The youth policies of Malawi and Lesotho in part perform transnational governmentality. They clearly reflect the aspiration of national governments and their 'development partners' to control youth (for the nation) as much as to assist them, and to produce neoliberal subjects to serve national and international economies. The extent to which each policy manifests governmentality may reflect the degree of international influence, Malawi being more tightly tied to transnational networks in the construction of policy than Lesotho. Thus the Malawi policy, produced with UN support, both closely reflects neoliberal interests and inscribes governmentality as the means to entrench these. In Lesotho, by contrast, strong 'disciplining' language can be more easily justified by the state.

Neither youth policy examined is, however, a pure and coherent manifestation of governmentality. The internal inconsistencies reflect a wider tendency for youth policies to be fragmented, contradictory and theoretically inconsistent (Bogenschneider and Gross, 2004; Zeldin, 2004). Two explanations are probable. First, youth policy is seldom prioritised by governments (Wallace and Bendit, 2009), or even by youth themselves, and the outcomes are typically limited. This perhaps explains why the Malawi government, despite resisting international neoliberal agendas in other policy areas, has been unconcerned about neoliberal influence on youth policy. While the lives of young Africans are impacted in many ways by neoliberalism, youth policies may play only a minor role in this.

Second, youth policies are not simply outcomes of coherent national or international agendas. The UNESCO guidelines, while clearly concerned with producing neoliberal subjects, are not themselves wholly consistent or market-oriented. Governments respond to many influences, even youth themselves, who are at times able to exercise considerable influence (Zeilig, 2008). The involvement of diverse individuals and organisations in producing the two policies is apparent from the texts. Those involved have different agendas and views as to what is best for young people (Yohalem et al, 2006). This is not to suppose a power-neutral pluralistic policy process, but ideas creep into policies that do not support a neoliberal future. Indeed, youth policies serve some positive functions, bringing young people onto the political agenda and addressing some of their concerns, particularly around access to livelihoods. Thus, youth policy may indeed be understood as a form of transnational governmentality, albeit a very uneven one, and the spatial matrix through which youth policy is produced is porous, allowing some space for resistance, critique and alternative youth policies and practices to emerge.

**Notes**

[1] Interview, December 2007.

[2] The United Nations *Convention on the rights of the child* (UN, 1989) is often interpreted as prohibiting the use of corporal punishment. Moreover, dependence on donor funding meant Lesotho's NGO Coalition on the Rights of the Child felt compelled to accept funds to work on corporal punishment, even though this was not its top priority (Interview, NGOC, April 2008).

**References**

Alatout, S. (2006) 'Towards a bio-territorial conception of power: territory, population, and environmental narratives in Palestine and Israel', *Political Geography,* vol 25, no 6, pp 601-21.

AYCEOs (Alliance of Youth Chief Executive Officers) (2000) *National youth policies: a working document from the point of view of 'non-formal education' youth organisations – towards an autonomous, supportive, responsible and committed youth,* Chief Executive Officers of World Alliance of Young Men's Christian Associations, World Young Women's Christian Association, World Organisation of the Scout Movement, World Association of Girl Guides and Girl Scouts, International Federation of Red Cross and Red Crescent Societies and the International Award Association.

Besley, T.A.C. (2010) 'Governmentality of youth: managing risky subjects', *Policy Futures in Education,* vol 8, no 5, pp 528-47.

Bogenschneider, K. and Gross, E. (2004) 'From ivory tower to state house: how youth theory can inform youth policy making', *Family Relations,* vol 53, no 1, pp 19-25.

Brooks, R. (2008) 'Young people and political participation: an analysis of European Union policies', *Sociological Research Online,* vol 14, no 1.

Chisholm, L., Harrison, C. and Motala, S. (1997) 'Youth policies, programmes and priorities in South Africa: 1990–1995', *International Journal of Educational Development,* vol 17, no 2, pp 215-25.

Corbridge, S., Williams, G., Srivastava, M. and Véron, R. (2005) *Seeing the state: governance and governmentality in India,* Cambridge: Cambridge University Press.

Cupers, K. (2008) 'Governing through nature: camps and youth movements in interwar Germany and the United States', *Cultural Geographies,* vol 15, no 2, pp 173-205.

Dean, M. (2010) *Governmentality: power and rule in modern society* (2nd edn), London: Sage.

Driver, F. (1985) 'Power, space, and the body: a critical assessment of Foucault's Discipline and Punish', *Environment and Planning D: Society and Space,* vol 3, pp 425-46.

Eldon, S. (2007) 'Governmentality, calculation, territory', *Environment and Planning D: Society and Space,* vol 25, pp 562-80.

Ferguson, J. and Gupta, A. (2002) 'Spatializing states: toward an ethnography of neoliberal governmentality', *American Ethnologist,* vol 29, no 4, pp 981-1002.

Foucault, M. (1980) *Power/knowledge,* Brighton: Harvester.

Foucault, M. (1991) *Discipline and punish: the birth of the prison,* London: Penguin.

Foucault, M. (2007) *Security, territory, population: lectures at the Collège de France, 1977-78,* Basingstoke: Palgrave Macmillan.

Foucault, M. (2008) *The birth of biopolitics: lectures at the Collège de France, 1978–79,* Basingstoke: Palgrave Macmillan.

Fraser, N. (2009) *Scales of justice: reimagining political space in a globalizing world,* New York: Columbia University Press.

Garmany, J. (2010) 'The embodied state: governmentality in a Brazilian favela', *Social and Cultural Geography,* vol 10, no 7, pp 721-39.

Government of Lesotho (2002) *The national youth policy for Lesotho,* Maseru: Ministry of Gender and Youth, Sport and Recreation.

GTZ (Deutsche Gesellschaft für Technische Zusammenarbeit) (2005) *Comparative analysis of national youth policies,* Eschborn: Deutsche Gesellschaft für Technische Zusammenarbeit.

Hannah, M. (2000) *Governmentality and the mastery of territory in nineteenth-century America,* Cambridge: Cambridge University Press.

Herrera, L. (2006) 'What's new about youth?', *Development and Change,* vol 37, no 6, pp 1425-34.

Huxley, M. (2006) 'Spatial rationalities: order, environment, evolution and government' ['Les rationalités spatiales: ordre, environnement, évolution et gouvernement'], *Social and Cultural Geography,* vol 7, no 5, pp 771-87.

Huxley, M. (2007) 'Geographies of governmentality', in J.W. Crampton and S. Elden (eds) *Space, knowledge and power: Foucault and geography,* Aldershot: Ashgate.

ICNYP (International Council on National Youth Policy) (2002) *Training manual on the fundamentals of a national youth policy,* International Council on National Youth Policy.

Karger, H. and Stoesz, D. (2006) *American social welfare policy: a pluralist approach,* Boston: Pearson Education.

Kress, G. (1990) 'Critical discourse analysis', *Annual Review of Applied Linguistics,* vol 11, pp 84-99.

Laine, S. and Gretschel, A. (2009) 'Whose arena is the EU youth policy? Young participants' involvement and influence in the EU youth policy from their own points of view: case of the EU Presidency Youth Event in Hyvinkää, Finland', *Young,* vol 17, no 2, pp 191-215.

Lemke, T. (2001) 'The birth of bio-politics: Michael Foucault's lectures at the Collège de France on neo-liberal governmentality', *Economy and Society,* vol 30, no 2, pp 190-207.

Li, T.M. (2009) 'The law of the project: government and "good governance" at the World Bank in Indonesia', in F. von Benda-Beckmann, K. von Benda-Beckmann and J. Eckert (eds) *Rules of law and laws of ruling,* Farnham: Ashgate.

McNay, L. (1994) *Foucault: a critical introduction,* Cambridge: Polity.

Mitchell, K. (2006) 'Neoliberal governmentality in the European Union: education, training, and technologies of citizenship', *Environment and Planning D: Society and Space,* vol 24, no 3, pp 389-407.

Mizen, P. (2003) 'The best days of your life? Youth, policy and Blair's New Labour', *Critical Social Policy,* vol 23, no 4, pp 453-76.

Murdoch, J. and Ward, N. (1997) 'Governmentality and territoriality: the statistical manufacture of Britain's "national farm"', *Political Geography,* vol 16, no 4, pp 307-24.

Ngai, N.-F., Cheung, C.-K., Li, C.-K. (2001) 'China's youth policy formulation and youth participation', *Children and Youth Services Review,* vol 23, no 8, pp 651-69.

Philo, C. (1992) 'Foucault's geography', *Environment and Planning D: Society and Space,* vol 10, no 2, pp 137-61.

Raco, M. (2003) 'Governmentality, subject-building, and the discourses and practices of devolution in the UK', *Transactions of the Institute of British Geographers,* vol 28, no 1, pp 75-95.

Raco, M. and Imrie, R. (2000) 'Governmentality and rights and responsibilities in urban policy', *Environment and Planning A,* vol 32, no 12, pp 2187-204.

Republic of Malawi (2011) *National youth policy,* Lilongwe: Ministry of Youth Development and Sports.

Roger, C. (2008) 'Youth participation in society', *Asia Europe Journal,* vol 5, pp 469-77.

Rose-Redwood, R.S. (2006) 'Governmentality, geography, and the geo-coded world', *Progress in Human Geography,* vol 30, no 4, pp 469-86.

Schee, C.V. and Baez, B. (2001) 'HIV/AIDS education in schools: the "unassembled" youth as a curricular project', *Discourse,* vol 30, no 1, pp 33–46.

Share, M. and Strain, M. (2008) 'Making schools and young people responsible: a critical analysis of Ireland's obesity strategy', *Health and Social Care in the Community,* vol 16, no 3, pp 234-43.

Timmerman, G (2009) 'Youth policy and participation: an analysis of pedagogical ideals in municipal youth policy in the Netherlands', *Children and Youth Services Review,* vol 31, pp 572-6.

UNESCO (United Nations Educational, Scientific and Cultural Organisation) (2004) *Empowering youth through national policies,* Paris: Section for Youth of the Bureau of Strategic Planning, UNESCO.

UN (United Nations) (1985) *National youth policies in developing countries,* United Nations.

UN (United Nations) (1989) *Convention on the rights of the child,* New York: United Nations.

UN (United Nations) (1997) *World programme of action for youth to the year 2000 and beyond,* New York: United Nations, http://www.un.org/events/youth98/backinfo/ywpa2000.htm.

UN (United Nations) (2003) *World youth report: the global situation of young people,* New York: UN Publications.

UN (United Nations) (2009) *World population prospects. The 2008 revision: highlights,* New York: Population Division of the Department of Economic and Social Affairs of the United Nations Secretariat.

USAID (United States Agency for International Development) (2010) *Youth-policy.com,* http://www.youth-policy.com/index.cfm?page=index.

Wallace, C. and Bendit, R. (2009) 'Youth policies in Europe: towards a classification of different tendencies in youth policies in the European Union', *Perspectives on European Politics and Society,* vol 10, no 3, pp 441-58.

Yohalem, N., Wilson-Ahlstrom, A., Ferber, T. and Gaines, E. (2006) 'Supporting older youth: what's policy got to do with it?', *New Directions for Youth Development,* vol 111, pp 117-29.

Zeilig, L. (2008) *Revolt and protest: student politics and activism in Sub-Saharan Africa*, London: I.B. Tauris.

Zeldin, S. (2004) 'Preventing youth violence through the promotion of community engagement and membership', *Journal of Community Psychology*, vol 32, no 5, pp 623-41.

four

# 'Brighter futures, greener lives': children and young people in UK sustainable development policy

*Bethan Evans and Emma-Jay Honeyford*

## Introduction

In recent years, commentators have noted an increased focus on childhood in response to global fears of environmental degradation (Katz, 2008). This is part of a 'generalising tendency to futurity' (Horton and Kraftl, 2006, p 83) in policy engagements with children and young people (Mizen, 2003; Williams, 2004) evident across a range of policy contexts including child poverty (Prout, 2000), school design (Kraftl, 2011), obesity (Evans and Colls, 2009; 2011; Evans, 2010), youth criminal justice (Ruddick, 2006), childhood hope (Kraftl, 2008), aspiration and higher education widening participation policy (Brown, this volume, Chapter Six), and environmental and economic uncertainty (Katz, 2008). In the case of environmental policy, the 'futurity' which characterises such policy interactions with childhood and youth is inherent to an understanding of sustainable development as: 'Development that meets the needs of the present without compromising the ability of future generations to meet their own needs' (World Commission on Environment and Development, 1987, cited by Noorman and Uiterkamp, 1998, p 3). This 'futurity' presents multiple difficulties, apparent across diverse policy arenas and characteristic of attempts to govern the *future* (Anderson, 2010). These difficulties stem from the fact that pre-emptive and anticipatory policy is, as Anderson (2010, p 7) argues, faced with a paradox: how to navigate the 'passage between ontological modes' required to make 'a specific future present' and render that future actionable when 'any specific future – whether present in a climate change model or through a barely sensed apprehension about swine flu – is suspended between a here and now and an elsewhen or elsewhere'. This is where, as Evans (2010, p 34) argues, children, young people, youth and childhood become important since children and young people 'similarly traverse "ontological modes", existing simultaneously as children and young people *now* and adults not-yet-become' (original emphasis; see also Uprichard, 2008). Yet this positions

61

children and young people precariously within anticipatory and pre-emptive policy because, as children's geographers working across a range of different policy contexts have noted, the temporal logics which position children and young people as future adults allow an oversight of children's and young people's rights in the present (Ruddick, 2006; see also Katz, 2008; Evans, 2010; Evans and Colls, 2011).

The uncertainty that characterises anticipatory policy (Anderson, 2010) is writ large in sustainable development policy. Sustainable development remains a contested and complex term, with what has been termed the 'environmental paradox' – that is the mismatch between what is demanded of the earth in terms of future development and what the earth can provide in terms of finite resources (Williams and Millington, 2004) – a core cause of tension. Attempts to explain the lack of agreement over definitions of sustainable development, and hence the lack of agreement on appropriate policy have emphasised the plurality of concerns which such a broad term encompasses. While the plurality of voices and concerns covered by sustainable development is important, analysing sustainable development as a pre-emptive policy by exploring the different approaches to the future, and the different ways in which sustainable development policy attempts to traverse the ontological impasse between present action and future outcome, stands to make an important contribution to current debate about the 'diverse and parallel paths' (Raco, 2005, p 324) taken by sustainable development policies. Considering the ways in which different futures are imagined and acted on within sustainable development policy (and across other policy domains which are future-focused) is therefore important in order to fully appreciate the implications of such policies for social justice and is essential for any equality impact assessment. In particular, attention to futurity makes evident the need for questions of equality to take into account the relative rights of present and future subjects, to question how and by whom desired-for futures are imagined and whether those responsibilised for achieving such futures are able to fully participate in and challenge both the shape of, and routes to, such desired-for-futures (Kraftl, 2011).

In this chapter we do this by analysing the ways in which young people are positioned in sustainable development policy. Given the emphasis on the future in policy engagements with young people, analysing the position of young people in sustainable development policy provides a lens through which to explore the temporal logics governing such policy. In keeping with the aims of this book, we also focus on children and young people to draw attention to some of the implications of particular orientations to the future in contemporary policy for children and young people (Evans and Colls, 2011) since, as Mayall (2006, p 9) argues, 'policy on children is, to some extent, a reflection of the attitudes and values held about children and childhood in society as a whole'.

Our subsequent discussion is divided into the following four sections: first, drawing on recent work in geography we provide a brief outline of key debates concerning childhood/youth and sustainable development in relation to future-focused policy. We then present some background to the policy on which we base our discussion and situate this within broader policy concerning Education for Sustainable Development (ESD). We then present analysis of the document *Brighter futures, greener lives* (DCSF, 2008) before finally concluding.

## Childhood/youth, sustainable development and the future

In this section we provide a review of key debates in geography concerning children and youth and sustainable development in relation to future-oriented policy. In particular, two points of contention are apparent in both bodies of work: first, questions of social justice, participation and rights in relation to policy, and second, the neoliberalisation of contemporary policy and the role of capitalist economic systems in 'planned for' futures.

### Children, youth and the 'future'

There is a long history within Children's Geographies of problematising the ways in which children and young people are positioned as 'adults in the making rather than children in the state of being' (Holloway and Valentine, 2000, p 5). There is a wealth of work which notes the implications of this positioning of children and young people as incomplete subjects for their rights and participation (Mayall, 2006). Following the New Social Studies of Childhood (NSSC), important work has countered this by demonstrating the multiple ways in which children and young people are active in shaping their lives and the lives of those around them (Holloway and Valentine, 2000). More recent work (see Brown, this volume, Chapter Six; Mizen, 2003; Williams, 2004; Ruddick, 2006; Katz, 2008; Kraftl, 2008; 2011; Evans, 2010; Evans and Colls, 2011) has furthered this critique, through exploring the anticipatory logics which underpin the association of childhood and youth with the future. This work has argued that, informed by models of child development, dominant Western conceptualisations of childhood and youth are imbued with anticipatory logics positioning children and young people as 'the literal embodiment of change over time' (James, 2000, p 23). These deterministic logics, epitomised in the growth curves used to plot, predict, and govern children's growth in relation to predicted health outcomes (see Evans and Colls, 2009; 2011; Evans, 2010), have meant that children and young people have been a core target for policy which has attempted to shape the future across a range of different arenas.

Yet children are present in these interventions not as children, but as traces of the adults they will become (Evans, 2010). As such, Ruddick (2006; 2007a; 2007b) argues that children present the limit condition to neoliberal notions of subjecthood, never able to be considered full 'subjects' since, as Katz (2008, p 7) explains 'childhood defines an always-incomplete state; when it is complete – if it ever is – it is no longer childhood'. Thus, rather than simply demonstrating that children are agents, there is a necessity to challenge the adult-centric concept of subjecthood that children and young people are being measured against and the implications of developmental, anticipatory logics for young people's rights in relation to policy (Ruddick, 2006).

This is particularly important in relation to young people's position in pre-emptive policy because there is the potential for their rights to be overlooked through a focus on the rights of the future adult (see Williams, 2004). Since the aim of anticipatory policy is to create a desired future through action in the present, there is a temporal delay in benefits while costs may be felt in the present. Action which has a detrimental short-term effect on children's and young people's lives may therefore be justified with reference to the benefits to future adults (Evans and Colls, 2011). Thus, in relation to attempts to reduce child poverty in the UK, Prout (2000, p 305) argues that 'the central focus is on the better adult lives that will, it is predicted, emerge from reducing child poverty … it is not on the better lives that children will lead as children' (see also Lister, 2003; Williams, 2004; Katz, 2008; Evans, 2010; Evans and Colls, 2011). This raises important ethical questions about social justice in policy which targets young people as future-adults. Moreover, the anticipatory nature of such policy also exacerbates questions of social justice and equity between different young people. As Anderson (2010, p 4) explains, 'anticipatory action is … imbricated with the plurality of power relations that make up contemporary democracies'. Because pre-emptive or anticipatory policy revolves around an anticipated dystopia (because of the effects of climate change, terrorism, obesity, swine flu and so on) it is assumed that the future must 'radically differ from the here and now' (Anderson, 2010, p 4). Thus, 'any type of anticipatory action will only provide relief, or promise to provide relief, to a valued life, not necessarily all of life. Certain lives may have to be abandoned, damaged or destroyed in order to protect, save or care for life'.

Here, debates about the neoliberalisation of contemporary policy and the inequity present within capitalist economies is important in considering the form of the hoped-for-futures which pre-emptive and anticipatory policy aims to create and the implications of this for the forms of youth which are thought to lead to the best adult outcomes. In this context, Katz (2008) argues that the continued dominance of capitalist systems is leading to a global (but often classed) commodification of childhood whereby parents compete to give their children an 'edge' by investing in their future through the right school, extra-curricular classes, and so on. Thus, she argues that 'the child as commodity is niche-marketed to secure success in the insecure future' with important implications for social justice and equity in children's and young people's experiences of childhood and youth and future prospects (p 10; see also Brown, this volume, Chapter Six).

## Sustainable futures

Similar debates circulate around sustainable development policy. Concerns about the commodification of childhood resonate with concerns about the role of market forces and the commodification of the 'environment' in sustainable development policy (Raco, 2005). This is part of a broader debate within which multiple interpretations of 'sustainable development' are proposed. Two broad, distinct approaches have been referred to by some theorists as 'strong sustainability' and 'weak sustainability', with 'strong sustainability' referring to approaches which associate an intrinsic value to nature and conceptualise the human relationship with 'nature' as egalitarian (Stern et al, 1993) and 'weak sustainability' used to refer to 'anthropocentric' and 'techno-centric' approaches (Kahn, 1999) where technological development is seen as the means to ensure life continues in a sustainable way without significant disruption. These two broad approaches hide a multiplicity of different positions regarding sustainable development which reflect the multiple 'domains of life' involved.

As such, different models of sustainable development incorporate, and emphasise different domains. For example, Krueger and Gibbs (2007, p 4) refer to sustainability as a 'three-legged stool', encompassing environment, equity and economy, whereas Palmer et al (1997, p 88) develop a four domain model including 'futurity', 'environment', 'equity' and 'public participation' (notably excluding 'economy'). While policy rhetoric emphasises the need to work across domains, as Krueger and Gibbs (2007) argue, one is often emphasised above the other. In part, this reflects the uncertainty and intractability at the heart of pre-emptive politics since attempts to govern the future always concern matters which remain not-yet-known (see Anderson, 2010; Evans, 2010). What unites different approaches is an agreement that the future will (must) differ from the present/past, but, as outlined above, the 'value' decisions which must be made about what forms of life can/should be sustained and the 'best' routes to achieve such change remain points of contention.

In particular, the role of capitalist systems as routes to, and their compatibility with, sustainable futures, remains a key point of divergence (Krueger and Gibbs, 2007). In policy terms, these different positions have meant that:

> in recent decades critical conceptions of the principles and practices of development ... have taken ... diverse and parallel paths. On the one hand ... Normative notions of sustainable development advocate equity, empowerment, and environmentally sensitive economic development. On the other hand ... Development has become anything but sustainable as the demands of enhanced capital accumulation override the broader needs of social reproduction. (Raco, 2005, pp 324–5)

In the UK, policy has been criticised for falling into the second of these categories since, as Eden (2000, p 112) argues, 'governments (both Conservative and Labour, so far) have consistently prioritized economic growth in national indicators and have been consequently criticized for this and for confining non-economic indicators largely to environmental impacts, rather than sociocultural or community impacts'.

These points of contention within sustainable development policy do more than simply reflect different interest groups in the present. The divergence between different approaches to sustainable development also reflects different approaches to the *future* and hence different judgements about whether actions taken in the present are justified by anticipated outcomes (that is, is a policy which ignores social injustice in the present justified by assurances that it will lead to a socially-just sustainable future?). Thus, Swyngedouw (2007, p 27) argues that 'the sustainable future desired by "sustainability" pundits has no name. While alternative futures in the past were named and counted (for example, communism, socialism, anarchism, libertarianism, liberalism), the desired sustainable environmental future has no name and no process, only a state or condition'.

When read in conjunction with literature on the role of children and young people within contemporary policy, this becomes particularly apparent, revealing the need for questions about social justice within sustainable development policy to consider the relative rights of present and future subjects, as well as the relative rights of different groups in the present (or future). In the remainder of this chapter we consider this in relation to sustainable development policy in the UK.

## Education for sustainable development

Our focus for discussion in the remainder of this chapter is the UK New Labour government paper *Brighter futures, greener lives: sustainable development action plan 2008–2010* (DCSF, 2008). This document aimed to bring together the previous Labour government's commitment to both children and to sustainable development and was written by the Department for Children, Schools and Families (DCSF) (to cover the period April 2008 to March

2010). The report aimed to set out a strategy through which the DCSF could deliver government policy in relation to 'children and their families in a way that is in harmony with sustainable development' (DCSF, 2008, p 2). The report is closely related to several other reports – *Securing the future: delivering UK sustainable development strategy* (DEFRA, 2005), *The children's plan: building brighter futures* (DCSF, 2007), *Every child's future matters* (SDC, 2007) and *Every child matters* (HM Treasury, 2003) – and was produced in the context of an international focus on Education for Sustainable Development.

The term 'Education for Sustainable Development' (ESD) was coined in the report of the World Commission on Environment and Development (WCED) in 1987. Since then, efforts have been made to develop what was more recognisably known as 'environmental education' into the broader concept of 'education for sustainable development' in an attempt to bring together education concerning social inequality, environmental degradation and economic depression into one single subject. In 2005 the United Nations launched the UN Decade for ESD, reflecting the high importance of ESD on international agendas (UNESCO, 2010). As with the breadth of the term 'sustainable development', the scope of ESD is similarly contested and open to multiple interpretations. The United Nations offers the following broad definition:

> Education for Sustainable Development represents a catalytic process for social change that seeks to foster – through education, training and public awareness – the values, behaviour and lifestyles required for a sustainable future. Thus, sustainable development can be seen not so much as a technical concept but as an educational one – not so much the end goal of a government policy but a process of learning how to think in terms of 'forever'. This means that ESD involves learning how to make decisions that balance and integrate the long-term future of the economy, the natural environment and the well-being of all communities, near and far, now and in the future. (UNESCO, 2005, n p)

In the UK the influence of international concern with ESD was evident in 2000 when ESD was inscribed as a cross-curricular component of the revised National Curriculum for England and Wales (note that the National Curriculum differs in Scotland). This was followed by the launch of the initiative *Sustainable schools* in 2006 (Teachernet, 2009). *Brighter futures, greener lives* set out the strategy to deliver ESD in the UK. This strategy is based around five principles: 'living within environmental limits' (environment), 'ensuring a strong, healthy and just society' (equity), 'achieving a sustainable economy' (economy), 'promoting good governance' (participation) and 'using sound science responsibly' (innovation). In keeping with moves to 'cross-domain' thinking (Krueger and Gibbs, 2007), the DCSF stresses that for a policy to be considered sustainable it must respect all five principles yet, as Krueger and Gibbs (2007) note is often the case, some of these principles are emphasised over and above others and there are multiple points of contention between these different domains which remain unacknowledged. In the remainder of this chapter we explore these tensions.

## Brighter futures, greener lives?

The two main aims of *Brighter futures, greener lives* reflect the dual position of young people within pre-emptive policy since the DCSF aimed to 'ensure children's wellbeing' (DCSF, 2008, p 2), presumably as children in the present, and 'to ensure that children have the skills and knowledge they will need to live in a changing world' (DCSF, 2008, p 2). These dual aims run throughout the report and cut across the five principles of sustainable development, with children's wellbeing being viewed as linked to the quality and quantity of their access to 'natural', 'green' environments. This is seen to be an issue of equity in determining differences in children's wellbeing and life chances and the DCSF (2008, p 17) saw it as its responsibility, 'working with other government departments ... to create an environment fit for children ... [to] *support* our children to have happy and safe childhoods'. This is premised on an approach such as that furthered by Malone (2001, p 7), who argues that improving young people's wellbeing in the present should be at the heart of sustainable development policy rather than an emphasis on the future since 'it is evident that the quality of the environment children grow up in determines the quality of their lives. Therefore, discussions around improving children's quality of life should be inextricably linked to emerging discourses of sustainable development.' In this respect, the intergenerational equity outlined by the Brundtland definition of sustainable development (WCED, 1987) informs *Brighter futures, greener lives*, and repeated reference is made to the responsibility of adults to fulfil their 'duty of care to children' (p 5), to lead 'change in the system' and to 'lead by example' (p 10). In this respect, *Brighter futures, greener lives* is based on the assumption that 'while it is the young who will most bear the consequences of economic, social and environmental decisions and actions that are currently being made *or avoided*, it is knowledgeable, concerned and caring adults who must take responsibility for setting in train the changes that are needed for us all to get off our destructive paths' (Davis, 1998, p 117).

Yet while these aims clearly focus on children's wellbeing as children in the present, the futurity with which children are approached in pre-emptive policy means that this concern with children's wellbeing in the present is often secondary to a concern about future adulthood. For example, the DCSF (2008) describes young people as 'the next generation of consumers and stewards of the planet' (p 9), and frames 'empowerment' and equity in terms of 'the number of children and young people on the path to success' (p 10). This framing of young people as future consumers of resources reflects concerns outlined above that UK sustainable development policy is premised on a 'weak sustainability' approach and is increasingly neoliberalised (Raco, 2005). Thus, intergenerational equity is understood as an imperative to ensure that capitalist systems and lifestyles can be maintained in the future: 'our duty to ensure that we have not exhausted the earth's natural resources by the time they have grown up, or failed to deal with climate change placing their economic prosperity, and lives, at risk' (p 5).

The principle 'achieving a sustainable economy' (DCSF, 2008, p 4) emerges as dominant throughout *Brighter futures, greener lives* and frames, or is presented as a route to achieve, some of the other principles of sustainable development (for example, equity, participation and so on). Thus, as the DCSF (2008, p 4) explains, sustainable development requires a commitment to 'building a strong, stable and sustainable economy which provides prosperity and opportunities for all, and in which environmental and social costs fall on those who impose them (Polluter Pays), and efficient resource use is incentivised'. The 'sustainable future' which is imagined here is therefore one within which market forces regulate sustainable behaviour. As such, ESD is seen as a tool with which children and young people can be prepared to contribute to a growing economy. Thus, intergenerational equity is framed as a 'duty to ensure they [future adults] are prepared to tackle the type and scale of the challenges they will face in their lives' (p 5) and equal access to quality education is seen as important in order to provide 'access to skilled employment ... which meets the needs of the economy well into the future' (DCSF, 2008, p 15). This is reinforced by the ways in which the principle 'using sound science responsibly' is framed as a means to achieve technological development as a route to sustainable development and economic prosperity.

This weak model of sustainable development has important implications for the models of childhood and youth present here. As Lister (2003) argues, the emphasis is not just on future adults, but on the productivity of future 'citizen workers'. Such an agenda reflects the broader approach to children and young people noted by Lister (2003) and Katz (2008) as one within which childhood has become an accumulation strategy to contend with fears of economic futures. This is also reflective of wider debates about the role of capitalist economic systems in bringing about, and as part of, sustainable futures. Here, concerns focus on the extent to which ESD reproduces social inequalities and the emphasis on ensuring success as future citizen workers contrast with alternative approaches which emphasise the importance of ESD encouraging 'young people to interact effectively with people different from themselves and take action in transforming structures of local and global oppression and *inequity* into ones that bring about social and economic justice' (Palmer et al, 1997, p 843).

These concerns also resonate with critical work which questions the extent to which children and young people are allowed to actively participate within policy (Hill et al, 2004). As mentioned above, participation is one of the core principles of *Brighter futures, greener lives* and the DCSF (2008, p 5) states that 'children have often gone unheard in this debate although ... they have as much at stake – if not more – than those making the decisions that will affect their future'. As several children's geographers have noted, this reflects a broader agenda within contemporary policy in which participation has been held up as a panacea for countering the exclusion of children and young people from policy debate. Concerns have been raised about the extent to which projects are 'concerned with what adults can do to help youth rather than how youth themselves can take action' (Ryan, 2007, p 247) and whether government consultation with children and young people is truly participatory or tokenistic decoration (Hill et al, 2004; McNeish and Gill, 2006; Kjorholt, 2007). Within *Brighter futures, greener lives,* the principle 'promoting good governance' is referred to as ensuring 'effective participative systems of governance in all levels of society'. While this is positive, it is extremely vague and there is little discussion of what type of participation is appropriate or how participation was undertaken in the production of these guidelines. What is present is brief mention of some consultation with children concerning their environmental attitudes. Direct quotes from children (see Table 4.1) are included in the report, although these are not referenced in the subsequent discussion and there is no justification for them being there.

**Table 4.1:** 'What children told us in our sustainable schools consultation in 2006'

- 'Too many cars driving when you are trying to get to sleep'
- 'Children want to walk but they can't because of the cars'
- 'There seems to be no respect for the world whatsoever'
- 'Too much waste and packaging'

*Source:* DCSF (2008, p 6).

Here, there is again a tension between the involvement of children as children and their involvement as future adults. The emphasis on future adults within the document when discussing children as active participants in sustainable development, means that a construction of childhood as a period of innocence, passivity and vulnerability is continued. This construction of childhood is implicit within the very definition of sustainable development (as a form of intergenerational justice) and is furthered by environmental campaigns that present children as the victims of unsustainable development. While the affective potential of the vulnerable child (see Evans, 2010) has power and therefore has been important in such campaigns, there is a downside to this since it limits the extent to which children can be seen as active participants in the present. As McNeish and Gill (2006) argue, policy which acts to construct childhood as a period of vulnerability serves to *exclude* children from participation.

As such, participation by children is largely framed in terms of a *pedagogical* approach which will help develop skills for the future. Vargas (2000, p 386) suggests that ESD requires a 'different type of education and approach to teaching, both of which challenge public educators more than ever before'. This push for more participatory approaches to ESD is, in part, a result of the uncertainty and intractability of pre-emptive policy since the lack of any one 'right' answer about what/how sustainable development might be achieved is seen to present a challenge to traditional teaching methods. Thus, the DCSF states that 'we do not know what will be the skills needed for sustainable development, but we expect they will include ... making informed choices and participating in decisions' (2007, p 17). This resonates with Aldrich-Moodie and Kwong's (1997, p 14) suggestion that the best pedagogical approach is one which accepts that 'just as important as providing children with a balanced account of the environmental debate is an effort to prepare them as best as possible to take part critically and constructively in that debate'. However, in contrast to this openness in interpretation of sustainable development the emphasis on future economic prosperity within *Brighter futures, greener lives* (as discussed above) limits the potential to imagine futures that are not about the continuation of neoliberal forms of capitalism. Thus in a section titled 'Empowering and Educating Young People for Life in a Sustainable World' (p 15), emphasis is placed on the provision of 'a high quality learning route that provides access to skilled employment and higher education, and which meets the skills needs of the economy well into the future'. As such, participation is mostly about replicating existing values as opposed to allowing children and young people to participate in the imagination of alternative forms of sustainable future. As Kraftl (2011) argues, such limited forms of participation are doubly problematic since they fail to empower young people in any real way to question the forms of futures imagined, but through emphasising their participation (albeit limited) children are afforded a share in the 'burden of responsibility' for the success or failure of attempts to achieve such futures.

## Conclusions

There is increasing interest in the future within geography (Anderson, 2010) and it is clear that critical analysis of the ways in which futures are governed has much to offer critical work on sustainable development in providing an incentive to question both the forms of future imagined and the relative rights of present and future forms of life (Swyngedouw, 2007). Moreover, work on children and young people has much to contribute here since attention to children's and young people's position within contemporary, future-focused policy provides an important insight into the temporal logics which inform the shape of such policy. In our discussion of *Brighter futures, greener lives* this attention to childhood and youth has allowed us to interrogate the ways in which neoliberal, capitalist agendas inform the futures which are imagined *for* children and young people and *for* sustainable development. This has important implications for the ways in which children's participation is figured within ESD.

According to Hope et al (2007, p 323), 'on a national level, there appears to be ambivalence about *what* childhood is for and *who* it is for' (p 323). In this chapter we have aimed to open up this ambivalence to critical interrogation in relation to one particular sustainable development policy in the UK – the ESD policy of the New Labour government. The particular interpretation of sustainable development evident in *Brighter future, greener lives* is much narrower than that proposed by UNESCO (2010) and the emphasis on young people as future citizen workers is contextualised within the broader state neoliberalism which characterised New Labour's term in office as well as youth policies in many other geographical contexts (Mizen, 2003; also Ansell et al, this volume, Chapter Three, on transnational policy-making).

In relation to the issues raised in this chapter, there is a need to interrogate further the implications of the shared anticipatory logics that pervade dominant understandings of both economic and child development (Aitken et al, 2007) for young people's involvement in such policy in different places beyond the UK and North America. In so doing, as Aitken et al (2007, p 4) argue, there is a need to avoid reproducing 'problematic progressive and developmental terms that foist adult agendas on young people … [And instead] challenge not only the conventional wisdom on how places and economies change but also how young people develop through and within these changes and how they too are agents of change'. Within the UK, while it remains to be seen what changes will be implemented by the Conservative-Liberal Democrat Coalition government (which took power in May 2010) in relation to Education for Sustainable Development policy, it is likely that shifting understandings of the welfare state and increasing role of private finance in delivery of public services might impact on the 'value' judgements taken in imagining sustainable futures – particularly regarding the role of the market in sustainable development. The sweeping cuts to welfare support and public services, calls for more 'fact'-based education (BBC, 2011) and the instrumental, economic, approach to education as a route to future labour market success (evident in justifications for a significant increase in university tuition fees – see Brown, this volume, Chapter Six) which has characterised the Coalition government's term thus far, implies that young people's involvement in sustainable development policy will continue to be framed in terms of the production of successful, competitive, future citizen workers.

Several authors have noted (Mayall, 2006) that children and young people's participation in policy is often little more than tokenistic. What is evident is that when this is combined with a future-focused policy, children's participation *as children* is often overlooked not just in relation to the participation of current adults, but also in relation to the participation of *future adults*. Thus, Prout (2000, p 306) argues that '*on its own* a focus on futurity is unbalanced and needs to be accompanied by a concern for the present well-being of children, for their participation in social life and for their opportunities for human self-realisation' (Prout, 2000, p 306). While we agree with this, we also suggest, on the basis of our analysis in this chapter, that it is not only necessary to emphasise the rights of children and young people *as* children and young people, but that this must be accompanied by a broader critical interrogation of the temporal logics which frame children and young people's participation within contemporary policy and the other forms of futures which are brought to bear on children and young people through these logics. In particular, the *shared* temporal logics of childhood development and economic development require further interrogation to question the ways in which a commodification of childhood (Katz, 2008) plays an important role in the futurity with which children and young people are approached in contemporary policy, and also to challenge the implications of this for social justice.

## Note

[1] Although there are important distinctions between childhood and youth, and between children and young people (Evans, 2008), throughout this chapter we use these terms interchangeably. We do so because both children and young people are approached with similar temporal logics, understood as adults-in-the-making.

**Acknowledgements**

Thanks to Mark Jayne, John Horton, Peter Kraftl and Faith Tucker for comments on previous drafts of this chapter. Thanks also to former colleagues in Environmental and Geographical Sciences at MMU for conversations which helped shape the ideas discussed here.

**References**

Aitken, S.C., Lund, R. and Kjørholt, A.T. (2007) 'Why children? Why now?', *Children's Geographies*, vol 5, no 1, pp 3-14.

Aldrich-Moodie, B. and Kwong, J. (1997) *Environmental education*, London: The IEA Education and Training Unit and the IEA Environment Unit.

Anderson, B. (2010) 'Preemption, precaution, preparedness: anticipatory action and future geographies', *Progress in Human Geography*, vol 34, no 6, pp 777-98.

BBC (2011) 'Gove stresses "facts" in school curriculum revamp', *BBC News Online*, 20 January 2011, http://www.bbc.co.uk/news/education-12227491.

Davis, J. (1998) 'Young children, environmental education, and the future', *Early Childhood Education Journal*, vol 26, no 2, pp 117-23.

DCSF (Department for Children, Schools and Families) (2007) *The children's plan: building brighter futures*, https://www.education.gov.uk/publications/standard/publicationDetail/Page1/CM%207280.

DCSF (Department for Children, Schools and Families) (2008) *Brighter futures, greener lives: sustainable development action plan*, https://www.education.gov.uk/publications/standard/publicationDetail/Page1/DCSF-00339-2008.

DEFRA (Department for Environment, Food and Rural Affairs) (2005) *Securing the future: delivering UK sustainable development strategy*, http://www.defra.gov.uk/publications/2011/03/25/securing-the-future-pb10589/.

Eden, S. (2000) 'Environmental issues: sustainable progress?', *Progress in Human Geography*, vol 24, no 1, pp 111-8.

Evans, B. (2008) 'Geographies of youth/young people', *Geography Compass*, vol 2, pp 1659-80.

Evans, B. (2010) 'Anticipating fatness: childhood, affect and the pre-emptive "war on obesity"', *Transactions of the Institute of British Geographers*, vol 35, pp 21-38.

Evans, B. and Colls, R. (2009) 'Measuring fatness, governing bodies: the spatialities of the body mass index (BMI) in anti-obesity politics', *Antipode*, vol 41, pp 1051-83.

Evans, B. and Colls, R. (2011) 'Doing more good than harm? The absent presence of children's bodies in (anti)obesity policy', in L. Monaghan, E. Rich and L. Aphramor (eds) *Debating obesity: critical perspectives*, Basingstoke: Palgrave MacMillan.

Hill, M., Davis, J., Prout, A., and Tisdall, K. (2004) 'Moving the participation agenda forward', *Children and Society*, vol 18, pp 77-96.

HM Treasury (2003) *Every child matters*, https://www.education.gov.uk/publications/standard/publicationDetail/Page1/DfES/1081/2004

Holloway, S.L. and Valentine, G. (2000) *'Children's geographies: playing, living, learning'*, London: Routledge.

Hope, G., Austin, R., Dismore, H., Hammond, S. and Whyte, T. (2007) 'Wild woods or urban jungle: playing it safe or freedom to roam', *Education*, vol 35, no 4, pp 321-32.

Horton, J. and Kraftl, P (2006) 'What else? Some more ways of thinking and doing 'children's geographies', *Children's Geographies,* vol 4, pp 69–95.

James, A. (2000) 'Embodied being(s): understanding the self and the body in childhood', in A. Prout (ed) *The body, childhood and society*, Basingstoke: Palgrave Macmillan, pp 19-37.

Kahn, P.H. (1999) *The human relationship with nature: development and culture*, London: The MIT Press.

Katz, C. (2008) 'Cultural geographies lecture. Childhood as spectacle: relays of anxiety and the reconfiguration of the child', *Cultural Geographies*, vol 15, pp 5-17.

Kjorholt, A.T. (2007) 'Childhood as a symbolic space: searching for authentic voices in the era of globalisation', *Children's Geographies*, vol 5, pp 29-42.

Kraftl, P. (2008) 'Young people, hope and childhood-hope', *Space and Culture*, vol 11, pp 81-92.

Kraftl, P. (2011) 'Utopian promise or burdensome responsibility? A critical analysis of the UK Government's Building Schools for the Future Policy', *Antipode,* doi: 10.1111/j.1467-8330.2011.00921.x

Krueger, R. and Gibbs, D. (2007) 'Introduction: problematising the politics of sustainability', in R. Krueger and D. Gibbs (eds) *The sustainable development paradox: urban political economy in the United States and Europe,* New York: Guilford Press, pp 1-12.

Lister, R. (2003) 'Investing in the citizen-workers of the future: transformations in citizenship and the state under New Labour', *Social Policy and Administration*, vol 37, no 5, pp 427-43.

Malone, K. (2001) 'Children, youth and sustainable cities', *Local Environment*, vol 6, no 1, pp 5-12.

Mayall, B. (2006) 'Values and assumptions underpinning policy for children and young people in England', *Children's Geographies*, vol 4, no 1, pp 9-17.

McNeish, D. and Gill, T. (2006) 'Editorial. UK policy on children: key themes and implications', *Children's Geographies*, vol 4, no 1, pp 1-7.

Mizen, P. (2003) 'The best days of your life? Youth, policy and Blair's UK government', *Critical Social Policy,* vol 23, pp 453-76.

Noorman, K.J., and Uiterkamp, T.S. (1998) *Green households? Domestic consumers, environment and sustainability*, London: Earthscan.

Palmer, J., Cooper, I. and van der Vorst, R. (1997) 'Mapping out fuzzy buzzwords: who sits where on sustainability and sustainable development', *Sustainable Development*, vol 5, pp 87-93.

Prout, A. (2000) 'Children's participation: control and self-realisation in British late modernity', *Children and Society*, vol 14, pp 304-15.

Raco, M. (2005) 'Sustainable development, rolled-out neoliberalism and sustainable communities', *Antipode*, vol 37, no 2, pp 324-47.

Ruddick, S. (2006) 'Abnormal, the "new normal", and destabilizing discourses of rights', *Public Culture,* vol 18, pp 53-78.

Ruddick, S. (2007a) 'At the horizons of the subject: neo-liberalism, neo-conservatism and the rights of the child. Part one: from "knowing" fetus to "confused" child', *Gender, Place and Culture,* vol 14, no 5, pp 513-27.

Ruddick, S. (2007b) 'At the horizons of the subject: neo-liberalism, neo-conservatism and the rights of the child. Part Two: parent, caregiver, state', *Gender, Place and Culture,* vol 14, no 6, pp 627-40.

Ryan, M. (2007) 'Critical pedagogy and youth: negotiating complex discourse worlds', *Pedagogy, Culture and Society*, vol 15, no 2, pp 245-62.

SDC (Sustainable Development Commission) (2007) *Every child's future matters*, http://www.sd-commission.org.uk/publications/downloads/ecfm3_report_w.pdf.

Stern, P.C., Dietz, T. and Kalof, L. (1993) 'Values orientation, gender, and environmental concern', *Environment and Behaviour*, vol 25, no 3, pp 322-48.

Swyngedouw, E. (2007) 'Impossible "sustainability" and the postpolitical condition', in R. Krueger and D. Gibbs (eds) *The sustainable development paradox: urban political economy in the United States and Europe,* New York: Guilford Press, pp 13-40.

Teachernet (2009) *Sustainable schools*, http://www.teachernet.gov.uk/sustainableschools/index.cfm (last accessed April 2011 but no longer available online).

UNESCO (United Nations Educational, Scientific and Cultural Organization) (2005) *What is sustainable development?*, http://www.unesco.org/education/tlsf/TLSF/decade/uncomESDt05.htm (last accessed April 2011 but no longer available online).

UNESCO (United Nations Educational, Scientific and Cultural Organization) (2010) *UN decade for sustainable development*, http://www.unesco.org/en/education-for-sustainable-development/decade-of-esd/ (last accessed April 2011 but no longer available online).

Uprichard, E. (2008) 'Children as "being and becomings": children, childhood and temporality', *Children and Society,* vol 22, no 4, pp 303-13.

Vargas, C.M. (2000) 'Sustainable development education: averting or mitigating cultural collision', *International Journal of Educational Development*, vol 20, no 5, pp 377-96.

WCED (World Commission on Environment and Development) (1987) *Our common future: Brundtland report*, http://worldinbalance.net/intagreements/1987-brundtland.php.

Williams, F. (2004) 'What matters is who works: why every child matters to New Labour. Commentary on the DfES Green Paper Every Child Matters', *Critical Social Policy*, vol 24, no 3, pp 406-27.

Williams, C.C. and Millington, A.C. (2004) 'The diverse and contested meanings of sustainable development', *The Geographical Journal*, vol 170, no 2, pp 99-104.

# five

# Places to go, things to do and people to see: space and activity in English youth work policy

*Richard Davies*

## Introduction

This chapter is concerned with a specific ethical activity, that of youth work, and a specific location, England.[1] In particular, the chapter argues that the policy discourse about youth work has had too strong a focus on 'institutions with presence' and that this focus has a detrimental effect on the way effective youth work is conceptualised. As such it is not a work of 'social geography' or in fact any other discipline. Rather, it is concerned with the way in which policy-makers shape a particular arena of state activity. However, underlying the argument is the presumption that social geography (for example, work by Gregory and Urry, 1985; Crang and Thrift, 2000; Massey, 2005) opens up a new focus on the perception, conception, and impact of 'space' on human agency which has generated, and continues to generate, a number of new avenues of conversations with educators (see Pykett, Chapter Nine, and Cartwright, Chapter Two, this volume; Hung and Stables, 2011).

Youth work is primarily, in an English context, an activity of *informal education*. Emerging historically from the work of philanthropic volunteers, youth work is still predominantly provided by the voluntary sector (now constituted by both volunteers and paid employees), with a smaller, state-funded Youth Service managed by local authorities. Historically youth work bracketed the period between the end of compulsory schooling and marriage, and concerned itself with a diversity of issues often reflecting the concerns of the middle-class, religious values for the working-class poor (for example, temperance, manly or lady-like behaviour) or the requirement of the nation, for example, the fitness of young men for martial service (for a more detailed history of youth work see Gilchrist et al, 2001; 2003; 2006; 2009; for a specific history of the Youth Service see Davies, 1999a; 1999b). Contemporary youth work focuses on those aged 13–19 and vulnerable adults aged 19–25.

State involvement in youth work was initiated during the two world wars (1914–18 and 1939–45), and reflected a concern for the behaviour of young men and a recognition of the impact of absent fathers. Post-war the work of a state-funded Youth Service was consolidated by the *Albemarle Report* (Ministry of Education, 1960), which attempted to define a role for the state in the informal education of young people. Albemarle was followed by a series of government-sponsored reports (for example, DoES, 1969). Alongside, and informing the reports, was the changing culture of young people and especially working-class culture.

On its election in 1997, the New Labour government sought to develop a range of policies targeted at young people in the UK. While the first tranche was concerned with formal education, from 2000 onwards concern turned to informal contexts. The Connexions strategy (DfEE, 2000) was linked with the *Transforming youth work* agenda (DfEE 2001, DfES, 2002). This was followed by the *Aiming high* agenda (HM Treasury/DCSF, 2007; DCSF, 2010a). It is this decade from 2001 to 2010 which is the focus of this chapter (see also Brown, this volume, Chapter Six). It is worth noting that on its election victory in 2010 the Conservative-Liberal Democratic Coalition government signalled a transformation of the public sector, iconographically expressed in the term 'Big Society' (see Norman, 2010). It is uncertain what shape public policy will take in this era, but there will be a significant shift in the provision of youth work from direct delivery by the state to delivery by the voluntary sector. Although emerging in the later period of the New Labour government, the 'defence of youth work' campaign[2] has reacted to this shift. Its concern is what some see as a decimation of youth work, and it comprises a broad collective of practitioners and academics who wish to assert a traditional model of values in work with young people.

This chapter progresses through three claims. The first is that youth work is a particular type of activity, in part defined by its ethical character and in part through its distinction from a range of other activities involving adults and young people. The second is a consideration of recent examples of policy and practice in the light of spatiality and temporality, considering the way space is conceptualised, and the way space and time are segmented.[3] The third is a review of Alasdair MacIntyre's account of practices and institutions. This, it is argued, is a helpful way of articulating and evaluating the issue. Throughout the chapter, the underpinning claim is that policy discourses matter because, as Foucault reminds us, 'discourses ... systematically form the objects of which they speak' (Foucault, 1972, p 49). Taylor (2010, n p), in a recent open letter as part of the 'in defence of youth work' campaign, sees the language of policy as of major significance:

> ... with the accession of New Labour the drive to impose an instrumental framework on Youth Work gathered increasing

momentum. With Blair and Brown at the helm youth workers and managers have been coerced and cajoled into embracing the very antithesis of the Youth Work process: predictable and prescribed outcomes. Possessing no vision of a world beyond the present New Labour has been obsessed with the micro-management of problematic, often demonised youth. Yearning for a generation stamped with the State's seal of approval the government has transformed Youth Work into an agency of behavioural modification. It wishes to confine to the scrapbook of history the idea that Youth Work is volatile and voluntary, creative and collective – an association and conversation without guarantees.

Policy-makers and practitioners can, in fact must, create a social reality in order to work co-operatively together. Although Taylor and I begin and end in different places, nevertheless we both hold that English youth work has been insufficiently critical of the emerging shared discourse about youth work and the associated social reality it brings into being.

## Youth work: a distinctive ethical activity

Some commentators have seen youth work as essentially a process of informal education (see Jeffs and Smith, 1990), or a variant, such as 'life philosophy coach' (see for example, Young, 1999). Cartwright (this volume, Chapter Nine) gives a good account of that characteristics of this tradition of thought. However, this cannot be the whole story. Suppose Christine comes up to me to say Michael has split up with her. I do not primarily see this as an opportunity for her to learn what a self-serving bastard Michael is, although this may well be true and worth knowing. This is an occasion in which Christine, as a young person, seeks support from an adult she trusts and who she knows will accept her vulnerability without exploiting it.[4] This is the first aspect of youth work; as Sercombe (2010) puts it, at the heart of the relationship between the youth worker and the young people is a covenantal relationship of trust. We act above all, he reminds us, for the good of the young person. This obligation is limited only by our capacity to act, not by a preconceived idea of our role.

The second aspect of youth work is that it is a co-operative activity. At one level youth work requires voluntary engagement between the young person and the youth worker, which has been, historically, a central principle of youth work (Jeffs, 2001). However, by 'co-operative activity' I mean more than this, I mean youth workers work towards a shared understanding of our collective world. This requires me, as worker, as well as the young person, both to change our views. It is only by having this shared understanding of social reality that *we* can act co-operatively in the world.

The third aspect is the communal context of youth work; youth workers do not primarily think and work as dyads of young person and youth worker, but in groups. This is more than a pragmatic response to large number of young people and few workers. In a liberal democracy, we require both a commitment to personal autonomy, and to community. As Bauman (2000; 2003) points out, we need to value community because it is only within community that we find the resources necessary to identify a life worth pursuing.

The fourth, and final, aspect is the belief that there are better and worse ways of living life. We may be unsure as to the criteria for the 'better' life, but nevertheless, as youth workers, *we* act on the assumption that by engaging with young people in this way their lives will be better than they would otherwise have been. While some, perhaps all, of these aspects would be accepted by youth workers, they might not be expressed in the same language, which is intentionally reflective of MacIntyre's (1985) reconceptualisation of Aristotelian ethics, and particularly his account of a social practice. This will be returned to later. What such an account does mean, and here I think I can claim unanimity among youth workers, is that youth work is a specific and spatially-temporally bounded activity, and not just any activity involving adults and young people will do. Structurally and linguistically, we differentiate youth work by referring, on the one hand, to other professional groups who, as adults, often work with young people (for example, schoolteachers, social workers, mental health nurses), while on the other hand, we have also seen the rise in England of the more generic title 'working with young people' intended to identify work which is unspecified in role or function, and a related professional title, the 'youth professional' (CWDC, 2009). The very *presence* of such discourses affirms the distinctive nature of youth work.

## Youth work: spatial and temporal aspects

Youth work lends itself to discourses that are 'spatially and temporally rich'. One of the key markers of role and responsibility within the activity is one's age. This is not only true of the distinction between youth workers and young people, but within groups of young people. Further, there is some controversy within and beyond the profession of the most appropriate way of expressing these temporal distinctions and the legitimate implications of categories relating to age, for example adolescence (whether these are drawn from psychology, sociology or political science).

Spatially, one of the enduring distinctions in youth work practice is between 'centre-based' and 'detached' youth work. Centre-based youth work focuses on encouraging young people to spend their leisure time within the confines of a particular building, usually engaging in activities chosen from a menu of those made available. In accepting the option of entering a youth centre young people give up certain rights and are required to act in line with morally prescriptive ground rules (for example, no smoking or drinking, no swearing, no sexual intercourse on the stairs).

Detached work, on the other hand, emphasises youth workers' attempts to develop meaningful relationships with young people 'where they are'. This usually includes: public spaces; spaces where public access is encouraged, for example, shopping centres; and spaces where access is tolerated, for example, school grounds after school hours. However, there are also opportunities for youth workers to work, when invited, in more private spaces: private homes, squats and the like. Yet, this obviously spatial aspect risks disguising a more fundamental approach to the inevitable power relations between adults and young people expressed by these different approaches. Detached workers consciously divest themselves of the implicit powers resulting from age, status, and so on, and seek, in the liminal space so created, to form a situated and more equal relationship with young people.[5] Centre-based work, while affirming all the aspects of youth work outlined above, retains the trappings of power in which professional adults in our society are usually cloaked, although adult workers seek to use this power for the good of, and in partnership with, young people. In fact such a divesting of power is only possible for detached workers because of the shared understanding of the reality of public space; the enclosed materiality of the youth centre makes such acts impossible.[6]

## Three examples

To illustrate some of the above themes, three examples from policy and practice will be presented. These are only illustrations in that it is difficult to find a univocular analysis of policy; that is to say, it is possible to imagine other explanations of what is seen and heard. The three examples explore, respectively, conceptions of space, the segmentation of time and the segmentation of space in youth work policy and practice.

### Conceptions of space

The initial example develops an idea expressed in Massey (2005). Massey is discussing the actions of the conquistadors:

> Fabian suggests a further possible political repercussion of this reliance on [a Newtonian metaphor of space and time] ... which takes us back both to the temporal convening of special difference and, yet again, to the meeting of Moctezuma and Cortes:

'In the hands of ideologues such a time concept is easily transformed into a kind of political physics. After all, it is not difficult to transpose from physics to politics one of the most ancient rules which states that it is impossible for two bodies to occupy the same space at the same time. When in the course of colonial expansion a western body politic came to occupy, literally, the space of an autochthonous body, several alternatives were conceived to deal with that violation of the rule. The simplest one ... was of course to move or remove the other body.' (Massey, 2005, p 73)

Massey compares what she sees as the Newtonian model of space with a more diffuse, perhaps quantum, model in which different material bodies can co-exist in the same 'space'. In the classical view of Cortes, elimination of the 'other' is the only viable means by which one can enter into new space. Note that this is not a political or militaristic claim about what is needed in order to possess and own the land, but a conceptual issue about an individual's presence in space itself.

Consider, in this light, recent policy on so-called 'anti-social behaviour' by young people. While I do not want to claim that young people are always well-behaved in public spaces, or that adults are not intimidated by them, this falls short of the policy narrative. By 2010, *Aiming high: three years on* could link a decline in anti-social behaviour with the deliberate movement of young people from public spaces into youth centres:

> ... fewer young people are getting into trouble and communities are less worried about teenagers 'hanging around'. (DCSF, 2010a, p 5)

The policy narrative mirrors Cortes. The presence of young people in public spaces (be that streets, shopping centres, public squares) naturally means that such spaces are not also available to adult members of society. The issue, given this analysis, is not so much what young people do, but that they are present in particular, so-called public, spaces. In order to justify some state intervention in a liberal democracy two lines of justification are open: either one can claim to act in the young people's interest (because we know what is best for them), or identify their actions as hostile to the wider population. Deemed to be a *risk* to others, young people are seen to 'loiter' rather than 'stand around talking to friends', though it is unclear what the criterion is for preferring one description over the other. The pejorative tone of 'loitering' legitimates the action of the state, indicating as it does that the individuals are staying in this place for the purpose of some unsavoury activity. Deemed to be *at risk*, we see a concern that young people should move from open, outdoor spaces in order to be protected by attending a youth centre (see HM Treasury/DCSF, 2007; DCSF, 2010a). So we see a policy dynamic of, at best, young people being required to pass through space, pushed by adult state officials in either perpetual movement 'through' or encouraged to gravitate towards places seen as more appropriate for them.

## The segmentation of time

Let us continue reflecting on this example, and drawing on themes from Massey, by considering the segmentation of time. Obviously in the above example time is segmented into broad 'epochs' of *youth* (or young people) and *adults*. How is the epoch 'youth' seen to relate to the epoch 'adult'? Two dominant policy discourses have emerged. The first sees the two epochs as 'other'. Thus, adults do not see themselves as related directly to youth, but rather youth are, as Hersch (1999) put it, 'a tribe apart', or for Barham (2006) 'disconnected'. This, of course, moves both ways with both young people and adults seeming themselves as something 'other'. This discourse of 'otherness' is particularly prevalent in young people's engagement with the criminal justice system. The second discourse sees *youth* as developmentally prior to *adult* (or, as Massey sees this in relation to nation-states, 'more primitive'; see Massey, 2005, p 62) and, as such, in need of the support and direction of adults in the young people's interest. This discourse has, perhaps, dominated in relation to schooling. This is, of course, an element within broader considerations of the social construction of children and young people (see for example, Archard, 1993; James and James, 2004).

This distinction, into epochs, differs from youth work practitioners' consideration of their work, which tends to focus not on age segmentation, but either young people's ability or need. However, youth work discourses (and I think here particularly of the campaign to reduce the voting age in the UK, see British Youth Council, 2010) while in part focusing on the commonality of personhood, and reducing age to a rather abstract and inconsequential factor have also used this segmentation of otherness. This 'otherness' discourse sees young people as an equal, if different, constituency in UK politics that ought to have the vote. Thus, we see the 'naturalness' of this segmentation impacting not only in policy discourse of the state, but also picked up and used by practitioners.

## The segmentation of space

The historic longevity of the spatial division of youth work into centre-based work and detached work has already been considered. Given the variety of ways in which youth work can be sub-divided this longevity shows something of the deeper structure implicit in the practices of 'working with young people where we are' and 'working with them where they are'. The 'working with' is not just a spatial claim, but the spatiality embodies an ideology of power relations. Working 'where they are' shifts power from the adult worker to the young people; we are, if you like, invading *their home territory* (though of course this is often public space and the very use of this term expresses the 'Cortesian perspective' developed above). The general tenor of the last decade or so of youth work policy in England has been a move towards centre-based youth work as 'the place to go'[7] – a place which in numerous ways allows control by adults. Youth work can be seen to have recently shifted towards a form of 'out-of-school' school. *Youth matters* (HM Government, 2005, p 35) articulates this commitment to spatial presence:

> Many local areas are exploring alternatives to the traditional youth club approach, for example by investing in mobile facilities or youth shelters. However, these sorts of facilities remain underdeveloped, and their provision is not always in line with what young people actually want.

> We therefore propose to allocate capital funding worth £40 million ... This will help to pay for upgrading existing places to go for young people and provide new facilities where none exist.

The implication that detached work is a 'new' alternative, and that the reason young people rejected some of the shelters was that they wanted a youth centre, are subtle expressions of how policy-makers segment space. Five years later, in *Aiming high: three years on*, detached youth work is noted only in a couple of paragraphs and then only for its possible contribution to reaching the disaffected. In policy terms, the centre is the safe, useful place that reasonable young people will want to attend, and public space, like the forest of fairy tales, a place where feckless mobs roam.

## Theorising the spatial-temporal dimensions of youth work

Youth work is an 'everyday' ethical activity, and site of political activity (see Horton and Kraftl, 2009; for a specifically social geographical perspective on the ethical and the everyday, see Martin et al, 2007). At the common sense level this is reflected in the expectations that people have of youth workers (as well as teachers and others who work with the young). We do not want just anyone working with young people; we do not want them to be a danger to the young, but also we do not want them to encourage young people into certain types of behaviours that we consider unhealthy (see Roberts, 2009; Sercombe, 2010). While accepting this common sense view, in theorising about youth work I want to articulate the activity in more ethically exclusivist terms. In particular, ideas prevalent in the Aristotelian tradition developed by MacIntyre (1985) will be drawn upon.

The four aspects of youth work identified earlier were that it is:

- based on a covenantal relationship of trust;
- co-operative;
- grounded in community;
- directed towards the development of the 'better' life.

What I was moving towards in that description is to claim that youth work is a type of social practice (or to be precise, a series of social practices sharing a 'family resemblance'). MacIntyre (1985, p 187) identifies five characteristics of a social practice. It must be:

- complex;
- coherent;
- co-operative;
- involving agents having different roles;
- who work to achieve the same overall goods.

I assumed earlier, and continue to take it as an unproblematic claim, that youth work is a complex activity. By coherent, MacIntyre requires that the individual actions (say, for example, kicking a ball, or picking up a shopping basket) which form the behaviour of various agents within the social practice are related to each other; that is both that there is a relationship between the different actions of different agents, but also that my own actions relate to those I performed earlier and will perform later. What is more, this coherent and co-operative activity sees the various agents involved trying to pursue the same limited set of goods, specific to this social practice. Youth work practices are a little odd in this regard in that there are two sets of goods relating to each social practice. The first set of goods relate to the particular activity, so, for example, if one is playing a game, these goods are the goods of the game in question (scoring a goal, getting the tiddlywink in the cup, achieving checkmate, and so on). The second set of goods relate to the youth work element of the practice, the supporting of the young person in their pursuit of the 'better' life. Again there will be various types of goods: educational, social, psychological, emotional, and so on. One of the critical features of youth work practices are that they have these two sets of goods, that youth work is grounded in social practices, but with the specific intent of doing more than just engaging in that practice. It seeks to achieve this second set of goods. Of course, these two sets of goods are not independent; football is good as a base practice to achieve some youth work goods, whereas chess offers a different set of possibilities. The youth worker makes choices in terms of what is possible given the social practices available (or the practices they can initiate). This is my first critical point.

Engaging within a social practice requires agents to take up certain roles. In order for the community as a whole to successfully pursue the goods of the particular practice then individual agents need to perform their roles well. We can see this clearly in, for example, team games. Members of the team (in the case of soccer: strikers, defenders and goalkeeper) do not do the same work, but together they, through their various roles, pursue success. In youth work social practices the roles of youth worker and young person require a covenantal relationship of trust. Sacks' (2009, n p) exposition of such relationships is:

> There is a fundamental difference between contracts and covenants. In a contract, two or more individuals, each pursuing their own interest, come together to make an exchange for mutual benefit. When we pay someone to do something for us, implicitly or explicitly we make a contract.

> A covenant is something different. In a covenant, two or more individuals, each respecting the dignity and integrity of the other, come together in a bond of mutual responsibility to do together what neither can achieve alone. It is not about interests but about loyalty, fidelity, holding together when events seem to be driving you apart. A covenant is less like a deal than like a marriage: it is a moral bond.

Relationships, that is, that take as their model the relationships of the family and community, rather than the professional or business. Thus, youth work social practices are characterised by specific relationships between the main agents involved. This is my second critical point.

My third critical point is concerned with the relationship between social practices and institutions. MacIntyre (1985) claims, I think rightly, that institutions are necessary for the perpetuation of social practices. It is also seems right that institutions that no longer support vibrant social practices become redundant, having the appearance of life, but being dead. For example, the social practices of medicine are embodied within the institution of the hospital. We can imagine, however, that if the social practices of medicine were no longer relevant, if we had bodies and minds that were permanently healthy, then the institution of the hospital would be redundant, except perhaps as a theme park about the 'olden days', or a museum reminding us of what it was like to be sick. Some institutions locate social practices within particular places. Schools and hospitals are of this type, locating medical and educational practices respectively. These are 'institutions with presence' and include youth centres. What is more the spatial form of these institutions shape the nature of the social practices occurring. For example, medical practices are shaped in different ways in hospitals, local GP surgeries and sexual health clinics. Other institutions, for example marriage, are more difficult to locate spatially, they are literally embodied within the committed parties.

The fourth, and final, critical point is the way in which particular *material* institutions 'house' a range of social practice. I have referred to these elsewhere as 'geo-social spaces' (see Davies, 2003). Let us consider the school as a 'geo-social space' of this type. A school is primarily concerned with formal education, with the learning of a selection of key ideas from human history. Its primary relationship is that between the teacher and the pupil/student, and its key criterion of success is that of the pupil/student being able to muster the facts together in order to more adequately understand, and be able to act in, their world.[8] However, although this is the rationale for the building and the types of social relationships that develop within the school, this space is used for much more (see Collins and Coleman, 2008; Holloway et al, 2010 for geographically focused reviews of schools and space, and Hung and Stables, 2011 for an educationalist perspective). The state, in particular, sees the school as a useful vehicle for a range of other social practices, for example those concerned with public health, community cohesion or careers guidance.

## Drawing threads together

In recent policy we have seen a constant segmentation of space into centre-based and detached youth work, with the affirmation of one to the detriment of the other. We have also seen a particular segmentation based on age, and together these have constructed a social reality in which legitimate youth work practice has become centred on particular buildings, and located within 'institutions with presence'. What this chapter has suggested is that this focus on space and time is problematic for youth work, and whatever segmentation of spatiality and temporality is offered, whatever conception of space is shared, will distort it. We ought, in policy terms, to renew our focus on the nature of the activity itself and consider what follows in terms of space and time *from that focus*. It is worth reiterating that I accept MacIntyre's claim that social practices require some kinds of institutions for their perpetuations. What does not follow from this is that we need a focus on 'institutions with presence', in other words those institutions that require material form in bricks and mortar.

Let us return briefly to a social practices consideration of our three examples. These examples highlighted the exclusion of young people from public space as a result of a particular conception of space itself – of seeing them as 'other' – and, as a result, a policy focus on the space within which youth work occurs (youth centre or detached). The counter to this position, grounded in MacIntyre, is to focus on the social practices which provide a context for youth work (that is, those enabling us to pursue both sets of goods) and, emerging from this focus, a place to reconsider the institutions best suited to sustain such practices. At the heart of youth work as an activity is the development of young people's ability to live better lives and in part this requires a grounding in community. The 'Cortesian' perspective of space considered earlier is therefore anathema. Communal space must be shared and must be the context for effective youth work. However, this is not to claim that all those sharing that space need to be involved in the same social practices. Communal space, as in the example of the school, can be a geo-social space in which different groups engaging in different social practices can share the same physical space. What is required, as in a school, is a shared sense of community, a covenantal relationship between individuals within which young people and youth workers can locate themselves. Such an account of youth work also undermines discourses of 'epochs' and 'otherness' based on age. The focus becomes more on the roles individuals play within a range of social practices, and the contribution they can make to the successful pursuit of the goods achieved through those practices.

Such an account does not focus on spaces so much as a range of institutions that transcend space: families, fraternals and local communities. Geographical analyses (for example, by Massey, 2005) reveal that the policy discourses fail to capture this effectively and, what is more, their focus on buildings and what can be done within them blinds us (perhaps only temporally) to the possibilities a focus on activity affords. The difficulty for politicians is that such institutions are notoriously difficult to influence; space and time are more malleable to their hands.

## Notes

[1] It is worth noting that youth work is a devolved responsibility and takes different policy forms in the four jurisdictions of England, Northern Ireland, Scotland and Wales.

[2] See http://www.indefenceofyouthwork.org.uk/wordpress/.

[3] It is worth noting that this chapter focuses on the segmentation of time, though for theoretical (see Massey, 2005) and experiential reasons it is clear that time and space are intimately and inevitably linked.

[4] Of course I may hope that through the experience Christine learns more about Michael, herself and relationships in general, but this is not the sole – or even primary – driving force for my actions.

[5] By which I am not claiming that they become like the young people.

[6] By this I also mean that detached work is not to be seen as more democratic or more legitimate youth work (though this is sometimes claimed). Rather, that the spatial location of youth work is significant for what type of practice can occur.

[7] The policy strap line taken up and used on the websites of many youth services has been 'places to go and things to do' (or variants).

[8] I accept that this is a particular expression of the liberal aspiration which most, if not all, schools fall short of achieving. It may well be that the actual focus of many schools is social reproduction.

## References

Archard, D. (1993) *Children: rights and childhood,* Abingdon: Routledge.

Barham, N. (2006) *Disconnected: why our kids are turning their backs on everything we thought we knew,* London: Ebury Press.

Bauman, Z. (2000) *Liquid modernity,* Cambridge: Polity Press.

Bauman, Z. (2003) *Liquid love,* Cambridge: Polity Press.

British Youth Council (2010) *Our parliament, our vision: British Youth Council's general election manifesto,* http://old.byc.org.uk/media.php?parent_id=159&content_id=160.

Collins, D. and Coleman, T. (2008) 'Social geographies of education: looking within, and beyond, school boundaries', *Geography Compass,* vol 2, pp 281-99.

Children's Workforce Development Council (2009) *The young people's workforce reform programme,* http://www.cwdcouncil.org.uk/assets/0000/5441/Youth_Professional_Status.pdf.

Crang, M. and Thrift, N.J. (eds) (2000) *Thinking space,* London: Routledge.

Davies, B. (1999a) *From voluntaryism to welfare state: a history of the youth service in England, volume 1 1939–1979,* Leicester: Youth Work Press.

Davies, B. (1999b) *From Thatcherism to new labour: a history of the youth service in England, volume 2 1979–1999,* Leicester: Youth Work Press.

Davies, R. (2003) *Education, virtue and the good life: the ability of schools to inform and motivate students' moral activity,* unpublished DPhil thesis, Oxford.

DCSF (Department for Children, Schools and Families) (2010a) *Aiming high for young people: three years on,* London: TSO.

DfEE (Department for Education and Employment) (2000) *Connexions: the best start in life for every young person,* London: DfEE.

DfEE (Department for Education and Employment) (2001) *Transforming youth work,* London: DfEE.

DfES (Department for Education and Skills) (2002) *Transforming youth work: resourcing excellent youth services*, Nottingham: DfES Publications.

DoES (Department of Education and Science) (1969) *Youth and community work in the 70s: the Fairbairn-Milson report*, London: HMSO.

Foucault, M. (1972) *The archaeology of knowledge and discourse on language*, New York: Pantheon Books.

Gilchrist, R., Jeffs, T. and Spence, J. (2001) *Essays in the history of community and youth work*, Leicester: National Youth Agency.

Gilchrist, R., Jeffs, T. and Spence, J. (2003) *Architects of change: studies in the history of community and youth work*, Leicester: National Youth Agency.

Gilchrist, R., Jeffs, T. and Spence, J. (2006) *Drawing on the past: essays in the history of community and youth work*, Leicester: National Youth Agency.

Gilchrist, R., Jeffs, T., Spence, J. and Walker, J. (2009) *Essays in the history of youth and community work: discovering the past*, Lyme Regis: Russell House Publishing.

Gregory, D. and Urry, J (1985) (eds) *Social relations and spatial structures*, Basingstoke: Macmillan.

Hersch, P. (1999) *A tribe apart: a journey into the heart of American adolescence*, New York: Random House.

HM Government (2005) *Youth matters*, London: TSO.

HM Treasury/DCSF (2007) *Aiming high for young people: a ten year strategy for positive activities*, London: HMSO.

Holloway, S., Hubbard, P., Jones, H. and Pimlott-Wilson, H. (2010) 'Geographies of education and the significance of children, youth and families', *Progress in Human Geography*, vol 34, no 5, pp 583-600.

Horton, J. and Kraftl, P. (2009) 'Small acts, kind words and not too much fuss: implicit activisms', *Emotion, Space and Society*, vol 2, pp 14-23.

Hung, R. and Stables, A. (2011) 'Lost in space? Located in place. Geophenomenological exploration and school', *Educational Philosophy and Theory*, vol 43, no 2, pp 193-203.

James, A. and James, A.L. (2004) *Constructing childhood: theory, policy and practice*, Basingstoke: Palgrave Macmillan.

Jeffs, T. (2001) '"Something to give and much to learn": settlements and youth work', in R. Gilchrist and T. Jeffs (eds) *Settlements, social change and community action*, London: Jessica Kingsley.

Jeffs, T. and Smith, M. (1990) *Using informal education*, Buckingham: Open University Press.

MacIntyre, A. (1985) *After virtue*, 2nd edn, London: Duckworth.

Martin, D., Hanson, S. and Fontaine, D. (2007) 'What counts as activism? The role of individuals in creating change', *Women's Studies Quarterly*, vol 25, pp 78-94.

Massey, D. (2005) *For space*, London: Sage.

Ministry of Education (1960) *The youth service in England and Wales: the Albemarle report*, London: HMSO.

Norman, J. (2010) *The big society: the anatomy of the new politics*, Buckingham: University of Buckingham Press.

Roberts, J. (2009) *Youth work ethics*, Exeter: Learning Matters.

Sacks, J. (2009) 'Credo: Obama renews a covenant and inspires fresh hope. Why America sees itself as "one nation under God"', *The Times online*, http://www.timesonline.co.uk/tol/comment/faith/article5575945.ece.

Sercombe, H. (2010) *Youth work ethics*, London: Sage.

Taylor, T. (2010) *In defence of youth work*, 2nd version, http://www.detachedyouthwork.info/in_defence_of_youth_work.htm.

Young, K. (1999) *The art of youth work*, Lyme Regis: Russell House.

# Part II
# Education and employment policies: learning beyond schools and schools beyond learning

# six

# The place of aspiration in UK widening participation policy: moving up or moving beyond?

*Gavin Brown*

## Introduction

The thirteen years that New Labour held power in Britain (1997–2010) witnessed profound changes in the form and character of the British welfare state. During this period, as Raco (2009) has charted, British welfare policy became increasingly focused on the creation of 'aspirational citizens' who would take individual responsibility for 'bettering' themselves through upwards social mobility. He suggests that this 'existential politics' of aspiration has replaced an earlier 'politics of expectation' in which the state was the primary provider of welfare provision. The protests by school and university students regarding the Conservative-Liberal Democrat Coalition government's proposals to raise the cap on university tuition fees in England from 2012 demonstrate the extent to which many young people's aspirations have been raised to the point where they expect to undertake higher education, but also the limits on realising those aspirations in a time of austerity.

Like Raco (2009), I believe that this policy shift has had significant political and material consequences for people living in the most deprived areas of Britain and their experience of social and spatial (in)justice. Despite New Labour's talk of 'raising' people's aspirations, this political shift had the effect of *lowering* the expectations of what the state could provide for them. This neoliberal reconfiguration of welfare provision (and the consequent shift in the terms of debates around 'social justice' to promote individual rather than social responsibility for change) underpinned many aspects of education and youth policy under the New Labour governments. It can be seen in the promotion of private sector sponsorship of state schools through the academies programme (Purcell, 2011), which was intended to improve student attainment, behaviour and aspirations. It also inspired the provision of extended school services at either end of the traditional school day to promote children's involvement in structured extra-curricular activities and equip them with skills and aspirational dispositions (Holloway and Pimlott-Wilson, 2011). This chapter examines one key area of education and youth policy where the creation of future aspirational worker-citizens was central – policy initiatives concerned with widening participation in higher education through interventions to raise the aspirations of young people from low income families and certain minority ethnic groups who had long been under-represented among successive cohorts of university students.

The chapter begins with a short overview of the history of British widening participation policy since 1997, suggesting that there have been three distinct phases in the implementation of this policy over this period. The chapter focuses on the second of those phases, in which the emphasis was on interventions designed to change the aspirations of young people from low income families. The second section of the chapter examines how interventions around young people's aspirations during the period 2001–10 simultaneously operated in relation to multiple spatial scales. The third section examines the spatiality of specific interventions by widening participation practitioners to influence young people's aspirations in practice. Through understanding how these interventions developed and are practised, it is possible to formulate more critical approaches to developing young people's aspirations (that are all the more important given the current Coalition government's cuts to widening participation funding). The final section of the chapter offers an alternative spatial language to describe widening participation interventions.

## A brief history of recent widening participation policy

The publication of the *Dearing Report* (NCIHE, 1997) into the future of British higher education spurred the New Labour government to widen participation in higher education to include young people from social backgrounds that were under-represented in the university sector – principally those from low income families, some minority ethnic groups and young people with disabilities. Although there have been a series of policy initiatives going back several decades to enable 'non-traditional' students to participate in higher education (Kettley, 2007), the investment in widening participation since 1997 has been unprecedented. However, it can be argued that there have been three distinct phases to this policy strand, each motivated by different political discourses. Initially, during the first term of the Blair government (1997–2001), widening participation was promoted through a discourse of *equality*. The focus was on raising young people's attainment in school examinations so that all young people could have equal access to higher education to pursue the education and careers that they desired. The second phase, covering the remaining years of the Blair and Brown governments (2001–10), witnessed a shift from a policy of enabling young people's existing aspirations to promoting interventions that would 'raise' their aspirations in very specific ways. In this phase, the policy discourse shifted, from the promotion of *equality*, towards a greater drive for *social control* (Archer, 2007). The third phase, coinciding with the election of the Coalition government in May 2010, is still developing, but appears to be articulated around a politics of *fairness*. Key motifs from each phase will be briefly examined.

It has become something of a cliché to note that Blair came to power promising to prioritise 'education, education, education'. Throughout New Labour's first term in office, the priority in education and youth policy was on raising the attainment of young people from lower socio-economic groups. Although ministers frequently talked about harnessing young people's aspirations (through widening participation interventions such as the *Excellence in Cities* programme) throughout this period, the egalitarian promise of these initiatives was to enable all young people to achieve their existing aspirations rather than to direct them towards specific forms of education and employment. This is exemplified by the following extract from a speech given by the then Secretary of State for Education and Employment early in 2000:

> "We intend [the *Excellence in Cities* programme] simultaneously to meet the needs and aspirations of all young people, whatever their gifts and talents, and to remove systematically the barriers to their success, whether these be inside or outside the school." (Blunkett, 2000)

Central to the second phase of recent widening participation policy was the imperative to raise (and, thereby, change) the aspirations of young working-class people so that they would consider progressing to higher education (Warrington, 2008). This is not to overlook the promotion of vocational education for less academically able students, but to suggest it was always of secondary importance to the promotion of higher education. The emphasis shifted from enabling the existing aspirations of young people towards directing them to very specific ends. This chapter primarily focuses on the spatialities of widening participation interventions during this phase, so the rhetoric of *social control* will not be examined in great detail here. However, some overview of the structures and processes through which widening participation policy was enacted in this phase is useful.

From August 2004, aspiration-raising initiatives were primarily delivered through the Aimhigher programme. Aimhigher was jointly funded by the Higher Education Funding Council for England (HEFCE) and the Department for Business, Innovation and Skills (BIS).[1] English higher education institutions were expected to deliver their own activities to support the progression to higher education of 'non-traditional' student groups (as a condition of continued public funding). Funding for Aimhigher was removed by the Conservative-Liberal Democrat Coalition government in July 2011.

Although participation rates in higher education by 18- and 19-year-olds from all social classes have increased since 1997, they remain highly differentiated – for the academic year 2009/10, HEFCE (2010, p 7) predicted that 19 per cent of this age cohort living in the most disadvantaged areas of England would enter higher education, compared to 57 per cent of their peers growing up in the least disadvantaged areas of the country (see Archer, 2007).

The election of the Coalition government in May 2010 has heralded a third phase in the promotion of widening participation since 1997. The precise details of how the Coalition will approach widening participation remain to be seen as the impact of the increase in higher education tuition fees from 2012 plays out. From its inception, the Coalition has claimed a commitment to 'increas[ing] social mobility' and 'attract[ing] a higher proportion of students from disadvantaged backgrounds' (HM Government, 2010, pp 31-2). However, it has distanced itself both from New Labour's early discourse of *equality* and from the later focus on individual *aspirations*, articulating instead a politics of *fairness* that is still positioned within a liberal framework of extending individual choice.

If New Labour saw education as adding value to young lives, hence its focus on *raising aspirations*, the Coalition government draws (perhaps unsurprisingly) on that aspect of their respective approaches to education where the Conservative and Liberal Democrat parties most overlap – namely that individuals should get out of education the fruits of what they bring to it. In other words, the appeal to *fairness* in education is motivated not by a desire for *equality* (of either opportunity or outcome) but a belief that every young person has the right to go as far as their abilities will allow them (Bangs et al, 2010). The second of the three policy discourses just identified is now explored: interventions to raise the aspirations of young people from low income backgrounds.

## National aspirations; local interventions

In contrast to much work by educationalists (Gewirtz, 2001; Kettley, 2007), Green and White (2008, p 214) have outlined how *place* influences the terrain of opportunities that shape young people's future adult lives: 'place influences "subjective" geographies of opportunity, and … "objective" geographies of opportunity vary by location'. A geographical study of young people's aspirations must incorporate an examination of how place influences those '"subjective" geographies of opportunity', but it must also pay attention to the multiple scales at which policy interventions designed to affect young people's aspirations operate. This section of the chapter focuses on policy discourses about young people's aspirations (during the period 2001–2010); comparing the national-global ambitions of these policies with the ways in which they identified young people with 'low aspirations' as living in particular types of local places and targeted their interventions at this scale. In so doing, this work addresses Ansell's (2009) critique of Children's Geographers for over-relying on micro- and local scale studies at the expense of investigating the impact of wider policy discourses on children's lives.

Throughout the 2000s, New Labour ministers repeatedly asserted the idea that the British public was already highly aspirational and that the proper role of government was to harness those aspirations, and to inspire people to take responsibility for bettering themselves and society (Gewirtz, 2001). This rhetoric was used to justify a comprehensive restructuring of the delivery of education and welfare services, attempting to realign their provision such that the emphasis was on preventing anticipated future social problems rather than pursuing redistributive policies to tackle existing systemic social inequalities (Evans, 2010).

In a speech presented at the University of Greenwich in late 2007, Prime Minister Gordon Brown set out his vision for an education system orientated to producing aspirational future citizen-workers in the service of Britain's national economic competitiveness:

> "I make no apology therefore for saying that education is the best economic policy … That is why it is my passion. That is why I want to see a Britain where every child can go to a world class school, supported by high aspirations and surrounded always by excellent opportunities … And that is why too I want a Britain where every young person can see ahead of them a goal in life, the support they need to get there, and it is a Britain therefore where effort is rewarded, ambition fulfilled, potential realized, a Britain of high aspirations." (Brown, 2007)

In this extract, ambitions for the global competitiveness of the national economy are folded together with ambitions for individual young people situated within their local schools. Various scales are melded together here, for example in the aspiration for 'world class schools' where both the local and the global are fused in one imagined place.

In June 2008, Bev Hughes MP (then the Minister for Children, Young People and Families) acknowledged that the government's 'aspirations agenda' signified a major shift in thinking about the state's responsibility for young people's futures – "[it] requires us to think again about our expectations, to challenge preconceptions and change the terms of reference around young people" (Hughes, 2008). The promotion of a politics of aspiration in youth policy (not just in Britain) has led to young people increasingly being expected to take personal responsibility for their own social mobility (Davidson, 2008; Jeffrey, 2010). However, the dismantling of state welfare provision and related structural changes have simultaneously served to make it harder for young people to access the resources they need to achieve the social mobility that is imagined for them (Mizen, 2003; Lister, 2006). In a period of global recession, the efforts of young people to 'obtain [the] social goods associated with "adulthood"' (Jeffery, 2010, p 496), such as stable employment and housing, are being undermined and they are finding it harder to complete the transition to adulthood, finding themselves trapped instead in perpetual 'youth'.

During the early 2000s, widening participation interventions were targeted at individuals who were understood to inhabit (a particular type of) 'local' place. In this context, social mobility was presented as being predicated on overcoming (and physically moving away from) the problems associated with particular small-scale local territories (Cameron, 2006). These 'local' spaces were understood, implicitly, as predominantly urban, containing close-knit, inward-looking communities comprised of low income, poorly educated populations over-reliant on welfare benefits (Raco, 2009). As a result, widening participation interventions were directed at the local scale, with ministers advocating that "[w]e must focus on 'making it happen' locally" (Hughes, 2008). This was not just an imperative to focus interventions where they were most needed, it was consolidating an assumption that young people from low income families would not travel for higher education. Of course, the introduction of university tuition fees made this more likely.

Although most English universities recruit students at a national scale, most have also focused on working 'locally' to recruit non-traditional students. In a review of widening participation practice, HEFCE (2006, p 40) identified that, for many universities, the schools and neighbourhoods targeted for widening participation interventions by most universities were 'intensely local', with only a minority of elite institutions engaging in this work beyond their regional location. Universities typically target their widening participation work on 'deprived' areas in their locality. However, HEFCE (2006) noted that there was inconsistency across the sector in terms of how universities identify such neighbourhoods. This lack of a consistent targeting methodology can allow middle-class students to benefit from widening participation initiatives – for example, the children of gentrifying families living in otherwise socially deprived areas of inner cities, according to indices of multiple deprivation. Furthermore, by locating educational inequalities as 'local', the broader national and global relationships that cause these inequalities are left unchallenged.

The association of working-class young people with the 'local' scale serves to fix them in place, drawing attention to their distance from the cosmopolitan habitus of higher education, even as the ultimate aim of widening participation initiatives is to enable their mobility beyond these communities (Taylor, 2008). Indeed, it can be suggested that New Labour policy discourses needed to present the lives of these young people as being fixed in place in order to justify the prioritisation placed on enabling their social and spatial *mobility*. After all, these are the young people identified by Gordon Brown (2008) as belonging to 'the poorest and the most left behind families'.

In the context of recent widening participation policy and practice, local place became a convenient proxy for social class. It facilitated the targeting of interventions on those young people deemed to have inappropriately low aspirations without ever directly acknowledging their social class. Specific scalar orientations became attached to different expressions of aspiration in this policy discourse: 'high' aspirations (for future professional careers) were presented as expansive, mobile and operating at the national and global scales; while, 'low' (or 'inappropriate') aspirations were considered insular and fixed at the local and domestic scales.

## Understanding aspiration-interventions in practice

Many widening participation practitioners understood the New Labour government's motivation for 'raising aspirations', but were critical of the focus on raising aspirations (rather than attainment). Even an audit report on national widening participation activity by the National Audit Office (2008, p 6) acknowledged the false premise of prioritising aspirations without addressing inequalities in attainment:

> The attainment of qualifications by students at secondary school or college plays a critical role in gaining access to higher education. Low achievement by some pupils in secondary schools is the principal reason for the difference between rates of participation in higher education for different groups. Notably, all applicants with the necessary qualifications are equally likely to accept a higher education place as others with the same level of attainment, regardless of their family background.

This statement tells only part of the story. The higher education participation rates by young people from different social backgrounds vary significantly. Young people from more affluent families remain more likely to attend research-intensive universities to undertake competitive degree courses (Corver, 2010; HEFCE, 2010). Those institutions with low to medium grade tariffs for admission to their degrees have carried the weight of increasing and widening participation in the English university sector. I interviewed an Aimhigher Coordinator working in two inner London boroughs with very diverse populations. In common with other London-based practitioners (but less so those in the East Midlands), she noted:

> "... that for a lot of the kids the aspiration is not the thing that's lacking. A lot of my schools are very good at this now. ... What we find is that the reason that a lot of people are not making it onto both FE and HE courses is because they're not getting the grades." (Interview with Alison)

By promoting a politics of aspiration recent education policy has privatised responsibility for the relatively low educational attainment of young people from low income families within working-class homes, rather than addressing those inequalities perpetuated by the education system.

Policy initiatives designed to raise the aspirations of young people were primarily intended to move their ambitions up a perceived hierarchy of acceptable future careers. However, in practice, these interventions also operated to increase the intensity of young people's aspirations – making them adhere more strongly to those imagined futures. Universities continue to engage in this work through a fairly standard suite of activities; these include student mentoring schemes, taster days and masterclasses that offer a flavour of undergraduate life, and intensive (frequently residential) summer schools. These activities are considered effective because they utilise the 'higher education environment to change learner attitudes, aspirations and misconceptions' (HEFCE, 2006, p 23).

One-off activities can inspire individual teenagers, but increasingly universities have been encouraged to engage young people in sustained programmes of activities that build cumulatively on each other for maximum impact (HEFCE, 2006, pp 24-5):

> "I know from looking at lots of evaluations of students and talking to previous [widening participation] students who are now in HE and ... there's so many of them talk about a wow event that just turned their lives." (Interview with Neville, widening participation practitioner, East Midlands)

Many of the practitioners interviewed recognised the power of 'wow' moments and gave examples of times when they had witnessed young people being powerfully affected by such activities. In events of this kind practical activities utilising those resources that are available in universities (but less frequently in schools) are mobilised to provoke 'wow' moments that attempt to stimulate, affect and move young people's aspirations. These intense moments of surprise and revelation are designed to generate enthusiasm and can have profound impacts on how young people perceive what might be possible (in their future lives). Residential summer schools, campus visits and encounters with student mentors serve to provide young people with time and space away from those people and places that can depress their ambitions. At their best, widening participation activities provide young people with opportunities to think differently about their futures.

In many ways these activities sat comfortably within the scope of the New Labour's promotion of an existential politics of aspiration. Most of the practitioners interviewed recognised that the focus of policy on raising young people's aspirations was initiated to meet the needs of the national economy and to expand the development of a highly skilled workforce. But a few practitioners, such as Doug who manages widening participation initiatives in the East Midlands, articulated an alternative case for widening participation that was founded on a commitment to radical class politics and redistributive understandings of equality:

> "Well, we'd all like to think it's about social justice and, you know, it's a moral thing to do. But of course, ultimately, a lot of these initiatives are driven by the needs of the economy, and I think that's top of the agenda – it wouldn't be done if it was just a social imperative.... So it's about competitiveness. It's a recognition that India and China have basically developed their economies based upon, you know, well, people with higher level skills than we have in this country.... But many of us working in WP [widening participation], of course, do it because it's an ideological commitment ... because we believe in it and we believe in equality."

Doug's comments suggest that despite the increasingly tight guidance provided by Aimhigher and other government agencies regarding the targeting and delivery of aspiration-raising activities, there is still considerable 'wriggle room' for practitioners, allowing them to deliver educational activities for young people that are motivated by alternative conceptions of social justice and, hence, alternative outcomes.

Faced with these dilemmas, many of the widening participation practitioners interviewed chose to orientate their activities in a way that resisted the government's individualising politics of aspiration. Although they continued to primarily work with young people as individuals (rather than fostering collective peer support and a culture of mutual aid), they sought to enable them to make informed choices about the higher education and careers available to them, rather than disciplining their aspirations to satisfy the needs of the national economy. For some practitioners the aim of their work was to enable working-class teenagers to achieve social mobility (but only if they wanted to); while, for others, the emphasis was on making a small contribution to greater social equity and helping to level the playing field of educational outcomes and life chances for these young people.

## The challenge of (re)orientating aspiration-interventions

The focus of widening participation policy on 'raising' the aspirations of working-class young people implied that their existing aspirations were inappropriate and deficient (Brown, 2011). In this final section of my chapter the possibilities for thinking differently about how to act on young people's aspirations are explored. An aspiration is an affective stance that is orientated to the future. It is a dream or ambition for what might be achieved in times to come (Nilsen, 1999). While it is useful for young people to imagine what they want their future lives to become and, crucially, to develop the ability to plan concretely for the realisation of those aspirations (Brannen and Nilsen, 2007), it is useful to bring spatiality and geographical concepts back into thinking about their aspirations. I want to do this in two ways – first, to think about how aspirations might be mobilised in a way that acknowledges young people as active social agents; and, second, to think about ways in which their aspirations can be orientated spatially as well as temporally.

In proposing interventions that mobilise young people's aspirations, I am partly advocating a return to the initial phase of widening participation work seen in the early years of the 1997 New Labour government, when the emphasis was far more on enabling young people to achieve the aspirations they already had. But it is also useful to think about how and where young people's aspirations are orientated and how widening participation interventions seek to (re)orientate them. Alongside all the talk of 'raising aspirations' (orientating them higher), government ministers and widening participation practitioners have often also spoken of the need for 'broadening [the] horizons' of young people (orientating them further or in new directions). While talk of raising aspirations can imply that young people hold deficient aspirations that need dragging up to an acceptable standard, talk of broadening horizons can also imply a more hopeful (and less derogatory) exposure to unseen, unconsidered options and opportunities. More problematically, perhaps, a focus on 'broadening horizons' also implies that work (with and) on young people's aspirations requires that they should be exposed to and engage in reconfigured spatial relations and orientations. There is an implicit association between social mobility and geographical mobility that underpins many existing widening participation initiatives, but such issues are seldom directly and openly discussed.

Despite the tendency in widening participation policy to project an image of the young people who are the objects of these interventions as being fixed in particular types of multiply deprived local places, a Cabinet Office report published towards the end of the final New Labour government

(Social Exclusion Task Force et al, 2008) recognised that not all deprived communities are the same and that important variations in the social and *spatial* relations within different communities can have significant impacts on young people's aspirations. This report acknowledged that socially-deprived young people growing up in ethnically mixed inner-city neighbourhoods that are shaped by transnational diasporic connections that extend far beyond the local territory, often have higher aspirations than their peers living in equally impoverished, but more physically and socially isolated areas such as small towns bearing the scars of prolonged deindustrialisation or large peripheral social housing estates on the edge of cities. These lessons have yet to be explored in depth in either widening participation policy or practice.

In considering how young people's aspirations might be (re)orientated, I am calling for widening participation initiatives that foster a sense of what Massey (2005, p 15) has described as '"outwardlookingness" ... a positivity and aliveness to the world beyond one's own turf'. Such work would focus on enabling young people to encounter possibilities beyond their familiar local circumstances rather than primarily encouraging them to aim higher up the career ladder. It is expansive, rather than hierarchical in its approach and ethics. For Ahmed (2006, p 8), a focus on orientations draws attention to starting points and:

> how we proceed from 'here,' which affects how what is 'there' appears, how it presents itself ... The starting point for orientation is the point from which the world unfolds: the 'here' of the body and the 'where' of its dwelling.

In these terms Green and White (2007, p ix), in their work on the geographies of young people's aspirations, argue that it is vital that widening participation interventions are developed in ways that are sensitive to the histories and geographies of specific places, their demographics, current and historical patterns of employment, and local cultural norms. At first glance, there might appear to be a disjuncture between Massey's outward-looking attention to place-beyond-place and the (potentially) more inward-looking focus of Green and White on the specific dynamics of particular localities. However, it is important to attend to the local specifics in order to think critically about how these are produced 'beyond place' and to develop strategies for enabling young people to experience life beyond their home territories. In addition to sympathetically paying attention to where young people are coming from, my call for greater attention to how young people's aspirations are orientated also draws critical attention to how widening participation and other youth policies serve to direct young people in 'in some ways rather than others' (Ahmed, 2006, p 21). Since the early 2000s, widening participation policy has been too tightly tied to particular types of social mobility and an orientation to 'reaching certain points along a [preferred and expected] life course' as a social good (Ahmed, 2006, p 21). By thinking more spatially about the orientation of young people's aspirations, this chapter seeks to highlight the benefits of thinking not just about what lies ahead, but also what lies beside (Sedgwick, 2003) and beyond.

In practice, many of the best widening participation initiatives do seek to expose young people to opportunities that they might not otherwise have come into contact with (either directly through their own life experiences and those of close family and friends, or through representations in the media). As Alison commented, in relation to her work with young people in inner London:

> "For some of them it really is about talking, just broadening their aspirations if you like. They've got a tiny narrow view, and of course they do because they're young and they don't have that life experience. Sometimes it's about tweaking the edges of that view and pulling it further and going 'well, let's just take a peek around the corner and see what else there is'." (Interview with Alison)

Green and White (2007) have outlined a range of relatively mundane and easily achievable interventions that might help to broaden the horizons of young people living in inward-looking, socially isolated neighbourhoods. These include providing young people with subsidised travel and training in how to use public transport to travel beyond their local territory. More than this, they advocate arranging 'visits/trips to unfamiliar places, [and] bringing people from other districts into the local area' (Green and White, 2007, p 80). Through this simple support, young people can be enabled to break through the 'wall in the head' (Hanley, 2007) that can be generated by growing up in monocultural, physically isolated locations.

For most university-based widening practitioners, the major implication of working to enable young people to broaden their horizons is to resist the temptation to focus on recruiting 'local' students to their local university. As Janet confessed:

> "We very strongly encourage local students to go somewhere else. You take your university hat off, and then you say, 'well think about the enrichment that that offers'. Everybody knows, don't they, that students who stay at home all the way through their degree course, they're missing out on all sorts of things, not least of which is the ability to grow their own independence." (Interview with Janet)

However, even when this is not possible, and young people feel compelled by family and financial constraints to remain at home and study at their local university, universities can still play an important role in helping them to continue to broaden their horizons by participating in study abroad and work experience placements. In these ways, students from widening participation backgrounds can still be enabled to experience 'place beyond place' (Massey, 2005), even if they remain living at home and studying locally. At the risk of making a professionally indulgent point, school and university geographers have a useful role to play here in engaging young people with the world beyond their home communities.

Doing widening participation work in this manner, however, still does not (necessarily) overcome one of the fundamental paradoxes that confront both the most reflexive practitioners working in the field and the young people they work with. Work that broadens young people's horizons by opening up new vistas, new connections and new ways of orientating themselves to the world can still have the effect of disrupting existing social networks and relationships to place in ways that can be deeply unsettling (Brown, 2011). Progression to higher education for young people from families and neighbourhoods where few people have preceded them along that life path can risk alienating them from peers and family members who no longer understand the world they (aspire to) inhabit. This can be a daunting possibility, and too often existing widening participation work does not equip young people to navigate these complex emotional geographies. However, experiencing and learning to appreciate the value of place beyond place can also serve to disrupt simplistic equations between social mobility and spatial mobility. It can offer young people new resources for exploring new ways of being without forsaking existing relationships and attachments to place.

## Conclusions

There have been three distinct phases in British widening participation policy since Blair's New Labour government was first elected in 1997. In each phase, widening participation policy and practice has sought to work on young people's aspirations for the future in different ways. This chapter has focused on the second of these phases, which focused on raising the aspirations of young people from low income and directing them towards higher education as a means to professional employment that might contribute to future national economic competitiveness.

Since the Conservative-Liberal Democrat Coalition government was elected in May 2010, the policy context for widening participation work in England has changed rapidly. Funding for the Aimhigher partnerships ceased in July 2011. For the academic year 2012–13, the cap on university tuition fees in England has been lifted and, for many universities, fees will treble to £9,000 per year. To charge this new maximum tuition fee these universities will be expected to offer scholarships and other incentives for students from low income families. The long-term impact of these changes on the efforts to widen participation in higher education remains open to question.

In critically examining this phase of recent education policy, this chapter makes two key arguments and one suggestion. Together these contributions extend recent debates in geography and the critical social policy about the 'politics of aspiration' (Archer, 2007; Davidson, 2008; Raco, 2009). My first argument is that recent widening participation policy was orientated to multiple spatial scales simultaneously – it aspired to improve national economic performance globally, but was targeted at particular types of local places. Different expressions of aspiration were ascribed to different spatial scales in this policy discourse: 'high' educational and career aspirations were promoted as expansive and operating at the national and global scales; while 'low' aspirations were considered insular and fixed at the local scale. In these policy debates local place became a proxy for social class and facilitates the targeting of widening participation interventions on those young people with 'low aspirations' without ever directly acknowledging their social class. This reinforced a wider tendency to rescale neoliberal policy interventions away from state-led action to tackle systemic inequalities and towards the development of individual aspirations.

My second argument is that, in practice, widening participation interventions that sought to work on young people's aspirations operated through a particular range of spatial practices. Frequently, widening participation practitioners take the young people they work with out of the school and community settings with which they are familiar to distance them from those people and places that may serve to limit their ambitions and to expose them to possible futures they may never have encountered or contemplated before. By working in this way, some widening participation practitioners enact modest forms of resistance to the individualised neoliberal politics of aspiration which underpin widening participation policy. In practice, they are seeking to broaden young people's horizons, rather than to raise their aspirations.

The modest proposal made in this chapter is to capitalise on this resistant tendency in widening participation practice. Although it is beyond the scope of this chapter to fully flesh out alternative proposals for how future widening participation policy could operate, it has been argued that recent debates in geography (and related disciplines) about the value of experiencing 'place beyond place' (Massey, 2005) and why our orientation to the world matters (Ahmed, 2006) could offer useful tools to inform this work. Such an approach could usefully be informed by critical pedagogies of hope (hooks, 2003; Freire, 2004) used in various forms of informal education and youth work (see Davies and Cartwright, this volume, Chapters Five and Nine). To talk of broadening the horizons of young people from low income families does not denigrate their existing aspirations, or assume that they are always already lacking. There is, of course, a danger that this approach would still leave many young people 'left behind' in disadvantaged communities, and that they would still experience these places as isolated and 'local'. However, by working not just with individual young people, but within the social networks that matter to them, such an approach could have the effect of developing a broader awareness among community members that they live in a multiply-connected place. It offers young people (and their communities) the possibility of more hopeful encounters with unseen, unconsidered options and opportunities, and it values the power of happenstance over the narrowly prescribed futures envisaged by recent widening participation policy.

## Note

[1] Aimhigher was the responsibility of the erstwhile Department for Education and Skills (DfES) until June 2007 and then the Department for Innovation, Universities and Skills (DIUS) until June 2009.

## References

Ahmed, S. (2006) *Queer phenomenology*, Durham, NC: Duke University Press.

Ansell, N. (2009) 'Childhood and the politics of scale: descaling children's geographies', *Progress in Human Geography*, vol 33, no 2, pp 190-209.

Archer, L. (2007) 'Diversity, equality and higher education: a critical reflection on the ab/uses of equity discourse within widening participation', *Teaching in Higher Education*, vol 12, no 5-6, pp 635-53.

Bangs, J., Macbeath, J. and Galton, M. (2010) *Reinventing schools, reforming teaching: from political visions to classroom reality*, London: Routledge.

Blunkett, D. (2000) *North of England speech on the future of education*, 6 January 2000, http://www.dfes.gov.uk/speeches/speech.cfm?SppechID=34 (last accessed April 2011 but no longer available online).

Brannen, J. and Nilsen, A. (2007) 'Young people, time horizons and planning: a response to Anderson et al', *Sociology*, vol 41, no 1, pp 153-60.

Brown, G. (2007) *Speech on education presented at the University of Greenwich*, 31 October 2007, http://www.number10.gov.uk/Page13675 (last accessed April 2011 but no longer available online).

Brown, G. (2008) *Speech on education and social mobility*, 23 June 2008, http://www.number10.gov.uk/Page16181 (last accessed April 2011 but no longer available online).

Brown, G. (2011) 'Emotional geographies of young people's aspirations for adult life', *Children's Geographies*, vol 9, no 1, pp 7-22.

Cameron, A. (2006) 'Geographies of welfare and exclusion: social inclusion and exception', *Progress in Human Geography*, vol 30, no 3, pp 396-404.

Corver, M. (2010) *Using UCAS data in policy-making*, paper presented at the UCAS Research Forum, 3 June, http://www.ucasresearch.com/documents/ucasdata_policymaking.pdf.

Davidson, E. (2008) 'Marketing the self: the politics of aspiration among middle-class Silicon Valley youth', *Environment and Planning A*, vol 40, no 12, pp 2814–30.

Evans, B. (2010) 'Anticipating fatness: childhood, affect and the pre-emptive "war on obesity"', *Transactions of the Institute of British Geographers*, vol 35, no 1, pp 21-38.

Freire, P. (2004) *Pedagogy of hope*, London: Continuum.

Gewirtz, S. (2001) 'Cloning the Blairs: New Labour's programme for the resocialization of working-class parents', *Journal of Educational Policy*, vol 16, no 4, pp 365-78.

Green, A.E. and White, R.J. (2007) *Attachment to place: social networks, mobility and prospects for young people,* York: Joseph Rowntree Foundation, http://www.jrf.org.uk/sites/files/jrf/2126-attachment-to-place.pdf.

Green, A.E. and White, R.J. (2008) 'Shaped by place: young people's decisions about education, training and work', *Benefits*, vol 16, no 3, pp 213-24.

Hanley, L. (2007) *Estates: an intimate history*, London: Granta.

HEFCE (Higher Education Funding Council for England) (2006) *Higher education outreach: targeting disadvantaged learners*, Bristol: HEFCE, http://www.hefce.ac.uk/pubs/hefce/2007/07_12/.

HEFCE (Higher Education Funding Council for England) (2010) *Trends in young participation in higher education: core results for England*, Bristol: HEFCE, http://www.hefce.ac.uk/pubs/hefce/2010/10_03/.

HM Government (2010) *The Coalition: our programme for government,* http://www.cabinetoffice.gov.uk/media/409088/pfg_coalition.pdf.

Holloway, S.L and Pimlott-Wilson, H. (2011) 'The politics of aspiration: neo-liberal education policy, 'low' parental aspirations, and primary school Extended Services in disadvantaged communities', *Children's Geographies*, vol 9, no 1, pp 79-94.

hooks, b. (2003) *Teaching community: a pedagogy of hope*, New York: Routledge.

Hughes, B. (2008) Speech on 'the aspiration agenda: social mobility and the Greater Manchester challenge', 27 June 2008, http://www.dcsf.gov.uk/speeches/speech.cfm?SpeechID=811 (last accessed April 2011 but no longer available online).

Jeffrey, C. (2010) 'Geographies of children and youth I: eroding maps of life', *Progress in Human Geography*, vol 34, no 4, pp 496-505.

Kettley, N. (2007) 'The past, present and future of widening participation research', *British Journal of Sociology of Education*, vol 28, no 3, pp 333-47.

Lister R. (2006) 'Children (but not women) first: UK government, child welfare and gender', *Critical Social Policy*, vol 26, pp 315-35.

Massey, D. (2005) *For space*, London: Sage.

Mizen, P. (2003) 'The best days of your life? Youth, policy and Blair's UK government', *Critical Social Policy*, vol 23, pp 453-76.

National Audit Office (2008) *Widening participation in higher education*, London: TSO.

NCIHE (National Committee of Inquiry into Higher Education) (1997) *Report of the national committee*, https://bei.leeds.ac.uk/Partners/NCIHE/.

Nilsen, A. (1999) 'Where is the future? Time and space as categories in analyses of young people's image of the future', *Innovation*, vol 12, no 2, pp 175-94.

Purcell, K. (2011) 'Discourses of aspiration, opportunity and attainment: promoting and contesting the Academy schools programme', *Children's Geographies*, vol 9, no 1, pp 49-61.

Raco, M. (2009) 'From expectations to aspirations: state modernisation, urban policy, and the existential politics of welfare in the UK', *Political Geography*, vol 28, pp 436-44.

Sedgwick, E.K. (2003) *Touching feeling: affect, pedagogy, performativity*, Durham, NC: Duke University Press.

Social Exclusion Task Force, Department for Children, Schools and Families, and Department for Communities and Local Government (2008) *Aspirations and attainment in deprived communities*, London: Cabinet Office.

Taylor, Y. (2008) 'Good students, bad pupils: constructions of "aspiration", "disadvantage" and social class in undergraduate-led widening participation work', *Educational Review*, vol 60, no 2, pp 155-68.

Warrington, M. (2008) 'Decisions and transitions: meeting the needs of the "knowledge economy"', *Environment & Planning C: Government & Policy*, vol 26, pp 924-37.

# seven

# School choice versus social cohesion: examining the ways education policies shape children's geographies in the UK

*Susie Weller*

## Introduction

Over the past two decades children's geographies within Britain have been shaped, in part, by an education system founded on quasi-market principles. As a result children, particularly those in urban areas, may attend a school some distance from home. Little attention has been afforded to the implications of such policies on children's geographies and, more specifically, on their opportunities to create neighbourhood social capital by making connections with and within the spaces surrounding their homes and beyond. Drawing on a four-year study that explored the significance of social capital for children and parents during the transition to secondary school, this chapter explores the articulation between families' responses to school choice policies and children's geographies. In so doing, it reflects critically on the spatial connotations of, and tensions between (national) school choice policies and wider drives by the New Labour government to promote (local) cohesion. It is hoped the chapter will contribute to the sub-disciplinary field of 'Children's Geographies' which has, over the past decade or so, taken a variety of spatial perspectives to elucidate important issues in the diverse lives of children and teenagers across the world (for example Holloway and Valentine, 2000; Aitken, 2001; Matthews, 2003).

## The education market and geographies of inequality

Notions of choice have been apparent, to some degree, within the British education system for over 60 years, although parental choice has been most profusely promoted over the past two decades with the privatisation of the education system (Taylor, 2001a; Ball, 2006). The increased emphasis on choice in social policy along with individualisation, marketisation and privatisation was born out of an era of neoliberalism under the Conservative government of the 1980–90s, which sought to increase public sector efficiency (Weekes-Bernard, 2007). For schools, such drives centred on moving away from the comprehensive school model of the late 1960s to a quasi-market system that positioned schools as market competitors and parents as consumers. The 1980 Education Act advocated parental expression of choice and put in place arrangements for parents to appeal against decisions on school allocation. Subsequent measures (outlined in the 1988 Education Reform Act) applied to England and Wales, but a similar approach was taken in Scotland and Northern Ireland (Chitty, 2009).

The 'third way' ideology of the New Labour government (1997–2010) saw the continuation of quasi-market principles, tempered by state intervention to tackle inequalities particularly in disadvantaged areas (Paterson, 2003; Tomlinson, 2003). As part of a drive to raise standards New Labour set about modernising the comprehensive system by diversifying further the types of school available (such as specialist, faith, single-sex, community, and schools part-funded by industry) with the aim of catering for children's differing abilities and interests, along with the concerns and choices of parents (Chitty, 2009). New Labour's approach to school diversity centred on two principles: school specialisation, and collaboration between schools including the sharing of expertise. Policies to promote fairness in the admissions process were also introduced, along with the lessening of local authority control over schools, and a new emphasis on partnerships between schools, parents and the public and private sectors (Rogers, 2007). Among the plethora of policies that have bolstered the choice agenda key initiatives include: the 2001 *Schools achieving success* White Paper and 2002 Education Act that promoted the further specialisation of schools and the establishment of new schools such as Academies,[1] and the 2005 *Higher standards, better schools for all* White Paper that included emphasis on more choice and support for parents. The new Conservative-Liberal Democrat Coalition government appears to be augmenting such policies through, for instance, the introduction of independent, publicly funded 'free schools' operating outside local authority control and set up in response to parental demand (DoE, 2010).

Critics such as Tomlinson (2003) argue that the modernisation of the comprehensive system is essentially 'a return to a system of overt or covert selection and 'choice' for a few at the expense of the many' (p 200) that has led to the polarisation of schools and dichtomisation of families into 'winners' and 'losers'. Research suggests middle-class families are more confident and comfortable than working-class families with being consumers of education and that their social, economic and cultural capital can confer advantage in the competition for places at well-resourced schools (Ball and Vincent, 2001; Ball, 2006). Although emphasis has been placed on class differences, spatial inequalities have been afforded less attention despite differences in the policies implemented in the devolved UK regions[2] and differing markets at the local level (Taylor, 2001a; 2001b; 2002; Chitty, 2009). Some have accredited geographers with foreseeing the spatial implications of a market-oriented system and with placing due emphasis on geographies of school choice and allocation (Taylor, 2002; Holloway et al, 2010). Related work also exists in other international contexts (for instance Witten et al, 2003; André-Bechely, 2007; Butler and van Zantan, 2007; Noreisch, 2007) and while this chapter examines the local implications of national policies on school choice it is important to acknowledge that analogous experiences exist in other regions where neoliberal approaches to education predominate. With the stress on *parental* choice, however, the connotations of such policies on *children's* everyday geographies have hitherto been under-researched.

Forming a central tenet of New Labour's 'third way' approach, social capital has become an increasingly popular concept in policy debates surrounding both school choice and social cohesion (Baron et al, 2000; Forrest and Kearns, 2001; Hetherington et al, 2007). Definitions of social capital employed by influential theorists vary, with authors such as Coleman (1988) and Putnam (1995) viewing social capital as a positive force for community cohesion. Putnam (2000) differentiates between 'bonding' and 'bridging' social capital, with the former denoting inward-looking connections among homogeneous groups that enable people to 'get by', while the latter refers to outward-looking connections among heterogeneous groups that permit people to 'get ahead'. Alternatively, Bourdieu (1986) considers the interaction between different forms of capital (namely cultural, economic and social) regarding social capital as a source of inequality, not equally available to all (Adkins, 2005). Seeking to contribute to the growing body of work on children's social capital, this chapter is framed by an understanding of social capital as the resources that individuals and collectives derive from their social networks; it is through social interaction that social capital is developed. While recognising that conceptualisations of 'neighbourhood' and 'cohesion' are complex and contested, this chapter focuses on local interaction at the neighbourhood level and solidarity in terms of the propensity towards having, at least some, networks grounded in the locality (Forrest and Kearns, 2001). By focusing on the implications for children's geographies it is hoped that the chapter will contribute to the growing international literature that elucidates the connections between neoliberal approaches to education and wider geographies of cohesion and/or segregation (for example Witten et al, 2003; André-Bechely, 2007).

## 'Locality, schools and social capital' project

This chapter draws on a project that explored the significance of social capital to children and parents during the transition to secondary school. The study formed part of the Families & Social Capital ESRC Research Group;

a five-year programme of work that examined family change and social capital in different UK contexts.[3] The project employed a mixed-method approach combining large-scale quantitative data analysis with in-depth qualitative accounts that focused on the experiences of a diverse sample of children and parents residing in areas where access to well-resourced schools was limited. The five main research sites comprised: two inner-London boroughs with ethnically and socially diverse populations; a White working-class inner-city area in central England; a new town in southern England with a predominantly lower middle-class population; and an affluent outer London suburb. Twelve primary schools, identified on the basis of ward and school characteristics, provided the locus for initial fieldwork.

Conducted between 2003 and 2005 during the New Labour administration, fieldwork comprised two phases. During the first 'pre-transfer' phase 588 children (two cohorts in 2003 and 2004) in the final year of primary school (aged 10–11 years) completed questionnaires that explored their role in choosing schools, anticipated changes in, for instance, friendships and school journeys, and their interests, spatial freedoms and aspirations for the future. Concurrently, 76 parents (primarily mothers) were interviewed in their homes to determine their experiences of 'choosing'[4] schools, concerns about their child's imminent move, parental networks, practices and values. From the 12 primary schools children moved to 103 secondary schools, rendering the tracking of every participant problematic. The second 'post-transfer' phase, therefore, focused on a sub-sample of children. Follow-up questionnaires were completed by 81 children aged 12–14. Focus groups were carried out with 75 children across a variety of schools in order to glean peer group perspectives. These data were complemented with individual interviews comprising a diverse sample of 20 children that enabled more in-depth discussion of personal experiences. Such qualitative data provided rich accounts enabling grounded critical analysis of the implications of key policy drives on school choice on the everyday lives of participants, along with reflection on the ways in which children, parents and schools responded to the 'choice agenda'.

## Implications for everyday geographies

The chapter began by exploring some of the implications of school choice policies and families' responses to such policies on children's geographies. Many children in Britain attend a primary school relatively close to their homes, while the distance travelled to secondary school varies widely. National data suggests that in 2008 the average length of a journey to primary school was 2.5 km increasing to 5.5 km at secondary school (ONS, 2010). In our study just under half of the parents interviewed (n = 76) explicitly stated the distance travelled or the nature of the journey impacted on their 'choices'. Indeed, many feared particular/unknown geographies and had concerns about the accessibility and cost of transport, and their child(ren)'s safety especially given the restricted geographies of many children at primary school. Research on parental choice has highlighted class differences with middle-class families often regarded as 'active choosers', seeking places at well-resourced schools outside their immediate vicinity whereas working-class families are seen to place value on 'community', often favouring schools and networks rooted in their locality (Ball, 2006; Brown, this volume, Chapter Six). In our study children who travelled further to secondary school were likely to have parents who considered a greater number of possible schools, were less concerned that their children maintain local links, and were often, although not exclusively, from middle-class backgrounds. Indeed, some actively pursued places at more distant schools in an effort to (re)structure their child(ren)'s networks. Differing education markets at the local and regional level were therefore implicated in the likelihood of children attending their nearest secondary school.

For many children travelling to their new school marked a significant shift in their independent mobility. In Year Six, 48 per cent (n = 588) travelled to school without an adult, while 66 per cent expected to do so at secondary school. Girls were just as likely to anticipate travelling long distances as boys (see Table 7.1).

**Table 7.1:** Anticipated length of journey to secondary school by gender

| Distance (n = 588) | Girls (%) | Boys (%) |
|---|---|---|
| Short walk (less than 1 mile) | 35.3 | 31.8 |
| Long walk (1–2 miles) | 23.3 | 22.2 |
| Too far to walk (more than 2 miles) | 28.2 | 28.0 |
| No answer | 13.2 | 18.0 |

**Table 7.2:** Anticipated length of journey to secondary school by research site

| Distance n = 588 | Main research sites (%) | | | | | Additional areas[a] (%) | | |
|---|---|---|---|---|---|---|---|---|
| | Inner-South London | Inner-East London | Inner-city, Central England | Southern New Town | Outer London suburb | Inner-London | Inner-London | Inner-London |
| Short walk (less than 1 mile) | 37.5 | 42.0 | 26.5 | 32.7 | 25.3 | 0 | 0 | 0 |
| Long walk (1-2 miles) | 17.5 | 24.4 | 26.5 | 26.9 | 23.0 | 0 | 0 | 0 |
| Too far to walk (more than 2 miles) | 28.1 | 18.3 | 27.5 | 26.0 | 43.7 | 100.0 | 100.0 | 0 |
| No answer | 16.9 | 15.3 | 19.6 | 14.4 | 8.0 | 0 | 0 | 100.0 |

[a] A small number of participants lived in three areas just outside the main research sites.

There was, however, a significant difference (p<0.007) between the distance travelled and a child's area of residence (see Table 7.2).

Children from our affluent outer London site were more likely to travel further than children living in inner-city East London. Echoing the work of Burgess et al (2006) this reflected middle-class parents' desire for selective schools in neighbouring local authorities. In our study educationally ambitious migrants, often from middle-class backgrounds overseas but living in disadvantaged areas, also sought schools outside the vicinity. Several children described a substantial commute of up to 18 km, often undertaken on public transport without an adult. Many of these children spoke of the positive effects on their confidence as a result of their long or complex journey. Nonetheless for some the move to secondary school signalled a decline in their independent mobility, with 28 per cent (n = 588) of those who travelled to primary school unaccompanied making the journey to secondary school by car. It is apparent that children's independent mobilities can both expand or contract with respect to the freedoms afforded.

Aside from simply growing older the period surrounding secondary school transition signalled a time when parents often felt forced to afford their children more independent mobility as Oba, a Nigerian, socially mobile mother from inner-London conveyed:

> "No, they don't go out on their own now but when they go to secondary school it will change ... she'll have to and she'll go out on her own."

Children from working-class backgrounds and those seeking places at sought-after schools outside of the immediate locality were most likely to have the greatest autonomy and, in general, families living in our inner-city sites were more likely to actively encourage their children to become street-savvy. The transition was regarded as an important time for gaining 'street literacy' and practising to be streetwise. Cahill (2000) describes street literacy as acquiring and using knowledge about, and constructing the self through, experiences of the local environment, and this notion certainly applied to many children in our study, with journeys planned and practised during the weeks leading up to the transition. Importantly, older children, often siblings, friends and family acquaintances, were drawn upon to help negotiate new geographies. Lady Loud, a Black-British, working-class girl from inner-London, travelled by bus to her school 5 km away. She initially sought the support of her older brother, but then found new friends with whom she could travel:

"On the first day my brother took me and then on the second day after I decided that I was going to go into school with some of my friends."

Existing networks can play an important role in providing resources or social capital thus broadening children's spatial and social horizons (Morrow, 1999; Edwards et al, 2006; Holland et al, 2007; Weller, 2007a; 2007b). Here the significance of children's own social capital, neglected by many influential authors, becomes apparent.

Some children noted symbolic markers of their new-found independent mobility. For instance Alan, a White-British, working-class boy in inner-London was given his own front door key when he moved to secondary school. While seemingly trivial the need for many parents to afford their children greater freedom as a result of their move to secondary school often had a profound effect on their opportunities to negotiate local geographies. For some this increased independence also impacted on their leisure-time. Jazzy B, a Black-British, working-class girl from inner-London provides a case in point:

"In primary school my Mum used to drop me everywhere and take me places but now I can go there by myself. She still sometimes, when it's late, she still sometimes picks me up but I can go places by myself now."

Despite many children gaining independence during this period, this did not always apply to all aspects of their lives. Discussions with highly ambitious middle-class parents often drew attention to some contradictions, for while some were happy to allow their children to travel long distances to school alone or with friends, many did not afford their children similar spatial freedoms within the local neighbourhood. Matthew, a White-British, middle-class boy from outer-London travelled unaccompanied to his private school 10 km away. He was critical of his parents' emphasis on structured activities, and his local networks were limited to his involvement in the church. He did discuss occasional interaction with a local boy who also attended his school:

"Occasionally but not very often and it depends ... sometimes we come home together if we come home at the same time but, today for instance, he had cross-country and I had choir, so we came home at different times."

The friendship networks of children attending schools outside their immediate vicinity were often dispersed, rendering socialising outside of school challenging, particularly without the help of parents. In this respect the journey became, for some, a significant time to engage with local and wider geographies without an adult. Some of those attending more local schools also had restricted leisure-time independent mobilities. Kiera, a Vietnamese, working-class girl living in inner-London described such a scenario. Kiera was not permitted to go out without an adult during her leisure-time. The relatively short walk between home and school, therefore, represented her only opportunity to experience her local geography and develop neighbourhood social capital. Every day Kiera and her friends took a complex route to/from school stretching their geographies:

> "Basically, I live here and one of them is here and one down there so, basically, there's a triangle and [friend 1] comes and buzzes [rings door bell] her and she comes down and walks with her to me and then they buzz me and I come down and we walk to school together ... 'cos at 3.00pm is when the school dismiss and then I go out and wait for my friends and then we walk together the long way so we can talk to each other."

Echoing Catling's (2005) notion that engaging in the local area is often a social activity Kiera's new-found freedom represented a small but very real change allowing her to construct a relationship with the local area independent of her family (Weller and Bruegel, 2009).

Accounts from both children and parents, therefore, suggest that school choice policies and families' responses to such policies (re)shape children's geographies in multifarious ways. Some were able to expand their knowledge and experience of their neighbourhood developing further local networks, while others were exposed to new localities and more dispersed networks. Moreover, broader education policies that separate primary and secondary education and the location of such schools essentially bring to the fore concerns about children's independent mobility and the need to be streetwise. For many, journeys, near and far, constituted valuable learning experiences (Cartwright, this volume, Chapter Nine). Nonetheless, while spatial mobility has frequently come to be seen as significant to social mobility it was often children from middle-class backgrounds, whose parents had economic and relevant social capital, who were experiencing geographical mobility (see Brown, this volume, Chapter Six).

## Connotations for cohesion

This chapter now focuses on school choice policies, families' responses to such policies and wider geographies of cohesion. Based on his work in the US Putnam describes neighbourhood schools as 'unique sites for building social capital' (2000, p 362); a notion also echoed by Witten et al (2003) in their research in New Zealand. To some extent such a view has been reflected in recent policies in the UK, including measures that extend schools into community hubs for a range of family services and, more specifically, the 2007 duty placed on maintained schools in England to promote community cohesion.

During the process of selecting schools, primary school playgrounds transformed into 'hot beds' of information. Parents, particularly although not exclusively in the more affluent site, drew on their social networks to obtain additional information about schools outside the immediate vicinity not easily available through formal measures (Ball, 2006). Parents with access to such networks valued the role they played in aiding the process. In the main, however, these were not sites of solidarity and, while information was shared, parents were all too aware that their children were in competition with one another. A support organisation working in one of our inner-London sites suggested that the instrumental use of social capital to gain places at well-resourced schools did little to foster long-term local solidarity:

> "The whole system process doesn't encourage you to work together.
> It's almost 'well, if I don't tell you when the open day is or when
> the application form has to be in, then I might get a place'."

Those without experience of the British education system or for whom English was an additional language were most disadvantaged by a system bolstered by particular forms of social capital.

School choice policies also brought to the fore divisions within neighbourhoods. School admissions criteria based on the distance between a child's home and school segregated some localities, resulting in feelings of resentment among neighbours. JP, a White-British, working-class boy from inner-London described his feelings:

> "I would have liked to have gone to [school name] ... a good school
> ... one of the really high-rated schools ... I would have liked to
> have gone there but we were one street out ... can't go there."

Even in our more affluent research site parents spoke of local geographical inequalities and the impact of administrative boundaries. 'Black holes' represented a common term of reference to denote places that fell outside of the distance-based criteria of all the surrounding schools.

A small minority of, primarily middle-class, families used their economic capital, paying a premium to purchase a home within the catchment area of a sought-after school. Martha, a White-British, middle-class mother from outer-London, felt this was their only option:

> "We actually looked around in Year Five because we were thinking about secondary schools and we moved house in order to get the school we wanted ... had we stayed where we were we wouldn't have had a choice."

Alternatively, Rosemary, another White-British, middle-class mother from outer-London was conscious of the implications of moving house on her own community involvement, and instead used her economic and social capital to gain a place for her son at a private school:

> "We want to be involved in the community and you can't do that if you're only there for two or three years, then move on."

Although Rosemary and her family were involved in the life of their local church, her son spent much of his leisure time in structured activities at/after school. For some, going to a school further afield resulted in the shifting of their leisure-time activities and social networks to outside their immediate neighbourhood. While such families may contribute economic capital to the area, their social capital often lies elsewhere (Butler, 2002). This may result in some young people becoming disconnected from their local neighbourhood (Rogers, 2007). The strength of communities, Johnson (2003) argues, relies on families staying in areas and not moving out in search of schools. Such examples point to the connections between education policies and broader residential geographies including, for example, processes of gentrification (Butler and Robson, 2003; Thiem, 2009).

Less affluent families rarely had the same options and were, therefore, 'confined' to particular neighbourhoods and schools. A very small minority were able to relocate. Janet, a White-British, working-class mother from central England was determined to leave her disadvantaged estate to avoid her daughter gaining a place at the local school. Although the area to which she moved was also blighted by disadvantage it did have the benefit of being well-placed for a better-resourced school. Policies that promote parental choice play on the notion that in order to 'get on, you must get out', which has the potential to be damaging for areas already struggling with a range of challenging socioeconomic issues (Holland et al, 2007).

School reputation was very important for some families in shaping their 'choices'. Such reputations were often based on perceptions of the area surrounding the school and, therefore, the likely intake. Although Reay (2007) describes inner-city community schools as 'places on the margins', such a school was also apparent within close proximity of our affluent outer London site and was a place some parents feared being allocated. Indeed, school reputations were enduring. Lesley, a White-British, middle-class mother, discussed her perceptions of the school, having grown up in the area, moved away and subsequently returned:

> "Yeah I mean the [local school] may be fine but it's got a reputation and it won't change … and as much as people have said 'oh it's really good and the headmaster's really good' unfortunately it's tarred and … [It had that reputation when I was at school]."

Similarly, parental 'choices' were influenced by perceptions of with whom their children would be mixing (Ball, 2006). Lydia, a White-British, middle-class girl from inner-London attended a Roman Catholic school 9 km away. She lived in an affluent enclave situated within a disadvantaged area that she viewed as 'rough'. As a result she only socialised with her (middle-class) neighbours:

> "I wouldn't ever go down to [local area] on my own 'cos there's lots of rough people down there."

Rather, Lydia would have preferred to live in the area surrounding her secondary school, again signalling a disconnection from her locality; not brought about by, but reinforced through her family's choice of school.

When selecting schools some parents welcomed diversity (particularly ethnic) while others expressed racist overtones and were concerned about their child's 'place' within the school. Children participating in focus groups in urban schools, however, often embraced diversity, questioning the value of different school types, especially faith schools (Weller, 2009). Many were adamant that it was important to mix with others from different backgrounds, as Leena from East London argued:

> "I think church schools are all right but then you don't get to mix with people from other religions and find out about their religions."

Several, therefore, implicitly regarded faith schools as detrimental to the development of what Putnam refers to as 'bridging' social capital. In so doing, many challenged government policies that endorse the expansion of different school types including faith schools. For a significant proportion of children multi/non-faith schools were important spaces in which they could learn about and experience life in a cosmopolitan society.

Likewise, the chances of a child making friends with those of different ethnic and faith backgrounds[5] was dependent on the opportunity of doing so in their school (Table 7.3) and neighbourhood. For example, White children from more affluent areas were less likely to have any friends from a different ethnic background. Those attending Roman Catholic primary schools were more likely to be in ethnically homogeneous classes, compared to other children living in the area, but this was not the case for those at Church of England primary schools. Children with more than one minority ethnic friend came from even more ethnically diverse primary classes. In general White children whose secondary school friends were exclusively White came from primary classes that were 80 per cent White, while those with at least one secondary school friend of a different ethnic background came from a primary class in which only 66 per cent of the children were White; a result that was statistically significant (see also Bruegel, 2006).

**Table 7.3:** Example school-based characteristics making for significant differences (p<0.001) in the proportion of friends of another ethnicity

| Characteristic | Base[a] | % of friendships of same ethnicity |
|---|---|---|
| All | 814 | 57.0 |
| Ethnically diverse school | 111 | 25.0 |
| Ethnically homogenous school (i.e. White) | 245 | 80.0 |

[a] In the 2004 survey primary school children were asked to detail up to four friendships. The base, therefore, refers to the number of friends outlined by the 270 respondents.

The school a child attends shapes the nature of their networks and their opportunities for creating social capital. In terms of individual school policies and professional practice the primary schools in our study had very different approaches to supporting families through the admissions process for secondary school. One devolved all responsibility to parents themselves, while others made a concerted effort to help families make strategic selections. The greatest level of help documented involved a teacher who lived in his school's vicinity and knew both the parents and local education market well. Families were, therefore, able to tap into his social capital. It is, however, apparent that individualised notions of mobility implicitly advocated within policies on school choice and the marketisation of schools are in tension with wider drives to foster cohesion (Holland et al, 2007). Such policies have wider implications for social capital in neighbourhoods, given our previous work highlighting the role children play in facilitating social capital for families (Weller and Bruegel, 2009).

## Conclusions

This chapter has explored some of the implications of school choice policies, and families' responses to such policies on children's everyday geographies. In so doing, it has sought to contribute to 'Children's Geographies', using the concept of social capital to frame theoretically the implications of policy

on children's everyday lives. It has endeavoured to illustrate the connec[...]
between policies, individual geographies, and broader concerns abou[...]
state of neighbourhoods and communities, demonstrating that child[...]
geographies are not merely a matter for the individual but are inextricably
shaped by and connected to broader residential geographies and socio-
spatial concerns about cohesion and/or segregation. In so doing, it is hoped
that the chapter goes some way to respond to Thiem's (2009) call for more
outward-looking geographies of education.

It is apparent that from parents' perspectives that imagined, aspirational and
fearful geographies are implicated in the process of school choice. For many
children secondary school transition offers new opportunities to engage
independently with local and wider environments. Those attending schools
outside the vicinity appear to have access to wider geographies, although
for some this freedom was confined to the school journey. With their
families' social capital often situated outside their immediate vicinity, such
children are in danger of becoming disconnected from their locality; perhaps
an intentional or unintentional outcome of their families' choices. Those
attending more local schools tended to have networks rooted in the locality
and often had greater opportunities for socialising in the neighbourhood,
although the possibilities for developing 'bridging' social capital with those
from different class backgrounds may be limited. In highlighting such
differences this chapter has not sought to extol more localised forms of
social capital but to illuminate the tensions between school choice policies
and those that seek to promote cohesion at the local level.

Framed by notions of social capital our work suggests that school choice
policies can result in or enhance existing class and, sometimes, ethnic
divisions in neighbourhoods. The reliance on particular forms of, and
the instrumental use of, social and economic capital helps to reproduce
inequalities. More disadvantaged areas are often problematically seen to
be deficient in such forms of social capital and thereby less cohesive. Little
emphasis has been placed on the connotations of children attending schools
outside the vicinity on cohesion in more affluent or socially diverse areas.
While social capital is not just developed through schools, such institutions
are fundamentally important arenas in shaping the lives and networks
of children and parents alike, as authors such as Witten et al (2003) have
demonstrated in other international contexts. The concept of social capital
is particularly valuable within the context of education policy as it re-
introduces the 'social' into a system that prioritises and validates individual
'success' (Weller, 2009). Perhaps, the most useful dimension of the concept
is its emphasis on the value of social networks in providing resources for
families to negotiate policy terrains. Nonetheless, the interaction between
different forms of capital is fundamentally important.

Many parents, from a variety of backgrounds, simply wished for a 'good local school'. Indeed, authors such as Chitty (2009) suggest that in countries with more egalitarian education systems community cohesion is seen to be greater. As Ball (2006) argues policies can be 'awkward, incomplete, incoherent and unstable' (p 17) and it certainly appears that those promoting the choice agenda in education do little to foster local cohesion. This chapter has, however, been written during a period of significant economic and political change. Although reminiscent of the neoliberal policies of previous administrations, the Conservative-Liberal Democrat Coalition government of 2010 onwards presents its policy ideas as a more radical approach to reform. 'Free schools' represent a flagship initiative providing parents, teachers, and third and private sector organisations with the opportunity to establish new schools in response to parental demand. Such schools will be state-funded but independent of local authority control. While currently under development, lessons from similar free schools in Sweden (albeit a different social and policy context) suggest that a greater proportion of such schools are positioned in more affluent or gentrified areas, inferring that inequalities may continue to be perpetuated (Allen, 2010). Debate in the British media has also pointed to concerns about the impact of free schools on other local schools, as well as tensions between the needs of free schools and local community groups, perhaps contradicting some elements of the Coalition government's 'Big Society' plan that aims, in part, to empower local people and communities (BBC, 2010; Burns 2011). Further research into the implications of such initiatives on children's everyday geographies and wider geographies of cohesion will certainly be required.

## Acknowledgements

The study and analysis on which this chapter draws was undertaken with Professor Irene Bruegel who, very sadly, died shortly after the project had been completed.

## Notes

[1] Academies are schools with a particular specialism. They are publicly funded, along with support from, for example, the private sector and operate semi-independently.

[2] The devolved regions of England, Scotland, and Wales have similar educational histories but have followed different paths (Chitty, 2009).

[3] Comprising nine projects, the programme was funded by the Economic & Social Research Council (Award Reference: M570255001).

[4] Within the context of this research, 'choice' is used with caution as only 24 per cent of parents (n = 76) felt they had had a choice.

[5] For further discussion of the challenges of defining ethnic backgrounds, please see Weller (2010).

## References

Adkins, L. (2005) 'Social capital: the anatomy of a troubled concept', *Feminist Theory*, vol 6, no 2, pp 195–211.

Aitken, S.C. (2001) *Geographies of young people: the morally contested spaces of identity*, London: Routledge.

Allen, R. (2010) 'Replicating Swedish free school reforms in England', *Research in Public Policy: CMPO Bulletin*, no 10, pp 4–7.

André-Bechely, L. (2007) 'Finding space and managing distance: public school choice in an urban California District', *Urban Studies*, vol 44, no 7, pp 1355–76.

Ball, S. (2006) *Education policy and social class: the selected works of Stephen J. Ball*, Abingdon: Routledge.

Ball, S. and Vincent, C. (2001) 'New class relations in education: the strategies of the 'fearful' middle class', in J. Demaine (ed) *Sociology of education today*, Basingstoke: Palgrave, pp 180–95.

Baron, S. Field, J. and Schuller, T. (2000) (eds) *Social capital: critical perspectives*, Oxford: Oxford University Press.

BBC (2010) *Free school controversy*, http://news.bbc.co.uk/today/hi/today/newsid_9030000/9030968.stm.

Bourdieu, P. (1986) 'The forms of capital', in J.E. Richardson (ed) *Handbook of theory for research in the sociology of education*, New York, NY: Greenwood Press, pp 241–58.

Bruegel, I. (2006) *Social capital, diversity and education policy*, http://www.lsbu.ac.uk/families/publications/SCDiversityEdu28.8.06.pdf.

Burgess, S., Briggs, A., McConnell, B. and Slater, H. (2006) *School choice in England: background facts*, The Centre for Market and Public Organisation Working Paper No 06/159, Bristol: University of Bristol.

Burns, G. (2011) 'New school could spell disaster for Shepherd's Bush community group', *Fulham and Hammersmith Chronicle*, 16 February.

Butler, T. (2002) 'Thinking global but acting local: the middle classes in the city', *Sociological Research Online*, vol 7, no 3, http://www.socresonline.org.uk/7/3/butler.html.

Butler, T., and Robson, G. (2003) 'Plotting the middle classes: gentrification and circuits of education in London', *Housing Studies*, vol 18, no 1, pp 5–28.

Butler, T. and van Zantan, A. (2007) 'School choice: a European perspective', *Journal of Education Policy*, vol 22, no 1, pp 1–5.

Cahill, C. (2000) 'Street literacy: urban teenagers' strategies for negotiating their neighbourhood', *Journal of Youth Studies*, vol 3, no 3, pp 251-77.

Catling, S. (2005) 'Children's personal geographies and the English primary school geography curriculum', *Children's Geographies*, vol 3, no 3, pp 325-44.

Chitty, C. (2009) *Education policy in Britain*, Basingstoke: Palgrave MacMillan.

Coleman, J.S. (1988) 'Social capital and the creation of human capital', *American Journal of Sociology*, vol 94, pp 95-120.

DoE (Department of Education) (2010) *Free schools*, www.education.gov.uk/schools/leadership/typesofschools/freeschools.

Edwards, R., Hadfield, L., Lucey, H. and Mauthner, M. (2006) *Sibling identity and relationships: sisters and brothers*, Oxford: Routledge.

Forrest, R. and Kearns, A. (2001) Social cohesion, social capital and the neighbourhood, *Urban Studies*, vol 38, no 12, pp 2125-43.

Hetherington, M., Benefield, P., Lines, A., Paterson, C., Ries, J. and Shuayb, M. (2007) *Community cohesion for children, young people and their families: a rapid review of policy, practice and research in local authorities*, Slough: NFER.

Holland, J., Reynolds, T. and Weller, S. (2007) 'Transitions, networks and communities: the significance of social capital in the lives of children and young people', *Journal of Youth Studies*, vol 10, no 1, pp 97-116.

Holloway, S.L., Hubbard, P., Jöns, H. and Pimlott-Wilson, H. (2010) 'Geographies of education and the significance of children, youth and families', *Progress in Human Geography*, vol 34, no 5, pp 583-600.

Holloway, S. L. and Valentine, G. (2000) (eds) *Children's geographies: playing, living, learning*, London: Routledge.

Johnson, M. (2003) *Schooling in London: an overview*, London: IPPR.

Matthews, H. (2003) 'Coming of age for children's geographies', *Children's Geographies*, vol 1, no 1, pp 3-5.

Morrow, V. (1999) 'Conceptualising social capital in relation to the well-being of children and young people: a critical review', *The Sociological Review*, vol 47, no 4, pp 744-65.

Noreisch, K. (2007) 'Choice as rule, exception and coincidence: parents' understandings of catchment areas in Berlin', *Urban Studies*, vol 44, no 7, pp 1307-28.

ONS (Office for National Statistics) (2010) *Travel to school*, http://www.statistics.gov.uk/hub/travel-transport/index.html.

Paterson, L. (2003) 'The three educational ideologies of the British Labour Party, 1997–2001', *Oxford Review of Education*, vol 29, no 2, pp 165-86.

Putnam, R.D. (1995) 'Bowling alone: America's declining social capital', *Journal of Democracy*, vol 6, no 1, pp 64-78.

Putnam, R.D. (2000) *Bowling alone: the collapse and revival of American community*, New York: Simon and Schuster.

Reay, D. (2007) '"Unruly places": inner-city comprehensives, middle-class imaginaries and working-class children', *Urban Studies*, vol 44, no 7, pp 1191-201.

Rogers, C. (2007) *Bridging into family support: locality, school and social capital*, http://familyandparenting.web-platform.net/item/item/691.

Taylor, C. (2001a) 'The geography of choice and diversity in the "New" secondary education market of England', *Area*, vol 33, no 4, pp 368-81.

Taylor, C. (2001b) 'Hierarchies and "local" markets: The geography of the "lived" market place in secondary education provision', *Journal of Education Policy*, vol 16, no 3, pp 197-214.

Taylor, C. (2002) *Geography of the 'new' education: secondary school choice in England and Wales*, Surrey: Ashgate.

Thiem, C.H. (2009) 'Thinking through education: the geographies of contemporary educational restructuring', *Progress in Human Geography*, vol 33, no 2, pp 154-73.

Tomlinson, S. (2003) 'New Labour and education', *Children & Society*, vol 17, no 3, pp 195-204.

Weekes-Bernard, D. (2007) *School choice and ethnic segregation: educational decision-making among black and minority ethnic parents*, London: The Runnymede Trust.

Weller, S. (2007a) 'Managing the move to secondary school: the significance of children's social capital', in H. Helve and J. Bynner (eds) *Youth and social capital,* London: Tufnell Press, pp 107-25.

Weller, S. (2007b) '"Sticking with your mates?" Children's friendship trajectories during the transition from primary to secondary school', *Children & Society*, vol 21, no 5, pp 339-51.

Weller, S. (2009) '"You need to have a mixed school ..." exploring the complexity of diversity in young people's social networks', in J. Allan, J. Ozga and G. Smyth (eds) *Social capital, professionalism and diversity: new relations in urban schools,* Rotterdam: Sense, pp 175-92.

Weller, S. (2010) 'Young people's social capital: complex identities, dynamic networks', *Ethnic & Racial Studies,* vol 33, no 5, pp 872-88.

Weller, S. and Bruegel, I. (2009) 'Children's "place" in the development of neighbourhood social capital', *Urban Studies,* vol 46, no 3, pp 629-43.

Witten, K., Kearns, R., Lewis, N., Coster, H. and McCreanor, T. (2003) 'Educational restructuring from a community viewpoint: a case study of school closure from Invercargill, New Zealand', *Environment and Planning C: Government and Policy*, vol 21, no 2, pp 203-23.

# eight

# Lunchtime lock-in: territorialisation and UK school meals policies

*Jo Pike and Derek Colquhoun*

## Introduction

What children eat at school has emerged as one of the most significant public health concerns in the UK over the last decade. During the office of the New Labour government in the UK (1997–2010) and in particular following the re-election of the Blair government in 2001, school meals became the cause célèbre of public health practitioners, dieticians and celebrities alike. As a central component of government attempts to halt the year-on-year rise in childhood obesity (HM Treasury, 2007), waves of legislation introduced increasingly stringent standards stipulating precisely what kinds of foods should be served at lunchtime and throughout the school day via vending machines, in after school clubs and in what are colloquially known in the UK as 'tuck shops', where children and young people are able to purchase snacks during their morning break (Statutory Instrument 2359, 2007). The continued public interest in the topic of children's food intake is evident by the increasing proliferation of websites and column inches devoted to what children eat, where, how and who with, and extends beyond UK borders. In Australia, for instance, this interest is noted through an intensification of food-related anti-obesity initiatives implemented via schools (Leahy, 2010). Nutrition Australia continues to provide support and resources for schools delivering dietary interventions aimed at promoting healthier eating (for example, *Start right, eat right*) and various state governments have begun to regulate the kinds of food and drinks that can be sold in schools (NSW Department of Health & NSW Department of Education and Training, 2004; Stanton, 2009).

Leahy (2010) notes that while some interventions provide important pedagogical opportunities that coincide with agendas around sustainability and biodiversity, they are also central to federal government attempts to address rising rates of childhood obesity. This agenda, she suggests, is never far from view. In the US the *National School lunch program* and the *School breakfast program* are federal programmes which provide nutritionally balanced meals either free or at low cost to eligible children within public and non-profit schools and residential childcare. According to The National Academies Institute of Medicine (2009, p 1) 'in fiscal year 2007, the participating schools served about 5.1 billion lunches at a federal cost of approximately $8.7 billion'. Its report *School meals: building blocks for healthy children* recommends revising the nutritional standards for school meals and replacing them with nutrient targets to better reflect the nutritional quality of the meal 'as selected by the student' rather than simply that which is served by the provider. Once again these proposals are described as 'an important component of First Lady Michelle Obama's *Let's move!* initiative to solve the challenge of childhood obesity within a generation' (USDA, 2011, n p).

This international obsession with children's diet and food practices has not gone unnoticed by academics who have sought to identify the types of foods that children eat (Evans et al, 2010), the factors that influence their food choices (Holmberg et al, 2010) and the effects upon their health and wellbeing, while other studies explore the social significance of food and food practices in children and young people's lives including in residential settings (Dorrer et al, 2010), and within the family (Backett-Milburn et al, 2006; Wills et al, 2007; Rawlins, 2009; Curtis et al, 2010). In part, the academic interest in school food and children's diets stems from attempts to critique the current policy obsession with childhood obesity and to interrogate the wider social meanings around food practices which are often occluded from narrowly focused biomedical explanations of children's food intake. Nevertheless, the significance of food as a means to explore both the social context and the policy landscape of childhood and youth cannot be underestimated, since concerns over school food and its nutritional quality are emblematic of far wider anxieties around the physical and moral condition of youth (Lupton, 1996). As a vehicle to combat childhood obesity in the UK, school food was regarded as 'central to the nation's future health' (Blair, 2006) and consequently, the successful implementation of school meals reform carried with it the hopes and expectations incumbent upon the next generation. Our approach to school food said something about the ways in which we judge contemporary youth and implicitly, the fears we had for their, and consequently the nation's, future.

This chapter seeks to move beyond analyses that assess the impact or effectiveness of school food interventions, and extend those that critique the assumptions about children, young people and their parents that underpin such attempts (see Pike, 2008a; 2010; Rawlins, 2008). The chapter attends to the issue of school meals by addressing the ways in which the management of the school site and the emergent *spatial* practices within and around school communities have been implicated in the delivery of policy objectives, specifically those that aim to produce young people as healthy subjects. Drawing on Sack's (1986) concept of territoriality the chapter discusses the kinds of spatialised strategies that are deployed in relation to the 'school boundary' and the ways in which this boundary is policed to ensure the effectiveness of school meals policy. According to Sack, the notion of boundary is one of three interrelated facets that constitute what he calls 'territoriality' and he suggests that boundary functions as a way of demarcating specific spaces controlled by certain individuals or groups.

Territoriality is defined as 'the attempt by an individual or group to affect, influence, or control people, phenomena and relationships, by delimiting and asserting control over a geographic area' (Sack, 1986, p 19). In seeking to achieve control over specific territories he suggests that three techniques are employed. Firstly, classification by area, whereby an area or the things within it are classified as mine not yours. Secondly, communication by sign or marker where the extent of the territory is delimited by the boundary, for example, the school fence and school gates. Thirdly, by enforcing control over access to the area and the things within it (for example, by policing the boundary). Using school food policy as a lens, the chapter explores the following strategies of territorialisation: the locking in of children during school lunch breaks; the exclusion of particular types of parents from the school grounds; and the manipulation of the environment immediately surrounding the school.

## School meals in England

School meals in England were initially conceived as a means to ameliorate the malnourished state of potential army recruits which was exposed during the Boer War (Welshman, 1997). The 1906 Education Act enabled children to take advantage of the recently extended education system and to 'benefit fully from their education' (Passmore and Harris, 2004 p 221) as local education authorities were entitled, but not compelled to provide school meals for poorer children to augment existing provision by charities and voluntary organisations. The introduction of school meals in 1906 provoked opposition on the grounds that they would undermine the function of the family meal in strengthening family values and thus destroy family life, and that 'with the weakening of the spring of responsibility we could not hope for an elevation of the standard of self-respect' (Fuller, 1885, cited in Welshman, 1997).

Legislation in the post-war period consolidated what Morgan refers to as the 'golden era' of school meals (2006, p 380), characterised by a strong emphasis on the principles of welfare and state provision. The 1944 Education Act placed a statutory duty on local education authorities to provide school meals and basic nutritional standards were introduced in 1941, although the eventual aim of the 1944 Act was universal free school meal provision (Morgan, 2006).

During the Thatcher era, the 1980 Education Act removed the obligation on local education authorities to provide school meals at all except for those children entitled to free school meals. Nutritional standards were removed along with the obligation to charge a fixed price for school meals, and free school milk was abolished. This led to a reduction in the quality of school meals (Morgan, 2006) and indeed the current interest in school meals may be attributable to the deregulation of the 1980s and the removal of nutritional standards. Significantly, during this period changes to free school meal entitlement were brought about through legislation introduced in the form of the 1986 Social Security Act which, according to White et al (1992), reformed the welfare benefit system and removed free school meals entitlement from some 400,000 children.

The latest reforms to school meals policy can be located within the broader context of concerns over childhood obesity, diet-related illness, sustainable development and devolution (Morgan, 2006). In 2004, the *Choosing health* White Paper signalled the government's intention to establish a school meals review panel to examine standards for school lunches based on nutrients rather than food groups (see Food Standards Agency (2007) *The eatwell plate*), to extend standards to other school food, and to provide a mechanism for inspection of school lunches through the Office for Standards in Education (Ofsted).

Up until the general election of 2005, school meals in England had been subject to nutritional guidelines set out in 2001 which were based on the five food groups (DfEE,[1] 2001; Buttriss, 2005) and stipulated, for example, the number of portions of fruit and vegetables to be served every day, and placed limits on the availability of fried foods and the availability of table salt. In practice, compliance with these guidelines was inconsistent (Nelson et al, 2004). Consequently, the issue of poor quality food of low nutritional value, high in fat and salt, continued to trouble public health professionals. In February 2005, the television programme *Jamie's School Dinners* (Channel 4) directed public attention to the inadequate state of food served in schools. Media interest galvanised around the 'turkey twizzler' (Plunkett, 2005; Revill and Hill, 2005), an item that became synonymous with cheap processed food. The New Labour government produced its election manifesto in 2004, restating its promise to review school meals policy and increase spending on ingredients. This review led to the implementation of stricter standards for school lunches based on nutritional composition in line with the Caroline Walker Trust[2] guidelines rather than on food groups and these were functioning in primary schools from September 2008 and in secondary and special schools from September 2009.

## Implementation of school food policy

Under the new standards school lunches must contain a minimum amount of nutrients (such as zinc, iron, calcium and folate) and must not exceed the maximum amount of salt, saturated fat, fat and non-milk extrinsic sugars. Schools are legally obliged to comply with 14 different nutrient-based standards. The revised Ofsted inspection framework came into force in September 2009, and required schools to demonstrate compliance with the standards and to indicate how many pupils take a school lunch as a proxy measure for pupils' healthier lifestyles. As part of its commitment to reform school meals, in 2005 the UK government established the School Food Trust, a non-departmental public body with a remit to advise on all issues relating to school food including implementing the nutritional standards.

Nevertheless, for schools tasked with implementing the changes to school meals and ensuring compliance with the nutrient standards, a number of issues initially presented themselves. Firstly, the new regulations regarding school meals highlighted capacity issues within school kitchens and dining rooms. School kitchens were required to produce new-style menus requiring both cooking equipment and additional preparation space, infrastructure which many lacked following the introduction of compulsory competitive tendering in the 1980s (Morgan, 2006). Additionally, the technical capacity and knowledge of staff had been depleted over previous decades and some 'rebelled against the extra work involved in *preparing* meals rather than *opening* packets' (Kelly and Harrison, 2009, p 34). Secondly, pupils who took school meals provided a vital revenue stream for those schools that brought their catering 'in house' in the wake of the media exposé of the poor standard of school food in England. Indeed, some schools were required to buy themselves out of long-term contracts with existing suppliers in order to do this. Thirdly, changes to school meals brought some schools into conflict with parents. In Hull, where changes to school lunch menus were implemented four years before they became mandatory nationally, schools became engaged in defending such policy decisions to parents who complained that children were not eating the healthier food (BBC, 2007; Colquhoun et al, 2008). Finally, as the new healthier menus were introduced, the numbers of pupils taking school lunches plummeted as many pupils elected to bring a packed lunch from home (BBC, 2006; Paton, 2007).

For many pupils, the option of staying for a school meal was unappealing and the temptation to visit local eateries around the school proved a more attractive option. Given that school lunch uptake was regarded as a proxy indicator for the health of young people through the Ofsted inspection framework (Ofsted, 2009) and the politically charged nature of the school meals reforms, persuading children to stay on site and to eat school lunches became something of a priority. With this in mind the chapter proceeds to consider some of the spatial strategies that schools employed in order to achieve this end.

## Policing the school boundary

Sack (1986) suggests that the concept of territory cannot be simplistically aligned to a geographic area or space. Particular spaces become territories through a series of practices and strategies which are continuously enacted in order to maintain territorial status. Thus he argues that certain spaces can be thought of as territories at certain times, but not at others. For the purposes of this chapter, it is the continuous re-enactment of spatialised practices and strategies in relation to school food policies that create schools grounds as territories.

### 'The lock-in'

The most contentious approach to improving school lunch uptake has been euphemistically referred to as the 'lock-in', 'lock down', or more formally, according to the School Food Trust (2009), the 'stay on-site policy'. Eliciting comparisons with prison practices this approach involves banning children from leaving the school premises over the lunch period by locking them within the school grounds, either physically or symbolically. Such a practice can be regarded as an attempt to control access to the space in a way that is explicitly territorial and, as Sack suggests, 'territoriality can be used to contain or restrain' (1986, p 20). The School Food Trust, with ministerial support, set the national policy framework for this practice providing: a rationale for persuading students, parents and schools in general; a stay on-site guide; case studies from across the country; a template for a stay on-site policy; and implementation ideas for schools to make their stay on-site policies successful.

The impetus for much of this comes from the Government's cross-cutting review into obesity, *Healthy weight, healthy lives* (HM Government, 2008, p 15), which urges schools to consider such a policy:

> In particular, schools should consider the length of time available
> for lunch, and whether adopting a stay-on-site policy at lunchtime
> would be helpful in ensuring that all children are eating healthy food.

Schools who implement a stay on-site policy frequently cite childhood obesity as the main reason for their policy. In Glasgow for instance, uptake of school lunches for 11–16 year old pupils in the first two years of secondary school was a low 30 per cent in 2007 and therefore a pilot scheme (*The Big Eat In*) was implemented which saw up to 1,000 secondary children locked in their schools at lunchtime (Glasgow City Council, 2009). The scheme aimed to provide children with increased responsibility for improving their health through encouraging healthier eating habits and providing greater opportunities for extra physical activities at lunchtime. Of course, there was an implicit assumption with the *Big Eat In* that children were kept away from fast food outlets in the schools' neighbourhood at lunchtime.

However and unsurprisingly, there has been considerable parental opposition to 'lock-ins'. According to Andy Hibberd, the co-founder of the Parent Organisation, school stay on-site policies should be 'blocked and opposed' as 'very nanny-ish, totally unworkable and impractical [and also for] taking away parental choice' (Campbell and Asthana, 2008, n p). The notion of choice has been a central feature in the debate over school stay on-site policies. Some have suggested that the removal of choice at lunchtimes for children is indeed, nanny-ish, 'Orwellian' (Hickman, 2007) and that we could even see a 'mass breakout of kids desperate to get their hands on crisps, chips and fizzy drinks' (Narain, 2007, n p).

The impact of school stay on-site policies on local fast food outlets has not gone unnoticed. Children have significant buying power with the average weekly pocket money being about £8.40 (Clark, 2007) and, as we will illustrate later in the chapter, the area in close proximity to schools in particular has become a focus for children's spending. It is suffice to say at this stage that an additional reason for schools developing stay on-site policies has been the financial cost of providing healthier school meals and the potential profit made from these school meals.

The Children's Minister, Kevin Brennan, also called on schools to develop stay on-site policies to address the allegedly soaring numbers of children who are obese, citing the benefits as improved uptake of school lunches but also improved behaviour and community relationships (Campbell and Asthana, 2008). The number of schools developing and implementing a stay on-site policy is not clear. Rob Rees, the celebrity chef and Chairman of the School Food Trust, suggests a stay on-site policy leads to better behaviour and afternoon attendance/punctuality by students in the afternoon (Garner and Dutta, 2010). However, children who are locked in at lunchtime can, of course, take a packed lunch, or even not have lunch at all but still spend their lunch money at the fast food outlets on their way home.

### Practices of exclusion: junk food mums and sinner ladies

It was the practice of 'locking in' that prompted one of the more controversial incidents in the history of school meals in England, and which became known in the popular press as 'The Battle of Rawmarsh'. In September 2006 a group of women dubbed 'junk food mums' and 'sinner ladies' were discovered passing food through the school railings to their children at a comprehensive school in Rawmarsh, South Yorkshire, UK. The latter term is revealing in its attempt to imply a certain moral failing by substituting the term 'dinner ladies', used colloquially to mean lunchtime staff, with the term 'sinner ladies' to allude to the potentially corrupting effects of the food practices of these women. Following the introduction of a new 'healthy' lunch menu at the start of the new school year, the women decided to deliver food from nearby catering outlets to children at the school, taking orders and passing deliveries to pupils on the other side of the school fence. Tensions escalated within the local community as parents' rights to determine what their children should and should not eat were brought into conflict with the views of the head teacher of the school along with a raft of nutritional experts, health campaigners and other parents (Pike, 2010).

While the women were portrayed in the popular press as junk food loving anti-health campaigners, the women themselves protested that it was the policy of locking children in at lunchtime, the reduction of the school lunch break, along with the changes to the menu which prompted the action:

> Mrs Critchlow [a 'junk food mum'] said she was angry that Mr Lambert [the head teacher] had not consulted parents before changing the rules, which include swapping breaks of 15 and 45 minutes for two 30-minute breaks. She wanted Mr Lambert to have a full parents' meeting so that every parent could have a say in the matter. (Percival, 2006, n p)

Interestingly, schools are now inspected upon their level of engagement and communication with parents, including the extent to which the school takes account of parents' and carers' views and how well they are involved in contributing to decision-making about whole-school matters (Ofsted, 2009). While some parents who became involved in issues surrounding school meals became celebrated within the press, eventually becoming part of the school food establishment (see Merton Parents, no date), the actions of the junk food mums were regarded as counter to the prevailing ethos of the school and therefore considered to be irrational and disruptive:

> John Lambert, head teacher of the 1,100-pupil school, said: "I'm stunned. What these two women are doing is unbelievable. They are encouraging children whose parents give them money for a healthy, nutritious meal to spend it elsewhere. It is undermining something this school believes in wholeheartedly. The food these parents are handing out is not part of that healthy diet. We are determined to take a strong line over this." (Stokes, 2006, n p)

Those parents seen to support healthy school meals may be invited to participate in related activities through School Nutrition Action Groups (Higgs, 2004) or similar mechanisms. They may even become part of the school food establishment (see Merton Parents, n d). Those that do not support the school meals agenda remain excluded from the school, literally and metaphorically, on the other side of the fence. This may be regarded as an explicit act of territorialisation, as participation in school activities is dependent upon aligning oneself with the objectives of the school. Access to the area is therefore conditional upon conformity with the rules that govern the space. Sack suggests that:

> Territoriality can have normative implications as well. Setting places aside and enforcing degrees of access means that individuals and groups have removed some activities from people and places and included others. That is, they have established different degrees of access to things. (Sack, 1986, p 26)

Indeed, part of the normative work of these exclusionary practices can be seen in the ways that the women were represented in the media. The women were branded 'scrubbers' by Jamie Oliver and the popular press alluded to their notable deficiencies in terms of their morals, taste, intelligence and mothering abilities among other things. They were caricatured as obese and morally excessive, ill-educated and irrational. *The Yorkshire Post* was particularly savage:

> If the rest of the world had ever wondered what goes on in deepest South Yorkshire, then they now know, thanks to the 'Rawmarsh Junk Food Mothers'. Quite aside from the sheer stupidity (and lack of respect) of shoving burger 'n' chips to schoolkids through a fence by standing on graves, the good ladies of Rawmarsh have demonstrated that the problems in our education system go back a lot further than one generation.

> I am trying not to be personally abusive, because I wouldn't want to come across any of them on a dark night, but, honestly, what an embarrassing shower. (Dowle, 2006, n p)

The article continues to stereotype the women further by labelling them incoherent, poorly-educated, alluding to their lack of employment, and even suggesting that they wore 'saggy leggings', thereby reinforcing their class position and lack of taste (Lawler, 2002; 2005). Such caricatures serve to reinforce the distinction between rational, educated, affective middle-class motherhood and the irrational, badly dressed, poorly educated, unhealthy working-class mothers who are notable because of their deficiencies. Territorialisation enforces symbolic as well as physical boundaries. The transgression of these women across the school boundary represented not only a threat to the physical safety and security of the school, but to the symbolic values that were contained therein. At a time when the issue of school meals was receiving an unprecedented degree of attention from the media through the *Jamie's School Dinners* television series, and from policy-makers and government through successive rafts of legislation, local strategies and policies, the Battle of Rawmarsh became a significant feature of a cultural landscape in which school meals became associated with particular types of subjects: subjects who were successful, self-regulating, rational and moral.

## Beyond the school boundary: policing the proximal space around schools

Strategies of territorialisation extend beyond the school gates to the proximal space immediately outside the school boundary. This proximal space surrounding schools has been classed as an 'obesogenic environment' (Egger and Swinburne, 1997) in which the physical environment promotes weight gain or discourages weight loss. Typically, for children and young people this proximal space around schools is an area where many children gather after school or simply have to walk/cycle through on their way home. Of relevance to this chapter is the way in which the influence of school meals extends past the school boundary to the proximal space beyond through the control of fast food outlets. Recently, local councils have focused on the location of fast food outlets and their proximity to schools in their attempts to address childhood obesity. The assumption is that manipulating children's healthy or unhealthy behaviour by advocating a healthier lifestyle is insufficient and is not working: the obesogenic environment needs to be tackled. This is set out in the government's *Healthy weight, healthy lives*:

> One of the challenges that we face in promoting healthy eating is the availability of foods high in fat, salt and sugar in local neighbourhoods, including the prevalence of fast food restaurants and takeaways in some communities. Local authorities can use existing planning powers to control more carefully the number and location of fast food outlets in their local areas. *The Government will promote these powers to local authorities and PCTs to highlight the impact that they can have on promoting healthy weight, for instance through managing the proliferation of fast food outlets, particularly in proximity to parks and schools.* (HM Government, 2008, p 18, original emphasis)

Significantly, this obesogenic environment around schools has been the focus for National Institute for Health and Clinical Excellence (NICE) guidance (2010) for the prevention of cardiovascular disease at the population level, with two recommendations focussing on the provision and control of fast food outlets. The NICE guidance is specifically targeted at environmental health officers, local government planning departments, public health nutritionists and trading standards officers, and is concerned with empowering local councils to restrict planning permission for fast food outlets and to change 'classes of use' orders for new fast food outlets on the grounds of disease prevention.

This NICE guidance responds to efforts by local councils to control new applications for planning for fast food outlets over the last three years. New guidance was to limit the opportunities that young people have to eat 'fast food', thus reducing childhood obesity. In Waltham Forest, for instance, the local council declared a 400-metre 'exclusion zone' around the schools (an arbitrary 10 minutes' walk from school), leisure and youth centres and parks. Fast food outlets also had to be 440 metres from each other. This policing of fast food outlets within the proximal space near schools received national notoriety and several councils followed suit.

At about the same time, the School Food Trust (2008) published the results of a study they called *Temptation town* which graphically illustrated the number of fast food outlets up and down the country and produced a league table of the places where the fast food outlets were most concentrated. On average, secondary schools were surrounded by 24 fast food outlets; the most was Brighton and Hove with 46 fast food outlets near each secondary school. This research led the School Food Trust to develop its 'stay on-site policy' mentioned earlier in the chapter. At around the same time, in what was described as a 'landmark' and 'unprecedented' case (Borland, 2010), Tower Hamlets council was found in the High Court to have acted unlawfully by approving a planning submission for the establishment of a fast food outlet (called 'Fried and Fabulous') from a grocery store close to a school.

Other measures used to police the proximal space around schools include the banning of mobile catering vans within a certain distance of a school. Interestingly, these distances vary across local authorities between 65 metres in the case of ice cream vans in Hillingdon to 300 metres for vans near Glasgow schools. In the case of Leicester, all vans are banned within 400 metres *except* ice cream vans.

It goes without saying that these controls of the proximal space have come under attack from parents, children and small businesses in particular. These criticisms have focused on the perceived removal of choice from parents and children to be able to buy and eat what they would like to and the restraint of trade for small businesses.

## Conclusions

This chapter has attempted to illustrate some of the ways in which school spaces and the spaces surrounding schools are policed and regulated through processes of territorialisation in an effort to advance the school meals agenda and increase the uptake of 'healthy' school meals. According to Sack (1986, p 5), '[T]erritoriality is a primary geographical expression of social power' and, as such, attempts to demarcate school boundaries, to exclude and allow access, and to extend the healthy eating agenda beyond the school boundary to influence planning decisions within the local community can be seen as an effect of social power relations. The school represents a site with a distinct – although not always discrete – geographic territory. The school boundary can be regarded as porous (Holloway and Valentine, 2001; Pike, 2010) with the transmission of material bodies, food items, competing discourses and political rationalities seeping across the boundary, necessitating constant policing and surveillance to ensure that the integrity of the area within is maintained. The women of Rawmarsh provide an illustration of the consequences of such transgressions. It has been argued that school meals policy can be regarded as a biopolitical strategy (Leahy, 2010; Pike, 2010) and that school dining rooms represent a site in which power relations are continuously reshaped and contested (Pike, 2008b; 2010). What Sack's work offers is an opportunity to extend such analyses and foreground space as intrinsic to the operation of power relations and in particular, for this chapter, to explore in some detail the function of boundary in signalling ownership of territory and the rules applied within. It is the effects of such strategies and the ways that they limit or prescribe an individual's or group's field of action that is of particular interest, for as Sack (1986, p 18) points out:

> We need to know not only what territoriality is, but what it does. It is principally on helping to point to the important effects of a phenomenon that the value of a definition rests.

The chapter did not seek to evaluate the policy intentions of reforms to school meals but rather to draw attention to previously overlooked spatial implications and the utilisation of space as a strategy to ensure the success of contemporary school meals policy and 'the future health' of children and young people. At the time of writing it is not clear whether school meals will continue to remain at the heart of government's ambitions to improve the health and well-being of the nation, but it looks likely that reforms to the welfare and benefits system will reduce entitlement to free school meals. In this respect, at least, the present Conservative–Liberal Democrat Coalition government appears to proceed along a similar trajectory to the Thatcher government in the 1980s, reshaping school meals policy in a way that some considered to be a 'monstrously myopic mistake' (Morgan, 2006, p 381).

## Notes

[1] The government department responsible for schools has been relabelled the Department for Education and Employment, the Department for Education and Skills, the Department for Children, Schools and Families and, in 2010, the Department for Education.

[2] The Caroline Walker Trust (CWT) is a charitable body that advises and campaigns on nutritional issues, particularly those affecting children and the elderly. The CWT produced a series of nutritional guidelines recommending the minimum nutritional composition of school meals in 1992. These were revised in 2005.

## References

Backett-Milburn, K., Wills, W., Gregory, S., and Lawton, J. (2006) 'Making sense of eating, weight and risk in early teenage years: views and concerns of parents in poorer socio-economic circumstances', *Social Science and Medicine,* vol 63, no 3, pp 624-35.

BBC (2006) *Fewer pupils take school meals,* 6 November 2006, http://news.bbc.co.uk/1/hi/education/6115192.stm.

BBC (2007) *Pupils shunning healthier meals,* 3 September 2007, http://news.bbc.co.uk/1/hi/education/6972699.stm.

Blair, T. (2006) *Our nation's future,* Speech given in Nottingham, 26 July 2006, http://www.brandrepublic.com/News/663971/Nations-Future---Blairs-speech-full/?DCMP=ILC-SEARCH.

Borland, S, (2010) 'Judge declares fast food takeaway near school is 'unlawful'', *Mail Online,* 12 June 2010, http://www.dailymail.co.uk/news/article-1285939/Judge-declares-fast-food-takeaway-near-school-unlawful.html.

Buttriss, J. (2005) 'Government promises school meals will be transformed', *Nutrition Bulletin,* vol 30, no 3, pp 211-14.

Campbell D. and Asthana, A. (2008) 'Minister calls for lunchtime lock-in at schools to stop rush for chippie', *The Observer,* 6 July 2008, http://www.guardian.co.uk/education/2008/jul/06/schools.uk.

Channel 4 (no date) *Jamie's School Dinners.*

Clark, L. (2007) 'Lock in pupils at lunchtime to make them eat healthy food, says top cook Prue Leith', *Mail Online,* 16 October 2007, http://www.dailymail.co.uk/news/article-487962/Lock-pupils-lunchtime-make-eat-healthy-food-says-cook-Prue-Leith.html.

Colquhoun, D., Wright, N., Pike, J. and Gatenby, L. (2008) *Evaluation of 'eat well do well', Kingston upon Hull's school meal initiative*, http://www2.hull.ac.uk/IFL/pdf/IFL-R_finalreport.pdf.

Curtis, P., James, A., and Ellis, K. (2010) 'Children's snacking, children's food: food moralities and family life', *Children's Geographies,* vol 8, no 3, pp 291-302.

DfEE (Department for Education and Employment) (2001) *Healthy school lunches for pupils in primary schools*, Nottingham: DfEE.

Department of Health (2004) *Choosing health*, London: HMSO, http://webarchive.nationalarchives.gov.uk/+/www.dh.gov.uk/en/publicationsandstatistics/publications/publicationspolicyandguidance/dh_4094550.

Dorrer, N., McIntosh, I., Punch, S., and Emond, R. (2010) 'Children and food practices in residential care: ambivalence in the "institutional" home', *Children's Geographies,* vol 8, no 3, pp 247-60.

Dowle, J. (2006) 'Indigestible realities about the Rawmarsh mothers', 22 September 2006, *The Yorkshire Post*, http://www.yorkshirepost.co.uk/news/debate/columnists/indigestible_realities_about_the_rawmarsh_mothers_1_2390324.

Egger, G., and Swinburne, B. (1997) 'An "ecological" approach to the obesity pandemic', *British Medical Journal*, vol 315, pp 477-80.

Evans, C.E.L., Greenwood, D.C, Thomas, J.D., and Cade, J.E. (2010) 'A cross-sectional survey of children's packed lunches in the UK: food- and nutrient-based results', *Journal of Epidemiology and Community Health,* vol 64, pp 977-83.

Food Standards Agency (2007) *The eatwell plate*, http://www.food.gov.uk/multimedia/pdfs/eatwellplatelarge.pdf.

Garner, R., and Dutta, K. (2010) 'How do you make children eat healthily? Lock them in', *The Independent,* 8 February, http://www.independent.co.uk/news/education/education-news/how-do-you-make-children-eat-healthily-lock-them-in-1892253.html.

Glasgow City Council (2009) *Official launch of new healthy eating drive*, 16 September 2009, http://www.glasgow.gov.uk/en/News/Archives/2009/September/bigeatinlaunch.htm

Hickman, M. (2007) 'Key to healthy eating? Lock school gates, says Leith', *The Independent,* 17 October 2007, http://www.independent.co.uk/life-style/health-and-families/health-news/key-to-healthy-eating-lock-school-gates-says-leith-397061.html.

Higgs, J. (2004) 'The health education trust and the health of young people today and tomorrow', *Nutrition and Food Science*, vol 34, no 4, pp 156-60.

Holloway, S. and Valentine, G. (2001) '"It's only as stupid as you are": children and adults' negotiation of ICT competence at home and at school', *Social & Cultural Geography,* vol 2, no 1, pp 25-42.

Holmberg, L., Coveney, J., Henderson, J., and Meyer, S. (2010) 'What should primary health care practitioners know about factors influencing young people's food choices?', *Australasian Medical Journal*, vol 1, no 4, pp 259-66.

HM Government (2008) *Healthy weight, healthy lives: a cross-government strategy for England*, http://www.dh.gov.uk/en/Publicationsandstatistics/Publications/PublicationsPolicyAndGuidance/DH_082378.

HM Treasury (2007) *PSA delivery agreement 12: improve the health and wellbeing of children and young people*, London: HMSO, www.hm-treasury.gov.uk/media/C/F/pbr_csr07_psa12.pdf.

Kelly, P. and Harrison, L. (2009) *Working in Jamie's kitchen: salvation, passion and young workers*, Hampshire: Palgrave Macmillan.

Lawler, S. (2002) 'Mobs and monsters: independent man meets Paulsgrove woman', *Feminist Theory*, vol 3, no 1, pp 103-13.

Lawler, S. (2005) 'Disgusted subjects: the making of middle-class identities', *The Sociological Review*, vol 53, no 3, pp 429-46.

Leahy, D. (2010) 'What's on (or off) the menu in school?' *Text*, 9, http://works.bepress.com/deana_leahy/28/.

Lupton, D. (1996) *Food, body and the self*, London: Sage.

Merton Parents (no date) *Merton parents for better food in schools*, http://mertonparents.wordpress.com/.

Morgan, K. (2006) 'School food and the public domain: the politics of the public plate', *Political Quarterly*, vol 77, no 3, pp 379-87.

Narain, J. (2007) 'School children should be locked in at lunchtime to make them eat school dinners', *London Evening Standard*, 5 September 2007, http://www.thisislondon.co.uk/news/article-23411183-school-children-to-be-locked-in-at-lunch-time-to-make-them-eat-school-dinners.do.

National Academies Institute of Medicine (2009) *School meals: building blocks for healthy children*, Washington: National Academies Press.

Nelson, M., Bradbury, J., Poulter, J., McGee, A., Msebele, S. and Jarvis, L. (2004) *School meals in secondary schools in England, research report no 557*, London: National Centre for Social Research, King's College London.

NSW Wales Department of Health and NSW Department of Education and Training, (2004) *Fresh tastes@school: New South Wales healthy canteen strategy*, https://www.det.nsw.edu.au/policies/student_serv/student_health/canteen_gu/CMPlanner.pdf.

NICE (National Institute for Health and Clinical Excellence) (2010) *Prevention of cardiovascular disease at population level*, National Public Health Guidance 25, London: NICE.

Ofsted (2009) *The evaluation schedule for schools: guidance and grade descriptors for inspecting schools in England under section 5 of the Education Act 2005, from September 2009*, http://www.ofsted.gov.uk/resources/evaluation-schedule-of-judgements-for-schools-inspected-under-section-five-of-education-act-2005-sep.

Passmore, S. and Harris, G. (2004) *Education, health and school meals: a review of policy changes in the UK over the last century*, Nutrition Bulletin 29, London: British Nutrition Foundation.

Paton, G. (2007) 'Most pupils 'shunning school dinners' after Jamie Oliver campaign', *The Telegraph*, 9 July, http://www.telegraph.co.uk/education/educationnews/5787464/Most-pupils-shunning-school-dinners-after-Jamie-Oliver-campaign.html.

Percival, J. (2006) 'Fast food mothers confront head teacher', *The Times*, 18 September, http://www.timesonline.co.uk/tol/news/uk/article642649.ece.

Pike, J. (2008a) *Junk food kids and sinner ladies: spatial transgressions and the 'Battle of Rawmarsh'*, Presentation given at Royal Geographical Society Annual Conference, London.

Pike, J. (2008b) 'Foucault and primary school dining rooms', *Children's Geographies*, vol 6, no 4, pp 413-22.

Pike, J. (2010) *An ethnographic study of primary school dining rooms,* unpublished PhD thesis, University of Hull.

Plunkett, J. (2005) 'Children keep gobbling turkey twizzlers', *The Guardian*, 23 March 2005, http://www.guardian.co.uk/media/2005/mar/23/broadcasting.schoolmeals.

Rawlins, E. (2008) 'Citizenship, health education and the obesity 'crisis'', *ACME*, vol 7, no 2, pp 135-51.

Rawlins, E. (2009) 'Choosing health? Exploring children's eating practices at home and at school', *Antipode*, vol 41, no 5, pp 1084-109.

Revill, J. and Hill, A. (2005) 'Victory for Jamie in school meal war', *The Observer*, 6 March, http://www.guardian.co.uk/society/2005/mar/06/schoolmeals.

Sack, R.D. (1986) *Human territoriality, its theory and history,* Cambridge: Cambridge University Press.

School Food Trust (2008) *Temptation town*, http://www.schoolfoodtrust.org.uk/news-events/news/new-research-reveals-the-scale-of-junk-food-temptation.

School Food Trust (2009) *Stay on site guide*, http://www.schoolfoodtrust.org.uk/partners/projects/million-meals-resources/stay-on-site-guide.

Stanton, R. (2009) 'Who will take responsibility for obesity in Australia?', *Public Health*, vol 123, no 3, pp 280-2.

Statutory Instrument 2359 (2007), *The Education (Nutritional Standards and Requirements for School Food) (England)*, School Meals and Nutrition Bill 37, 2005.

Stokes, P. (2006) 'Mrs Chips takes orders for the school dinners run', *The Telegraph*, 16 September 2006, http://www.telegraph.co.uk/news/uknews/1528992/Mrs-Chips-takes-orders-for-the-school-dinners-run.html.

USAD (United States Department of Agriculture) (2011) 'USDA unveils critical upgrades to nutritional standards for school meals', http://www.fns.usda.gov/cga/PressReleases/2011/0010.htm.

Welshman, J. (1997) 'School meals and milk in England and Wales, 1906–1945', *Medical History,* vol 4, pp 6-29.

White, J., Cole-Hamilton, I., and Dibb, I. (1992) *The nutritional case for school meals,* London: School Meals Campaign.

Wills, W., Backett-Milburn, K., Gregory, S., and Lawton, J. (2007) '"If the food looks dodgy I dinnae eat it": teenagers' accounts of food and eating practices in socio-economically disadvantaged families', *Sociological Research Online,* vol 13, no 1, doi:10.5153/sro.1681.

# nine

# Informal education in compulsory schooling in the UK: humanising moments, utopian spaces?

*Isabel Cartwright*

## Introduction

Western approaches to education typically focus on formal education, characterised by a structured curriculum, formal setting and compulsory attendance. Yet much of what we learn happens more informally. It has been shown that informal *learning* can help increase individuals' self-confidence, improve their social skills and contribute to an increasing commitment to citizenship, social identity and social capital (Cullen et al, 2000). However, the attempt to facilitate informal learning – informal *education* – is a practice that is little known and, partly as a result of its emphasis on experiential learning, has lacked research. This situation is beginning to be addressed in research (Jeffs and Smith 1999; 2005; Deer Richardson and Wolfe, 2001; Batsleer, 2008) and work with young people based on this approach (Wood and Hine, 2009; Batsleer and Davies, 2010). However, the research and discussion that has taken place has stayed mainly within the youth studies field. There is little literature on informal education by geographers, yet informal education is intrinsically concerned with notions of space and place:

> Often they [informal educators] are visitors – entering environments over which they have little or no control ... schools, health centres and people's homes ... Their work is always influenced by the 'where'. (Jeffs and Smith, 2005, p 7)

Informal educators therefore place a huge emphasis on understanding communities. Like Children's Geographers (Matthews and Limb, 1999; Holloway and Valentine, 2000), they relate the social to the physical dimensions of public space and make themselves familiar with the places where young people spend time (Whelan, 2010). They are also concerned with how the 'where' affects the development of young people's identities and willingness to engage with learning.

Drawing on the author's work as an informal educator in schools in the London Boroughs of Newham and Hackney, this chapter critically explores informal education, and how it can work as a prism through which to critique UK education policy and dominant Western approaches to education and young people. It will examine the following four key principles of informal education (based on Jeffs and Smith's model of informal education, 1999; 2005) in relation to the potential space that informal education can inhabit within the context of UK schools: creating spaces within formal educational settings to work *with* young people; the importance of dialogue/conversation in creating emotional spaces and 'horizons'; the importance of everyday geographies in fostering learning; and the creation of community/citizenship.

## What is informal education?

Professional informal educators emerged during the nineteenth century, particularly associated with philanthropic organisations such as the YMCA and the Mechanics Institutes.[1] In terms of the development of thinking about informal education as a deliberate practice, the first full-length text was by Brew (1946). In 1966 Davies and Gibson published *The social education of the adolescent*, focusing on youth work as a key vehicle for informal education. In their study of *The impact of youth work*, Merton et al (2004, p 5) found 'widespread consensus that youth work's core purpose is the personal and social development of young people, provided through informal education'.

Informal education is a dialogical practice that seeks to foster learning in everyday settings, on a voluntary basis. Learning is regarded in the Freirean sense of educational activity, situated in the lived experience of participants which leads to greater consciousness and aims to make a difference in the world. Informal educators seek to facilitate agency, by attempting to create a space that enables reflection and self-development, so that young people feel their lives belong to them. Young (2006) identifies this process as enabling young people to develop critical thinking skills, rational judgement, the ability to inquire about what is 'good' and conducive to the 'good life'. Informal education therefore rejects the notion of setting 'learning outcomes'. Informal education draws on Dewey's philosophical approach (1902) which emphasised 'drawing out' understanding rather than 'pouring in' knowledge.

## Formal, non-formal and informal education: what's in a name?

Often set against schooling, informal education supposedly offers choice rather than compulsion, freedom instead of order, and empowerment not indoctrination (Jeffs and Smith, 2005). The reality is less simple, and these dichotomies risk obscuring the shared concern for learning. As Dewey (1916) argued, there are differences between formal and informal education, but one is not *better* than the other, they are simply not the same. Geography is key here. One of the differences between formal and informal education is the level of control sought over the physical environment. Schools organise their physical layout; teachers decide who will be in which class and what rules should be followed. Informal educators have far less control over their environment. They seek to foster learning through relationships. This means that informal education can be hard to 'see', and even harder to measure. The lack of a physically designated space for informal education can contribute further towards its invisibility and potential marginalisation.

The distinction is sometimes made between informal and non-formal education. The latter can be characterised as organised educational activity outside formal systems but with pre-planned content/curriculum, for example an after-school dance project or a photography course offered by a youth centre. Informal education is less structured and more spontaneous: the conversations a detached youth worker may have with young people in a park or on a street corner; the discussions a learning mentor has with a young person in the school corridor or playground that help to foster reflection and growth. The types of education are, however, a continuum, and as Lave and Wenger (1991) have argued we should avoid sharp dichotomies.

Much of what Jeffs and Smith (2005) define as informal education is also given other names, such as community education/learning in Scotland, social pedagogy in Germany and popular education in South America. In the UK, New Labour policies that emphasised 'positive activities' and recorded and accredited outcomes (DfES, 2005; HM Treasury/DSCF, 2007) arguably shifted youth work from the informal to non-formal sphere. Some youth work even falls within the formal sphere, as many youth workers now offer targeted programmes for young people 'at risk', some stipulating compulsory attendance. Increasing numbers of informal educators are also working outside traditional youth and community settings, in formal settings such as in schools (Jeffs, 2007). There is much debate as to whether such work is actually 'youth work' (Davies and Merton, 2009[2]) or whether it colonises youth work skills, and the informal education process, in order to 'manage' student behaviour (Jeffs, 2007).

This chapter will now explore whether the agenda of schools around formal academic achievement is always likely to squeeze informal education to the margins, and will question whether informal educators are likely to be valued only for helping to create the conditions for formal, rather than informal, learning. It will consider whether the 'voluntary principle' is automatically undermined by a setting which involves compulsory attendance, and whether informal educators in the current educational climate are likely to be expected to work to an agenda that fits with, or undermines, the key principles of the practice.

## An analysis of informal education's four key principles

*Creating spaces within formal educational settings to work with young people*

By seeking to inspire explorative thinking, informal education rejects the notion of setting 'learning outcomes' and seeks to create the space to work *with*, not *on* or *for* young people. It adopts a 'problem-posing' approach to education, encouraging critical analysis rather than what Freire (1972) describes as a 'banking' model, where the students are seen as repositories and the teacher the depositor of knowledge. This approach will be examined in relation to the author's experience of facilitating girls' groups in two different schools (see Boxes 9.1 and 9.2). Both schools were concerned about certain girls' 'risk-taking behaviour'.

Dewey defined the 'business of education' as an 'emancipation and enlargement of experience' (1933, p 240). Through building trusting relationships and working *with* the girls in School A (see Box 9.1) we were able to help them to explore their lives, to try new things and to deepen their understanding of the things they were already doing (thus enlarging their experience). By creating the space for the girls to see the world differently the girls were emancipated – set free to try new ways of being. Prioritising the *process* of working together – building trust and developing relationship, we worked with issues that concerned the girls and connected with their emotions. The way that informal education values the affective domain of learning helps to redress the balance of formal learning environments, which tend to primarily emphasise cognition and downplay the role of emotion in learning (McGill and Brockbank, 2004).

This educational space was created *within* the parameters of the school – largely taking place inside the school building and within the timetabled school day. The girls were *required* to attend, and it could be argued that they were 'getting out of lessons' by doing so. This sits uncomfortably with the idea of working 'with', and the 'voluntary principle' valued in informal education and youth work. However, these girls generally chose whether to attend even formal lessons, and certainly chose whether to 'engage' if they *were* in a classroom. Their attendance was therefore still an active choice. Real participation – engaging with the views of others, sharing your own, risking thinking about things differently, can only be voluntary. The educational space that this work created represents what Pykett (this volume, Chapter Two) explores when she considers a more 'outward-looking geography of education', concerned not only with the difference space makes to education, but also 'how education 'makes space' (Thiem, 2009, pp 155-7). It also relates to the kind of widening participation that Brown (this volume, Chapter Six) calls for, which fosters 'a positivity and aliveness to the world beyond one's own turf' (Massey, 2005, p 15).

---

**Box 9.1: Author's experience at School A**

The headteacher had a background in community schooling and appointed an Informal Education team. As a youth worker in the team I was asked to work with one of the learning mentors to establish the girls' group. We were not asked to set any fixed learning outcomes or follow any pre-set agenda other than to explore what the girls felt would be relevant and helpful to them.

We planned the first few sessions around getting to know the group, building trust and finding out what they would like to get out of it. We anticipated facilitating sessions on topics such as alcohol, drugs, smoking and sex education. We soon discovered that the group had two main concerns: their relationships with their mothers and their desire to 'do stuff' that was 'exciting'. The 'stuff' that some of them were doing that was exciting generally involved causing some kind of disruption in the local area in order to get chased by the police. They enjoyed this but were happy to try something that didn't get them into trouble.

Working *with* the girls we developed a programme which provided space for them to talk about what was going on in their relationships, as well as some techniques around communicating assertively, resolving conflict and building self-esteem. We also planned some canoeing sessions on the local dock and a trip around London on an open top bus (despite living only a few miles from the centre of London, several girls had never been).

Attendance was excellent and participation improved as the girls grew in confidence. The girls particularly enjoyed talking through their conflicts, and gaining ideas about how to handle them more effectively. One of the girls became a key member of the canoeing club and others started travelling into town, as the bus tour had helped them realise it 'wasn't too far away'. Our relationships with most of the girls endured for the rest of their time at school; several of them would catch moments with us at the gates, or at breaktime, to discuss what was going on in their lives. Years later we were still talking about the open top bus tour.

---

**Box 9.2: Author's experience at School B**

Before having met the group of girls, a learning mentor and I were asked to write a detailed scheme of work for the sessions with clear learning objectives based around risk-taking behaviour. This made it straightforward to show, via questionnaires at the start and end of the term, that we had met our objectives – X had learnt more about the risks of smoking; Y understood the dangers of early pregnancy. Attendance was good until some members fell out with each other. This culminated in a fight. Senior Management was concerned that we stick to our scheme of work, rather than divert time to exploring these conflicts. The emphasis was upon offering information and advice to the girls, so that they could make more informed life choices.

We felt more in control as workers, but sessions remained at the level of information, rather than emotion. We failed to connect at a deeper level with the girls and trust was never fully established. The sessions felt like mini Personal, Social and Health Education lessons. As an informal educator I should have been offering something different. The opportunity of being in a small group, with fewer curriculum objectives, could have provided a chance to explore things that mattered to the girls, things concerning their everyday experiences and their community, and to enter a journey with them, getting to know the reality of their lives and what they wanted from them.

The current concern with young people leading lives of 'heightened risk' (Furlong and Cartmel, 2007, p 8) has led to an increased desire for understanding 'protective factors' and why some young people have the 'resilience' to ward off risk. However, resilience is increasingly understood as not simply located at the level of individual agency but as a cultural and structural concept (Wood and Hine, 2009, p 7). The 'risk-taking behaviour' of the girls in both schools was intrinsically linked to events taking place in their family lives and local communities. In School B (see Box 9.2) our approach failed to acknowledge this. We did not adhere to the principle of working *with*, or locate our work in relation to the context of the girls' lives. Our attempt to 'deposit' information, work 'on' the girls and to modify their behaviour was not even very effective – as the fight illustrated. Yet this way of working, and the school's concern with the girls making 'choices', fitted with New Labour's notion of social inclusion. As Kraftl (2011) describes, this notion was caught between two poles, on the one hand, the emphasis was upon personal 'responsibilisation', but on the other, intervention in certain geographical communities is seen as necessary as some people may be unable to 'take responsibility'. However, the girls in School A were able to 'take responsibility' precisely because we worked in a more holistic way which enabled them to think about how they felt about themselves and their world, and therefore to think about, and own, the changes they wanted to make to it.

As Pykett (this volume, Chapter Two) argues, schools tend to rely on a conception of children as future, incomplete adults in the making – in need of development and therefore 'working on'. Informal education offers a critique of this: it seeks to work from the interests, strengths and rights of young people, and rejects this deficit model. However, if schools under the Conservative–Liberal Democrat Coalition government are to continue New Labour's neoliberal agenda of targets and testing, and expand the academy programme, as is proposed, the scope for informal educators to create spaces that seek to locate learning in the context of young people's lives may be seriously restricted.

### The importance of dialogue/conversation in creating emotional spaces and 'horizons'

Freire (1972) describes dialogue as a process through which people create new understandings which are: 'explicitly critical and aimed at action, wherein those who were formally illiterate now begin to reject their role as mere "objects" in nature and social history and undertake to become "subjects" of their own destiny' (Goulet, 1974, p viii). Informal education draws on this understanding of dialogue and seeks to enhance people's autonomy through creating greater awareness of power and oppression.

Informal education also values everyday conversation for the way it brings people together and helps people feel connected. By engaging in conversation informal educators show interest in people, and by valuing what they have to say, display respect. For conversation to work it requires trust. We have to be open to the possible truth in the words of the other. Conversation also involves interpretation, we draw on background knowledge – *she's really angry about the teacher sending her out, but we also know her mum is ill.* Conversation involves immediate responses – saying things in the heat of the moment and thinking out loud – and it requires an appreciation of this which involves tolerance (Jeffs and Smith, 2005).

In exploring the value of conversation Gadamer (1979) uses the geographical metaphor of the horizon. We each bring prejudices to encounters and have our own 'horizon of understanding'. In conversation we have to put our own prejudices and understandings to the test. We have to open ourselves to the full power of what the 'other' is saying. By doing this their ideas become intelligible, without necessarily having to agree with them. We experience a 'fusion of horizons'. Conversation is therefore not only a method of informal education, but also embodies a number emotions and virtues informal educators seek to foster:

- concern for others and co-operation;
- trust;
- respect for others – and ourselves;
- affection (Jeffs and Smith, 2005).

The importance of conversation in relation to working with young people is illustrated in the example given in Box 9.3. The setting is the Youth Centre where I worked on a sessional basis, while employed at the nearby school.

---

**Box 9.3: Author's experience at a Youth Centre**

The two young women sat at the edge of the community hall. They didn't join in any activities or mix with anyone. I started chatting to them. They told me about getting into trouble, about how much they hated teachers, their parents and the police. We talked for ages. I challenged a lot of what they were saying – did they hate *all* teachers? *why* might they be getting the reaction they were from so many people? did they *really* enjoy it? ... I wondered afterwards if I'd challenged too much. Had I really listened? I was glad when they came back to the club a few days later. We got into more conversations. They became regulars. I could never get them to join in with any activities and used to feel guilty just sitting and talking.

I began to see the girls at school; they'd call me over to have a chat. I was able to talk to one of their PE teachers about how much one of them loved football, and they encouraged her to join the girls' football team. That meant she was allowed out more (she'd been 'grounded' as a result of all the trouble she was getting into) and she started getting on better with her mum. Through football she established more friends. Her stories became less about who she hated and more about her frustrations, and hurt, and sometimes what she was enjoying.

---

Young people, perhaps particularly young women, do not always want to be 'organised' into an activity. They sometimes want to 'just sit and talk', and this process of 'giving voice' should not be underestimated:

> It may be daughters giving voice to their understandings of their mothers; it may be a young women's group giving voice to a sense of the importance of their history as Black women or young women asserting their rights for health care to be offered in appropriate and non-patronizing ways ... all these processes ... participate clearly in that movement from silence to speech, from object to subject. (Freire, 1996, p 58)

In the scenario described in Box 9.3, I had thought the girls were regulars at the club, but one of the staff members explained that if I was not around they did not stay for long. I realised that chatting to them *was* the work. Our 'horizons' did not necessarily 'fuse' but we established a 'kind of sacred circle' – it is within this circle that informal educators work with whoever, wherever they are, and whatever they have done, in order to create possibilities of transformation – healing hurts, repairing damage and encouraging reflection and growth (Sercombe, 2010, p 11).

Working through conversation in this way, you never know quite where it will lead. In this example the initial conversations opened up a journey of exploration with the girls that I would never have anticipated. The space that I had as an informal educator to 'be around', enabled conversation to develop into a series of discussions which essentially addressed Socrates' question – 'how should one live?'. In embracing the unpredictability of conversation informal education offers critical moments that cut against the grain of neoliberal education and offer young people the opportunity to articulate 'impulses of hopefulness' (Kraftl, 2008, p 81). Such critical moments can help young people to feel more in control of their lives and enable them to take steps towards a different vision of their lives. Therefore the value of these small, often seemingly superficial, interactions should not be overlooked. Their ability to affirm brings humanising moments into people's everyday lives.

### The importance of everyday geographies in fostering learning

Informal education is located amidst the routines and everyday geographies of young people's lives (Horton and Kraftl, 2006; Kraftl, 2008). It seeks to take education 'to the places where people already congregate, to the public house, the licensed club, the dance hall, the library, the places where people feel at home' (Brew, 1946, p 22):

> The needs and issues presented by young people cannot be considered outside of the physical and social contexts within which they exist. How, for example, can detached workers respond effectively to a young person who tells them that he carries a knife because he constantly fears for his own safety, if they do not have any understanding of the context within which that fear exists?' (Whelan, 2010, p 51)

As well as seeking to understand public space, and how it affects young people, informal educators seek to facilitate the social environment. Creating supportive *spaces* is a fundamental aspect of enabling informal education. Small interactions in carved out spaces, such as gaps between lessons and break times, may lead to a project being established, such as a 'transition' group, helping students adjust from primary to secondary school.

Informal educators often have this understanding as they often live amongst the community that helps to shape the identity of those they work with. 'Living in an area expands the type of knowledge a worker can gather about young people allowing them to observe how life is lived as well as how it is presented' (Lloyd-Jones, 2010, p 20). Schools have tended to value this local knowledge and the ability of informal educators to resolve conflicts, and reach out to 'challenging' and 'disengaged' students. However, this 'management' of young people is primarily valued as it helps maintain order and the 'production of tranquillity' (Isin, 2004, p 228). For informal education to flourish in schools, informal educators need to be given the freedom to work with young people based around their *interests* as well as their *needs*, and the needs of the formal educational agenda. If the latter is primarily concerned with attainment, as opposed to young people's broader ethical development, and the Conservative–Liberal Democrat Coalition government's emphasis upon the value of league tables suggests that this focus is only to gain in momentum, informal educators may need to seek spaces outside of schools to foster learning in young people's lives.

### The creation of community/citizenship

The idea of association – of joining together in companionship or to undertake some task – and the educative power of playing one's part in a group (Doyle and Smith, 1999, p 44) appears repeatedly in the literature of informal education. Clubs and groups are seen as places where individuals can learn about community and citizenship by practising it. However, under New Labour, youth workers were encouraged to increasingly manage 'case loads' of young people, and the development of the Connexions Service focused on one-to-one work with young people deemed 'at risk'. Jeffs and Smith (2002) criticised this increasingly individualised focus, arguing that this approach cloaked public issues as private troubles.

I would argue that the power of association may be articulated in unlikely settings, including schools. For another way to introduce democratic opportunities into schools (as well as youth work) is to facilitate projects which give young people opportunities to critique power in a broader context than the school institution, addressing local to global concerns. I will turn to an example that took this approach and embodies the four principles of informal education through group – not individual – work.

The film project '*Where is the Love?*' described in Box 9.4 stemmed not from a concern with deficiencies or control, but from a desire to build on young people's interests and encourage involvement in shaping their world. It evolved through conversation and was characterised by mutuality, working *with* the young people on *what, when, where* and *how* the project should emerge. It gave the young people an opportunity to engage in politics in a way that was entirely new to all of them. Several members continued involvement in local politics long after the completion of the project. All felt more critical and more capable. Helping young people to 'be more' requires educators to join young people on a journey in which they actually exercise their rights, rather than just learn about them. This kind of project goes *beyond* the lives and concerns of young people in disadvantaged communities at a local scale, and connects with global concerns – representing a kind of scale-jumping (Ansell, 2009).

This project's creativity lay not only in its use of the Arts, but also in its structure and processes. The model of working involved an informal educator (building on existing relationships with young people and the community and focusing on the overall *process*) a formal educator (who brought techniques such as story-boarding and helped gain support from the wider teaching staff) and an outside expert (the film maker, who trained the students to be directors and create a project that would be genuinely engaging for a wide audience). This involved a commitment on the part of the workers to cross professional borders and value each other as educators with different approaches and expertise. The journey was based on trust and respect, and the cross-fertilisation of educational approaches opened up a unique learning opportunity: 'disenfranchised young people gained the confidence to take elements of their everyday lives and, in the process of sharing them and discussing them … arrived at a new understanding of their world' (Patel, 2010, p 63).

---

**Box 9.4: Film project *'Where is the Love?'***

An international arms fair was taking place opposite the school. Despite being able to see tanks and gun-ships from classroom windows, little debate was taking place about the fair or wider issues around the arms trade. As an informal educator I felt committed to giving students the opportunity to understand and engage with these issues.

Working closely with one of the school's English teachers I sought external funding to run an after-school documentary film project. From a starting point of practical concerns – such as disruption to bus routes home – the students' research led them into an exploration of the moral questions surrounding the fair. They began to link issues of local concern, such as asylum seekers and refugees, with the global implications of the arms trade. It came as a shock to the group that the terms 'asylum seeker' and 'refugee', commonly used as derogatory labels in the area, actually applied to classmates.

---

Sessions often took place over the road from the school in a café – itself a hub of committed local activism. The students learnt from local people about the days of the docks being a thriving community, about how heavily bombed the area was [during the Second World War], and about the loneliness and isolation felt by many older people in the area. Meeting in the café was important: we felt freer, that we were genuinely learning with and from each other and those around us. We worked on the project for over six months. The actual film-making and group editing took place across only five days. This enabled in-depth research giving the young people time to form their opinions. When it came to filming the young people were clear about whom they wanted to interview and why, and what they wanted the film to say.

The young people enjoyed the wide coverage that the film received by ITV news, features in the local press, and screenings at the local youth parliament and at a range of conferences. It stimulated a feeling amongst the wider student body that their voices could be heard and inspired other students to take action on other issues of concern. The young people became confident as public speakers, better able to make decisions together and deal with conflict. This was a rare opportunity to work closely with peers who they would not necessarily have spent time with – an advantage of school-, rather than club-, based informal education.

The film was built into the school's pastoral programme, incorporated as a scheme of work for English and written into the National Citizenship Teacher Training Programme. The film also became central to local debate and was screened at a variety of council meetings, stimulating debate, and perhaps playing some part, in the (elected) Mayor of Newham's change of attitude towards the arms fair. *Where is the Love?* can be viewed on YouTube: see http://www.youtube.com/watch?v=KsBOYZk-VrY

There is concern among practitioners about 'political' projects such as this, and of bringing their own bias to the work. In the *Where is the Love?* project, we had to allay the fears of senior teachers about the 'political' nature of the project, and to remind ourselves that 'our values are our "bias". They are our humanness ... It is frequently people's "bias" that touches us most' (Smith, 1982, p 37). Informal education, then, with its concern with enabling young people to exercise their rights and its vision of making the world 'not only more understandable, but also a better, place' (Jeffs and Smith, 2005, p 108) carries a sense of hope and belief that individual and societal change is possible. It is this hopefulness that imbues informal education with utopian potential and that makes associational and politicised projects (like *Where is the Love?*) so powerful.

## Conclusions

As Pykett (this volume, Chapter Two) argues, school life arguably dominates the everyday worlds of young people in countries such as the UK. For informal educators, who have always sought to work amidst the routines and everyday geographies of young people's lives, schools provide potentially rich opportunities for informal educators to create spaces to work *with* young people. If bridges are built between the educational spheres, informal educators, with their emphasis on process, can create unique educational spaces when working *with* formal educators, with their subject specialism and teaching and learning expertise. Informal education in formal settings such as schools is always likely to be squeezed to the margins but, as the examples in this chapter have shown, a lot can be achieved from there. Informal educators can help to keep the margins porous – bringing in outside expertise and engaging the local community – enabling more contextualised learning that values the role of 'emotion work', and offers a model of citizenship that is active, radical and meaningful.

However, schools are hierarchical and tightly organised places. Indeed, one of the schools referred to in this chapter was modelled on Bentham's Panopticon, not in a metaphorical Foucauldian sense, but literally, in terms of its design, with a central rotunda and corridors with walls of glass leading form it, built to ensure maximum surveillance. In line with an increasing trend across the UK, the school moved away from its concern with reaching out to the community: removing the position of community tutor from its senior management team; forbidding students to leave the school site at lunch-time; reducing its community projects, and increasingly focusing instead on building (or, it could be argued, controlling) the school 'community', rather than developing its links with the community within which it was situated. The 'informal education team' within which I worked lost its title and the youth workers were asked to focus on classroom support and behaviour management, potentially undermining rather than adhering to the principles of informal education.

Therefore, unless schools return to a focus on their role within, and interaction with, the local community, the scope for informal education within schools will be limited. This approach was briefly attempted by New Labour in its *Extended schools* programme and *Building schools for the future* (BSF) initiative – which envisioned a role for schools in regenerating neighbourhoods – using the utopian language of 'transformation', 'dreams' and 'hopes' (Kraftl, 2011), but the political landscape has changed since the 2010 General Election. For informal education to flourish it requires a holistic vision of education which focuses on the wellbeing and happiness of young people, and a contextualised understanding of their lives. However, the cancellation of BSF by the Conservative–Liberal Democrat Coalition government, the recent changes to the Ofsted criteria (with less focus on school context) and the shift, as Kraftl (2011) argues, from the New Labour language of social transformation, to a focus on efficiency and austerity, suggests this is unlikely in the short term.

Amidst a policy context that continues to view young people through a deficit model (focusing on the risk posed *by* and *to* them), the utopian vision of informal education building literal and metaphorical spaces that encourage young people to reflect and try out new ways of being, serves as a counterweight to current education policy. However, spaces for informal education may have to be created outside of the school environment. With the Coalition government announcing that its Big Society community-builders will be trained in the ideas of Alinsky and Freire, some commentators may predict that it is within such initiatives that these spaces will be created. Yet, the reality seems to be that it is in resistance to the Coalition's policies that young people are establishing the kind of social capital and political engagement that the Big Society advocates.

**Notes**

[1] See http://www.infed.org.

[2] See also www.indefenceofyouthwork.org.uk.

**References**

Ansell, N. (2009) 'Childhood and the politics of scale: descaling children's geographies', *Progress in Human Geography*, vol 33, no 2, pp 190-209.

Batsleer, J. (2008) *Informal learning in youth work*, London: Sage Publications.

Batsleer, J. and Davies, B. (eds) (2010) *What is youth work?*, Exeter: Learning Matters Ltd.

Brew, J.M. (1946) *Informal education: adventures and reflections*, London: Faber.

Cullen, J., Batterbury, S., Foresti, M., Lyons, C and Stern, E. (2000) *Informal learning and widening participation*, DfEE report no. 191, London: DFEE, http://www.education.gov.uk/publications/standard/publicationdetail/page1/RR191.

Davies, B. and Gibson, A. (1967) *The social education of the adolescent*, London: London University Press.

Davies, B. and Merton, B. (2009) 'Squaring the circle: the state of youth work in some children and young people's services', *Youth & Policy*, vol 103, pp 5-24.

Deer Richardson, L. and Wolfe, M. (2001) *Principles and practice of informal education: learning through life*, London: Routledge.

Dewey, J. (1902) *The child and the curriculum*, Chicago: University of Chicago Press.

Dewey, J. (1916) *Democracy and education*, New York: Macmillan.

Dewey, J. (1933) *How we think*, New York: D.C. Heath.

DfES (Department for Education and Skills) (2005) *Youth matters: next steps*, London: DfES.

Doyle, M.E. and Smith, M.K. (1999) *Born and bred? Leadership, heart and informal education*, London: YMCA George Williams College/Rank Foundation.

Freire, P. (1996) *Letters to Cristina. Reflections on my life and work*, London: Routledge.

Freire, P. (1972) *Pedagogy of the oppressed*, Harmondsworth: Penguin.

Furlong, A. and Cartmel, F. (2007) *Young people and social change*, Maidenhead: McGraw-Hill.

Gadamer, H.-G. (1979) *Truth and method*, London: Sheed and Ward.

Goulet, D. (1974) 'Introduction' to P. Freire, *Education: the practice of freedom*, London: Writers and Readers Publishing Cooperative.

Holloway, S. and Valentine, G. (2000) 'Spatiality and the new social studies of childhood', *Sociology*, vol 34, no 4, pp 763-83.

Horton, J. and Kraftl, P. (2006) 'What else? Some more ways of thinking about and doing children's geographies', *Children's Geographies*, vol 4, no 1, pp 69-95.

HM Treasury/Department for Children, Families and Schools (2007) *Aiming high for young people: a ten year strategy for positive activities*, London: HM Treasury.

Isin, E.F. (2004) 'The neurotic citizen', *Citizenship Studies*, vol 8, no 3, pp 217-35.

Jeffs, T. (2007) 'Crossing the divide: school-based youth work', in R. Harrison, C. Benjamin, S. Curran and R. Hunter (eds) *Leading work with young people*, Milton Keynes: The Open University, pp 97-108.

Jeffs, T. and Smith, M.K. (1999) *Informal education: conversation, democracy and learning* (2nd edn), Ticknall: Education Now.

Jeffs, T. and Smith, M.K. (2002) 'Individualization and youth work', *Youth and Policy*, vol 76, pp 39-65.

Jeffs, T. and Smith, M.K. (2005) *Informal education: conversation, democracy and learning* (3rd edn), Nottingham: Educational Heretics Press.

Kraftl, P. (2008) 'Young people, hope and childhood-hope', *Space and Culture*, vol 1, no 1, pp 81-92.

Kraftl, P. (2011) 'Utopian promise or burdensome responsibility? A critical analysis of the UK Government's Building Schools for the Future Policy', *Antipode*, doi: 10.1111/j.1467-8330.2011.00921.x

Lave, J. and Wenger, E. (1991) *Situated learning: legitimate peripheral participation*, Cambridge: Cambridge University Press.

Lloyd-Jones, S. (2010) 'The experience of growing work', in A. Rogers and M.K. Smith (eds) *Journeying together, growing youth work and youth workers in local communities*, Dorset: Russell House Publishing Ltd, pp 13-24.

Massey, D. (2005) *For space*, London: Sage.

Matthews, H. and Limb, M. (1999) 'Defining and agenda for the geography of children', *Progress in Human Geography*, vol 23, no 1, pp 61-90.

McGill, I. and Brockbank, A. (2004) *The action learning handbook*, Abingdon: RoutledgeFalmer.

Merton, B., Payne, M. and Smith, D. (2004) *An evaluation of the impact of youth work in England*, Nottingham: DFES.

Patel, R. (2010) 'Creativity and partnership', in J. Batsleer and B. Davies (eds) *What is youth work?*, Exeter: Learning Matters Ltd, pp 61-72.

Sercombe, H. (2010) *Youth work ethics*, London: Sage.

Smith, M.K. (1982) *Creators not consumers*, Leicester: Youth Clubs UK.

Thiem, C.H. (2009) 'Thinking through education: the geographies of contemporary educational restructuring', *Progress in Human Geography*, vol 33, no 3, pp 154-73.

Whelan, M. (2010) 'Detached youth work', in J. Batsleer and B. Davies (eds) *What is youth work?*, Exeter: Learning Matters Ltd, pp 47-60.

Wood, J. and Hine, J. (eds) (2009) *Work with young people: theory and policy for practice*, London: Sage.

Young, K. (2006) *The art of youth work*, Dorset: Russell House Publishing Ltd.

# Part III
Intervening in 'everyday life': scales, practices and the 'spatial imagination' in youth policy and professional practice

ten

# A free for all? Scale and young people's participation in UK transport planning

*John Barker*

## Introduction

Although a long-standing and heavily contested concept (see Cox, 1998; Marston et al, 2005; Ansell, 2009), scale has been used by geographers and other social scientists to refer to different orders of social processes to explore many diverse aspects of the social world. Scale is neither natural nor pre-existing and levels of order of social action are socially organised and constructed (for example, in classic 'nested' scales like local, regional, national or global). However, there are ongoing debates as to how scales should be conceptualised and how scales are ordered, linked and relate. One strand of these discussions focuses on hierarchies of scale, for example considering whether each smaller scale (such as the local) is nested within larger scales (such as the national or global), or whether it is more appropriate to use a network metaphor where different scales interpenetrate each other (Ansell, 2009). Furthermore, debates continue surrounding the implications of these different conceptualisations of scale for understanding flows of power; for example considering the relative influence of 'local contexts' or 'global processes' on a place (Marston et al, 2005).

Children's Geographers have engaged substantially with scale theory, in particular considering the nature and limit of young people's spaces of perceptions, action and engagement. Much emphasis has focused on the local, as children's everyday lives are often played out and embedded in local contexts, and the local scale has often been conceptualised as offering more potential for young people's participation (Wyness, 2009). However, more recent discussions have critiqued the sole focus on 'engagements and entanglements' at the local scale, highlighting a need to 'upscale' Children's Geographies (see Hopkins and Alexander, 2010, p 142). This has begun to be achieved though an exploration and analysis of national, international and global scale processes that impact upon children and young people, and conversely the opportunities for children and young people to influence social action beyond the local (Katz, 2004).

However, while scale theory has been applied to many diverse contexts, it has not been much considered in relation to mobility. Mobility is increasingly central to many societies. Spatial mobility refers to the act of movement, circulation or flow through space, landscapes, places and territory, including longer-term movements such as migration as well as everyday travel movements (Beckmann, 2001). Different forms of mobility include: personal travel; travel of objects, such as goods and commodities; virtual travel, for example through the internet; and communicative travel, such as email and mobile phones (Urry, 2004).

Until recently, mobility was an undervalued concept in the social sciences (Law, 1999; Cresswell, 2004). Geographers have offered significant contributions to the development of the interdisciplinary 'new mobilities paradigm', which has explored a diverse set of mobility experiences, for example, cars, airports, motorway service stations, and cyberspace and virtual environments (Cresswell, 2004). Most discussions have focused on the experiences of adults, and only recently has research begun to consider children (for example, Fotel and Thomsen, 2004; Laurier et al, 2008; Barker et al, 2009; Horton et al, 2011). Children and young people have unique experiences of mobility since, unlike other social groups, they lack the ability to drive and have limited access to funds to pay for transport and are often dependent upon adults for mobility, frequently having limitations placed on their ability to use public transport.

While Children's Geographers (such as Valentine, 1997; Barker et al, 2009) have complemented the work of others (including Hillman et al, 1990) in identifying changing trends in children's mobility (most notably, a decline in independent spatial mobility and increases in adult escorting and car-based mobility), less has been written about mobility and young people (although see Harker, 2009). Evidence from the UK suggests that young people have distinct travel patterns. Young people are more likely than many other sections of the population to use and rely upon public transport (DfT, 2002a; 2006b), yet are also more likely than other groups to report difficulties accessing it (DfT, 2002b). Young people often struggle with the cost of travel, and report problems with the steep rise in fares once they become too old to be eligible for child concessions (DfT, 2006a).

Over the past 20 years, many countries across the world have struggled with increasing levels of mobility. Successive UK governments' policies in relation to mobility have, like in other countries (Kearns et al, 2003; Buehler, 2010), been complex and contradictory. Faced with ever growing car ownership and use, and associated problems of congestion, pollution and accidents, policy-makers and planners have become increasingly critical of the 'predict and provide' approach to road-based transport planning. Arguably, the policies have moved away from the provision of more road space through road building programmes (for example, the widespread cancellation of the *Roads to prosperity* programme of the 1980s–90s). Instead the focus in the UK and elsewhere has shifted to demand management, including a variety of initiatives such as road pricing (for example, the London congestion charge introduced in 2003), *Work travel plans*, *Homezones* and public transport initiatives. More radical responses, such as the anti-road protests at Twyford Down in Hampshire (1992–95) and more formal organisations such as Transport 2000 and the Environmental Transport Association, have also problematised the building of new roads, and the wider dominance of cars. Once more, these challenges are not unique to UK policy-makers and planners and have been discussed in other countries (see Buehler, 2010).

In the above context, and in response to growing evidence about barriers young people face in accessing transport, since 2005 young people's transport needs have moved up the UK political agenda. There has been a variety of responses to growing concerns over traffic congestion generated by the journey to school and young people's perceived anti-social behaviour on public transport, including the *Footsteps* training for primary school children, and the *Yellow school buses* and *Safer routes to school* programmes. Similarly, a number of policy initiatives during the New Labour (1997–2010) government indicated the importance of transport in enabling young people to access a wide range of activities. The 2006 Education and Inspections Act gave local authorities the duty to secure young people's access to a range of positive activities. Statutory guidance for delivering this duty included transport as one of the key barriers to access that must be addressed. The *Youth matters* document also acknowledged the need for affordable travel to enable young people to access different opportunities (DfES, 2006) and the *Aiming high for young people: a ten year strategy for positive activities* document recognised the issue of transport in making services 'attractive and accessible' for young people (see HM Treasury/DCSF, 2007, p 44).

These have been interesting developments. While it is clear that young people's transport needs and mechanisms to incorporate young people's participation in planning have moved up the political agenda, the New Labour government largely placed the responsibility for this at the level of *local* government. Local authorities were tasked to work with local transport providers and other stakeholders to develop locally-based solutions. What is less clear is how this has emerged and has been implemented at the local level. This chapter critically discusses a number of local transport initiatives in which young people have been involved in planning. It discusses young people's campaigns to lobby for transport improvements, and how their efforts have helped to form *national* governmental guidance. It also discusses some of the possible implications for young people, participation and transport policy of the change of UK government following the 2010

Election. In so doing, the chapter uses different analyses of scale to consider the relationship between national-level policy guidance, local strategic plans and grassroots activities.

## Methods

In 2007–08, the National Youth Agency[1] commissioned Brunel University to conduct research to explore potential solutions to the problems faced by young people using public transport. Drawing upon some of these data, this chapter explores three case studies of young people's campaigns to improve public transport in these locations (see Table 10.1). The sample was purposive – that is to say, the three case study locations were chosen to provide an illustration of the variety of transport initiatives undertaken at the local level.

**Table 10.1:** Case studies

| Case study | Description of campaign | Scale of campaign |
|---|---|---|
| 1 | 50p bus fare on all bus (and rail) journeys across the local authority for those aged 5–19 in full-time education (scheme terminated Sept 2010) | Across the entire local authority |
| 2 | Term-time free minibus running one night per week to enable young people from one small town to access a youth centre 8 miles distant | 10–15 young people using one youth club |
| 3 | Concessionary fares scheme (quarter fare for under 16s, half fare for 16–19 year olds in full-time education) linked with ID proof-of-age card and discount card | Across the entire local authority |

Several research methods were employed. Seventeen in-depth interviews were conducted with professionals from different local authority departments, including Transport and Planning, Children's Services, Youth and Connexions. Providers of activities for young people, and bus companies and other operators also participated in in-depth interviews in some locations. In addition, reflecting the concerns of similar research to explore young people's own perspectives (see Barker, 2003; Robson et al, 2009), nine focus group interviews (involving a total of 20 participants) were conducted with young people aged 13–19 years. The interviews focused upon young people's perceptions of barriers to using public transport and their views on local campaigns and transport initiatives. A number of relevant documents (such as Local Transport Plans and Children and Young People's Plans) were collected from local authorities and subjected to thematic analysis to consider whether and how young people or transport were included in strategic plans.

In order to protect individuals' anonymity, this chapter uses pseudonyms for young people and generic titles for professionals (which give some indication of their departmental location/organisation). The in-depth interviews were transcribed verbatim and the transcripts were analysed according to the original research aims. Rather than exploring the initiatives themselves (see Barker, 2008), this chapter considers the three case studies for what they tell us about young people's participation in planning and policy development, and the importance of exploring the significance of scale in analysing such campaigns.

## Young people's campaigns to identify local transport problems

One theme common to the three case studies was that each campaign had been set up not as the result of adult-initiated mechanisms to involve young people but through long-running campaigns involving the dedicated tenacity of committed young people. Young people's initial engagement in these campaigns had different origins, indicating that participation (a contested concept; see Graham and Fitzgerald, 2010), takes many forms and there is never one clear route to or through participation and campaigning. In one case study, young people were mobilised through their attendance at a youth club. In other places previously established formal networks and mechanisms for young people's participation (for example, Youth Councils, Youth Parliament, School Councils and other campaigns) provided various conduits for young people to discuss their travel problems. These established mechanisms helped young people to expand their capacity to become politicised and participate in campaigning for local transport improvements.

In all three examples, young people came together as transport (non-)users, often organically and informally at the grassroots level, rather than a process initiated from formal, imposed, top-down models of communication from adult planners, an approach which has often been critiqued (Wyness, 2009). That participation was generated in different ways among these three case studies reflects other examples of young people's political participation. As Skelton (2010) notes, while excluded from formal participation in political structures and processes, a more broader definition of politics which includes informal, micro-politics and participation is helpful in demonstrating how young people often have substantial interest and engagement in political processes.

However, participants commented that previously, processes of young people's participation often worked in parallel with rather than interfacing with or informing formal adult transport planning:

> "The only time there were discussions about transport was at our annual [youth council] conference. But it wasn't really moving things forward. There was no way of really feeding that back into transport planning." (Youth worker, case study 3)

This lack of joined-up thinking and opportunities for young people to influence transport planning reflected a lack of guidance within extant policy documents and guidelines about young people's participation in the planning of transport services. Between 2000 and 2006 a raft of legislation, guidance and initiatives, such as the above-mentioned 2006 Education and Inspections Act, focused upon children and young people's travel. However, very little in these documents considered children and young people's *participation* in the planning process. For example, guidance for starting up a Walking Bus (where children are walked to school under supervision from trained and insured parent volunteers) did not mention involvement of children (DfT, 2006c). Significantly, the guidance for Local Transport Plans indicated opportunities for local authorities to develop plans that link transport with wider agendas such as children's services for the priorities *for* children, although there was no mention of consulting with children as part of this (DfT, 2009). On the other hand, guidance for *School travel plans* (designed to promote walking and cycling to school in an effort to reduce car dependency) considered the need for 'consultation with teachers, parents, pupils, governors and other local people' (DfT, 2003, p 3). More generally, however, while these documents were innovative in identifying that young people have particular transport needs, young people were clearly conceptualised as passive recipients of adult-made transport plans rather than active stakeholders.

In these three case studies, young people were not deterred by this lack of consultation, and developed different strategies and campaigns to address their own transport problems:

> "Looking back, we had [the annual youth conference], the youth council and the 3,000 signature petition." (Claire, 16, case study 1)

> "There was a survey done with the youngsters, getting out on the street using the detached youth workers, to talk to youngsters, we did a survey in the centre itself. So that showed there was a need there." (Youth worker, case study 3)

> "We had recently conducted a community survey of young people, so that was a huge asset. That was evidence that there was need." (Officer, Youth and Connexions, case study 2)

The initial stages of these campaigns reflect many other instances of young people's involvement in the early phases of policy and planning, through the scoping and the identification of barriers and needs (for example, Porter and Abane, 2008; Robson et al, 2009; Dudek, 2011). Indeed, young people's engagement in these activities can help to ensure that planning represents their needs (Blanchet-Cohen and Rainbow, 2006). However, more recent discussions have critiqued the assumption that participation necessarily creates better evidence or data, and also challenged the notion that having research evidence designed and collected by young people ensures that the participatory process was genuine and that the results are representative of all young people (Robson et al, 2009).[2]

Through these exercises, young people identified different problems and priorities in their local areas. For example, in one location the most reported problem was the affordability of fares and the transition to adult fare at the age of 14:

> "It used to cost more for the bus, £7, than it did to go to the cinema, which was £5. When I was 14, that seemed an awful lot of money." (Larry, 18, case study 1)

However, there was no consensus among young people as to problems accessing transport. In other locations, young people stated it was a general lack of availability of services, especially in rural areas, or a lack of availability in evenings and weekends, preventing young people from engaging in part-time employment:

> "Yeah our [bus service] stops at an early time. When it's a bit late, and I need a bus, I can't, I have to walk. It's quite far [to the village]." (Yasir, 16, case study 3)

The local is significant here, as consultations identified that young people's transport problems and priorities were not aspatial, but varied in different contexts. That these campaigns focused at the local level enables an application of scale theory. In these case studies, the local was an important focus for the organisation, participation and political action of and for young people. However, the local scale of children's everyday action interlinks with other, competing versions of the local. For example, while the local for young people may be constituted around planning transport for accessing a local youth centre once a week, for transport planners working at the level of local authority, the local compasses transport provision for 300,000 people covering 1,500 square miles. One practical example of how two competing versions of local become connected (and indeed how the local for transport provision has a significant impact upon young people's lives) is that since there is no nationally agreed comprehensive and consistent policy on the age limit or level of concessionary fares, young people's fares vary across local operators and across locations (DfT, 2006a). Furthermore, as many local transport providers are now owned by national and international parent transport companies, young people's local transport experiences are connected with transport providers at local, national and international scales.

## Young people's sustained campaigns for local transport improvement

Although many different examples of young people's participation in policy and planning can be critiqued for being limited or tokenistic (see Hart, 1992), young people's participation in these three case study examples was more comprehensive. Indeed, reflecting that participation can be seen as a process (Blanchet–Cohen and Rainbow, 2006), young people's involvement in these case study campaigns was ongoing and sustained, sometimes over a number of years. Armed with their research evidence and through hard work and determination, young people helped to convince, often over long periods, local authorities (most often Transport Planning or Children's Services departments) and other partners (such as bus companies) of the need for improving young people's travel. These campaigns often involved young people securing long-term membership of relevant local transport committees and groups at the local authority level:

> "One young person [in the youth cabinet] took on the role of being the transport person, in fact he was coined Mr Transport by the group. He got himself invited to a transport meeting set up by the county council … he instigated a specific meeting with the bus operators, we had about five or six bus operator companies represented, we had a really good turn out." (Youth worker, case study 3)

However, not all of young people's interactions with adults were productive or successful, and their campaigns often received setbacks:

> "Three years ago [the youth council] was trying to [lobby for reduced fares], the bus company had another guy at the top, another chairman who people didn't respect or see eye-to-eye with. His verbal skills weren't great. He'd say 'I want this' and not compromise." (Peter, 19, case study 1)

Indeed, participants were often disappointed by previous formal attempts from young people to participate in transport planning:

> "We had a 3,000 signed petition [for cheaper fares for young people] which the bus company just disregarded completely. The comment from the bus company was 'so the young people think this is going to change anything?'." (Youth worker, case study 1)

Clear in the discussions with young people and adult professionals was that perseverance and ongoing, sustained lobbying was key to success:

> "I would say the thing to do is to set up a plan and to be very persistent, don't allow yourself to be channelled, not to allow young people to be brushed away or pushed off, or channelled into other things ... if it is a serious issue, then keep up the pressure. The wheels of local government turn very slowly. Keep the pressure building." (Youth worker, case study 1)

Each local campaign differed, in part depending upon the scale of the issues under consideration. Some campaigns run by young people focused upon particular small-scale locations or specific groups of young people with particular needs (for example, case study 2's small group of young people campaigning for a minibus to solve difficulties of accessing youth clubs). In others, young people had led much larger campaigns to introduce fare concessions across entire local authorities. Similarly, the campaigns differed due to the preferred strategies, skills and capacity of the young people involved in the campaign. Some young people focused on developing high-profile media campaigns, whereas others preferred lobbying public meetings. Once more, scale is significant here, as there are different levels and scales of social action within young people's spaces of engagement (Cox, 1998), and there are spatial variations in the ways in which these engagements are manifest and configured at the local level.

Critically, in each of these case studies, young people's campaigns were supported by adult advocates, including (but not limited to) youth workers:

> "You have to do some work with adults to make them more receptive to the things that the young people are suggesting, because otherwise I think they will just say no." (Youth worker, case study 3)

Recognition of the important role of advocates for children and young people (at a variety of spatial scales including the international, national and local) is not new, and has been recorded by others exploring young people's participation (Wyness, 2009). The processes of gaining and working with advocates is complex – for example, Porter and Abane (2008) discuss the challenges in building alliances and advocates in the transport context in Ghana. That advocates worked effectively in a supporting role with young people in the examples presented in this chapter suggest that these case studies can be seen as reaching the top rung of Hart's (1992) ladder of participation – 'child initiated, shared decisions with adults'. Indeed, as Maxey (2004) states, it is naïve to assume that, given the broader political, economic and social contexts which place adults in positions of power, young people can effectively campaign on their own without working with adults to achieve change (see Ansell, 2009).

As well as persuading transport planners and local authorities to consider seriously young people's transport problems, young people actively worked in partnership with transport planners and bus operators to advise on the implementation of solutions to address these issues:

> "Having a target of having young people involved, not just in a consultation – which could go into a drawer – but having a transport group, that will meet regularly and look at the issues around it, something more solid, something more long term." (Youth worker, case study 3)

Research participants were clear that these campaigns both resulted in services better meeting young people's needs, while also increasing the capacity for ongoing and sustained participation of young people in the transport planning process.

Therefore, these young people were effective lobbyists, helping to raise young people's transport needs up the political agenda at the local level, and successfully generating 'spaces of engagement' (Cox, 1998) for youth and youth politics at the local level. This section has shown the importance of the local here in an analysis of these young people's campaigns and their engagement with the political (Hopkins and Alexander, 2010). These spaces of engagement were spatially specific – the terrain and battles in which young people engaged were configured in different ways in different places. Interestingly, young people and adult planners identified that local, responsive planning was more appropriate and effective than national initiatives in responding to local young people's needs. The local was favoured as a lens for developing effective policy and practice.

It is important to remember that these case study examples were three positive examples of successful young people-led campaigns, and it must be noted that many other campaigns may have failed, and across the country, many young people's voices or experiences may have not been heard. Furthermore, although successful, more critically, these forms of young people's lobbying and campaigning can be seen to replicate the adult-focused political and lobbying structure (Wyness, 2009).

## Scale, local youth campaigns and national policy

These three case studies of young people's campaigns were progressive and innovative, and could, drawing upon the language of the New Labour government, be described as 'trailblazers', 'Beacon initiatives' or 'innovative examples of good practice'. These campaigns, although well-developed and often successful, were organic, sporadic and haphazard, had emerged from the grassroots and were fought at the local level. As previously discussed, with some important exceptions, the local level is typically the scale of operation of youth participation and politics (Ansell, 2009; Wyness, 2009). When the research began there was no systematic mechanism or guidance at the central government level to encourage local authorities, transport companies and other planners to consult or participate with young people in transport planning. However, these three case studies (combined with other forms of lobbying) had the *unintended* consequence of influencing the development of *national* government guidance for local authorities to develop solutions to young people's transport problems.

The young people involved in two of the three campaigns were invited to present and discuss their work at a number of national arenas, including the UK Youth Parliament, the national media and with UK government departments. Their campaigns were instrumental in influencing the formation of central government guidance, for example, the 2007 *Aiming high* document (HM Treasury/DCSF, 2007) which specifically identified the need for local authorities to give sufficient recognition to young people's transport needs and a requirement for joined-up planning between local authority Transport Planning and Children's Services departments. Similarly, 2008 government guidance drew upon examples of these case studies to specify some of the ways in which local authorities could engage with young people in transport planning. These are examples of how young people's participation can be institutionally sanctioned (Wyness, 2009).

Therefore, young people's local campaigns helped to influence national policy and guidance, helping to position young people more visibly and more centrally in the planning of development of transport policies which may affect them. Once more, scale is significant here. Although not intended, these were clear if rare examples of how young people can engage with decision-making processes and arenas beyond the local and enact change at different spatial scales (Blanchet-Cohen and Rainbow, 2006; Ansell, 2009). These examples demonstrate that local engagement is never just local. Local campaigns 'jumped scale' (Cox, 1998) or were 'upscaled' (Hopkins and Alexander, 2010), and young people's spaces of engagement were rescaled from the local to also encompass 'networks of association' at the national scale. While Children's Geographies may have conceptualised the local as the most significant scale for mapping young people's participation, these examples show how young people's agency can operate beyond the local (Graham and Fitzgerald, 2010).

More critically, although these three examples were successful in jumping scale and informing national policy, it must be recognised that such upscaling was rare. Indeed, it took the research team a significant amount of effort to find three successful young people-led campaigns. Furthermore, Whitty and Wisby's (2007) work discussing the factors which lead to the successful participation of young people in School Councils is useful here in helping develop a more critical viewpoint of these three case studies. Their critique suggests that young people's participation is much more likely to be successful if young people's views can be co-opted or incorporated into (and support) broader adult agendas. Conversely, more radical attempts to disrupt or challenge the status quo are ultimately unsuccessful. This perhaps leads to a more critical view of these three case studies as examples, which perhaps fitted into and supported existing government agendas and policy trajectories.

## Scale, the 'credit crunch' and the UK Coalition government

Politics at any level or scale is always in a state of flux, and the coming of the new Conservative–Liberal Democrat Coalition government[3] has reshaped the ending point of this chapter. In response to the recession, the government's stated aim of reducing the UK government budget deficit (actioned in part through the Comprehensive Spending Review of October 2010) has already impacted upon young people, transport policy and provision. In so doing, this is reshaping and repositioning youth and transport policies, and indeed the capacity for young people's participation.

This is perhaps an unfortunate and negative example of the linkages between different scales and how young people's local spaces are always influenced by and linked to global processes (Skelton, 2010; Foley and Leverett, 2011). Just as young people can move beyond the local to influence national policy, so national and international contexts influence young people's lives at the local level. Indeed given existing unequal power relations between adults, young people and children, influences on young people from beyond the local are more likely than vice versa, as Ansell (2009) comments, young people:

> "are arguably much more (deliberately) acted upon from a distance then they are able to act (deliberately) on others (people or institutions) at a distance." (Ansell, 2009, p 202)

Young people's everyday lives at the local level are already being influenced in myriad ways by the 'global recession', which has trickled through and been played out through the national and local level, and has indeed influenced young people and transport policy locally in a number of ways. At the local level, despite a well-fought, high-profile campaign by young people and their advocates, the initiatives in one of the three case studies has already ceased operation and the future of another is uncertain. At the broader scale of national policy formation, the Coalition government has already stated the aim of dismantling some of the statutory requirements and guidance which support young people's involvement in transport planning. The abolishment of some mechanisms to ensure joined-up planning and delivery of services for children and young people (such as the *Children and Young People's Plans*) and the ongoing uncertainty relating to others brings into question the incentives and requirements for effective opportunities for young people's participation. It remains to be seen whether the government's emphasis on rolling back central government bureaucracy combined with increased rhetoric on empowering 'local communities' and the notion of 'the Big Society', extends to young people who, as this chapter has shown, demonstrate capacity for social action and political engagement at the local level.

## Conclusion

In conclusion, this chapter has explored some of the different ways in which young people have successfully campaigned for transport improvements and to increase their participation in local transport planning. The chapter has illustrated the usefulness of the concept of scale in mapping the possibilities for young people's participation and social and political agency (as also explored by Skelton, 2010). The examples in the research demonstrate how, for transport planning, the local remains the most significant scale and arena for political participation by young people. However, scale theory demonstrates how scales are interlinked, and the examples in the chapter show how young people's lives, including their capacity to participate in transport planning, are influenced by (and to a far lesser degree, have capacity to influence) geopolitics, policy and planning at scales beyond the local. Young people's lives are not just lived at the local scale. As Hopkins and Alexander (2010) focus on 'upscaling', this paper recognises the need to consider links between scales, such as the local, the national and international.

The chapter has also offered contributions to debates around mobility, beginning to tease out some of the ways in which the new mobilities paradigm could benefit from further consideration of scale. Scale theory can help make sense of (and order) mobility experiences and different interlinkages between agents at different orders. In so doing, the conclusions of the chapter have currency beyond the UK examples considered here. A more general point suggests how the concept of scale helps us to map how, as a result of globalising processes, young people's local mobility (and involvement in local transport planning) is contingent upon local, national and international contexts.

## Notes

[1] The author would like to thank the National Youth Agency for funding the research.

[2] Indeed, one issue which there is not enough time to explore fully in this chapter is to critically consider which groups of young people participated in these case studies, and which were excluded. Young people do not form an homogeneous group (Horelli, 1998). As Wyness (2009) states, it is important for us to critically reflect on who was enabled to participate (typically intelligent, articulate, well-educated, middle-class young people) and who was excluded, and to consider the processes relating to this inclusion and exclusion.

[3] The 2010 UK General Election saw the Conservatives as the largest party in the House of Commons, although without an overall majority. In response to this, a Coalition government, consisting of 306 Conservative and 57 Liberal Democrat MPs, was formed, with the aim of running for a full five-year term of office.

## References

Ansell, N. (2009) 'Childhood and the politics of scale: descaling Children's Geographies?', *Progress in Human Geography,* vol 33, no 2, pp 190-209.

Barker, J. (2003) 'Passengers or political actors? Involving children in transport policy', *Space and Polity,* vol 7, no 2, pp 135-52.

Barker, J. (2008) *Accessing positive activities: innovative solutions for young people's bus travel,* Leicester: National Youth Agency.

Barker, J., Kraftl, P., Horton, J. and Tucker, F. (2009) 'The road less travelled: children and young people's mobility', *Mobilities,* vol 4, no 1, pp 1-10.

Beckmann, J. (2001) 'Automobility: a social problem and theoretical concept', *Environment and Planning D: Society and Space,* vol 19, pp 593-607.

Blanchet-Cohen, N. and Rainbow, B. (2006) 'Partnership between children and adults? The experience of the International Children's Conference on the Environment', *Childhood,* vol 13, pp 113-26.

Buehler, R. (2010) 'Transport policies, automobile use, and sustainable transport: a comparison of Germany and the United States', *Journal of Planning Education and Research,* vol 30, no 1, pp 76-93.

Cox, K. (1998) 'Spaces of dependence, spaces of engagement and the politics of scale, or: looking for local politics', *Political Geography,* vol 17, no 1, pp 1-23.

Cresswell, T. (2004) *Place: a short introduction,* Oxford: Blackwell.

DfES (Department for Education and Skills) (2006) *Youth matters: next steps. Something to do, somewhere to go, someone to talk to,* https://www.education.gov.uk/publications/standard/publicationDetail/Page1/DFES-0261-2006.

DfT (Department for Transport) (2002a) *Attitudes to local bus services,* London: HMSO.

DfT (Department for Transport) (2002b) *Accessibility of local services and facilities,* London: HMSO.

DfT (Department for Transport) (2003) *Travelling to school: a good practice guide,* London: HMSO.

DfT (Department for Transport) (2006a) *Young people and transport: their needs and requirements,* http://www.dft.gov.uk/pgr/inclusion/childrenandyoungpeople/youngpeo.pleandtransportheri1186.

DfT (Department for Transport) (2006b) *Public transport statistics bulletin GB: 2006 edition,* London: HMSO.

DfT (Department for Transport) (2006c) *How to set up a walking bus,* http://www.dft.gov.uk/pgr/sustainable/schooltravel/howtosetupawalkingbus.

DfT (Department for Transport) (2009) *Guidance on local transport plans,* http://www.dft.gov.uk/pgr/regional/ltp/guidance/localtransportsplans/.

Dudek, M. (2011) *Nurseries: a design guide,* London: Architectural Press.

Foley, P. and Leverett, S. (eds) (2011) *Children and young people's spaces: developing practice,* Basingstoke: Palgrave Macmillan.

Fotel, T. and Thomsen, T. (2004) 'The surveillance of children's mobility', *Surveillance and Society,* vol 1, no 4, pp 535-54.

Graham, A. and Fitzgerald, R. (2010), 'Progressing children's participation: exploring the potential of a dialogical turn', *Childhood,* no 17, pp 343-59.

Harker, C. (2009) 'Student im/mobility in Birzeit, Palestine', *Mobilities,* vol 4, no 1, pp 11-35.

Hart, R. (1992) *Children's participation: from tokenism to citizenship,* London: Earthscan.

Hillman, M., Adams, J. and Whitelegg, J. (1990) *One false move: a study of children's independent mobility,* London: Policy Studies Institute.

HM Treasury/DCSF (Department for Children, Schools and Families) (2007) *Aiming high for young people: a ten year strategy for positive activities,* London: Department for Children, Schools and Families.

Hopkins, P. and Alexander, C. (2010) 'Politics, mobility and nationhood: upscaling young people's geographies, introduction to special section', *Area,* vol 42, no 2, pp 142-4.

Horelli, L. (1998) 'Creating child-friendly environments: case studies on children's participation in three European countries', *Childhood,* vol 5, pp 225-39.

Horton, J., Kraftl, P. and Tucker, F. (2011) 'Spaces-in-the-making, childhoods-on-the-move', in Foley, P. and Leverett, S. (eds) *Children and young people's spaces: developing practice,* Basingstoke: Palgrave Macmillan, pp 40-57.

Katz, C. (2004) *Growing up global: economic restructuring and children's everyday lives,* Minnesota: University of Minnesota Press.

Kearns, R., Collins, D. and Neuwelt, P. (2003) 'The walking school bus: extending children's geographies?', *Area,* vol 35, pp 285-92.

Laurier, E., Lorimer, H., Brown, B., Jones, O., Juhlin, O., Noble, A., Perry, M., Pica, D., Sormani, P., Strebel, I., Swan, L., Taylor, A., Watts, L. and Weilenmann, A. (2008) 'Driving and "passengering": notes on the ordinary organization of car travel', *Mobilities,* vol 3, no 1, pp 1-23.

Law, R. (1999) 'Beyond "women and transport": towards new geographies of gender and daily mobility', *Progress in Human Geography,* vol 23, no 4, pp 567-88.

Marston, S., Jones, P. and Woodward, K. (2005) 'Human geography without scale', *Transactions of the Institute of British Geographers,* vol 30, pp 416-32.

Maxey, L. (2004) 'The participation of younger people within intentional communities: evidence from two case studies', *Children's Geographies,* vol 2, no 1, pp 29-48.

Porter, G. and Abane, A. (2008) 'Increasing children's participation in African transport planning: reflections on methodological issues in a child–centred research project', *Children's Geographies,* vol 6, no 2, pp 151-67.

Robson, E., Porter, G., Hampshire, K. and Bourdillon, M. (2009) '"Doing it right?" Working with young researchers in Malawi to investigate children, transport and mobility', *Children's Geographies,* vol 7, no 4, pp 467-80.

Skelton, T. (2010) 'Taking young people as political actors seriously: opening the borders of political geography', *Area,* vol 42, no 2, pp 145-51.

Urry, J. (2004) 'Connections', *Environment and Planning D: Society and Space,* vol 22, pp 27-37.

Valentine, G. (1997) '"Oh yes I can," "Oh no you can't": children and parents' understandings of kids' competence to negotiate public space safely', *Antipode,* vol 29, no 1, pp 65-89.

Whitty, G. and Wisby, E. (2007) 'Whose voice? An exploration of the current policy interest in pupil involvement in school decision-making', *International Studies in Sociology of Education,* vol 17, no 3, pp 303-19.

Wyness, M. (2009) 'Children representing children: participation and the problem of diversity in UK youth councils', *Childhood,* vol 16, pp 535-52.

# eleven

# Including young people in heritage conservation in southern Brazilian cities: the case of Pelotas

*Laura Novo de Azevedo*

## Introduction

Although the notion and practice of heritage conservation is widespread, with a set of internationally agreed principles defined by UNESCO and ICOMOS,[1] the questions of *what and whose 'heritage'?* still court controversy. One critique is that heritage conservation is an elitist practice both produced and consumed by only a few groups in society (Pendlebury and Townshend, 1997; Jokilehto, 1999). Even though the need for heritage conservation policies to respond to values of wider society has been exhorted in the academic literature (Avrami, 2000; Jokilehto, 2002; Turnpenny, 2004), the practice of heritage conservation is often perceived as contradictory. In the UK, research on attitudes to heritage have found that young people have a largely negative view of, and limited engagement with, heritage as conventionally defined (MORI, 2000) and much work is still needed to minimise the gap between what the group values as heritage, and heritage as defined by policy discourses (Roker and Richardson, 2003).

Within this context, and following a lack of understanding of the role of young people in Brazilian political life, the investigation presented in this chapter considers whether heritage conservation policy and practice in Brazil are inclusive of what young people value as heritage. The chapter suggests that despite some 'one-off' projects that seek to involve young people in traditional heritage conservation projects, this social group remains invisible in national heritage conservation discourses, with scarce possibilities for exercising active citizenship and stamping their own values in the adult world of heritage. This is particularly concerning since young people, here generically defined as anyone under the age of 24, form about half of Brazil's current population.

Currently, the official discourse or representation of heritage in Brazil is inscribed into four 'Books of Listed Heritage' *(Livros do Tombo).* The books focus upon four sets of values: (1) archaeological, ethnographic and landscape;

(2) historical; (3) fine arts; and (4) applied arts. Each of these categories contains tangible (for example, historic sites and objects) and intangible (for example, traditional knowledge and ways of doing) exemplars of national 'heritage'. Although this broad definition would allow for the argument that most of what young people and adults value as heritage could be included in one of the categories above, analysis of local policies and practices at Brazilian municipalities suggests a different story. The Brazilian Constitution (Senado Federal, 1988) not only guarantees the independence of state and municipal levels of government, but also requires them to develop their own legal system for the management of their cities. Considering Brazil's great regional cultural diversity, this is positive as it helps to ensure that local characteristics will not be overlooked as could occur if the conservation system followed a centralised model. However, it can also lead to limiting situations where local policies and practices fail to embrace the diversity proposed at the national level.

Following these considerations the chapter reflects upon an investigation conducted in the city of Pelotas, a medium-sized city in southern Brazil. The chapter discusses an analytical framework to identify the extent to which local policy includes young people's values: (1) by directly classifying what the group considers as heritage, (2) by generating practical benefits for the group through actions of heritage conservation, and (3) by providing avenues for the group's meaningful participation in decision-making processes. While the discussion of the first two topics focuses upon products of local policies, the third topic considers the potential to adopt a dialogical approach (Freire, 1970) for including young people in decision-making. Based on the in-depth study of Pelotas, general recommendations for the development of more inclusive heritage conservation policies are outlined in the conclusion. These are starting points for bridging the gap between the exclusive character of heritage conservation and the current requirements for the inclusion of young people.

## The exclusive character of the 'inherited' heritage

Many groups in society do not recognise the *official* versions of heritage as theirs, and thus feel that they have nothing to contribute to the process or to the definition of heritage. They may perceive heritage as something *of* and *for* 'other people', characterising a lack of sense of ownership and responsibility (Azevedo, 2000). Young people are one generically defined group seldom included in the process of policy-making (Matthews, 2001, p 470). Indeed, young people remain largely anonymous from heritage conservation policy and practice (Agyeman, 1995; Gardner, 2004; Turnpenny, 2004). Where consideration is offered to this group it is generally couched in relation to the need to preserve heritage *for future generations*. Although the discourse underlying UNESCO and ICOMOS standard-setting documents reflects the need to respect, promote and represent the cultural diversity of society in the definition of heritage it is still permeated by ideas of heritage *of* the past and *for* the future. For example, the *Recommendation concerning the safeguarding and contemporary role of historic areas* (UNESCO, 1976, p 145) states that 'the study of historic areas should be included in education at all levels … so as to inculcate in young minds an understanding of and respect for the works of the past and to demonstrate the role of this heritage in modern life'.

The strong focus on the past might be attached to the definition of the word *heritage* as 'features belonging to the culture of a particular society, such as traditions, languages or buildings, which still exist from the past and which have a historical importance' (Walter, 2005 p 379). For example, the definition found in the *Young roots* project – a UK programme designed to engage young people aged 13–25 with their heritage – reinforces the *past* character of the word by stating that 'heritage is what we have inherited from the past and value enough to share and sustain for the future' (Heritage Lottery Fund and National Youth Agency, 2007, p 422). In Brazil, however, the definition of the word patrimony [*patrimônio*], the Portuguese equivalent of 'heritage', is less strongly linked to the idea of the past or inheritance, being also related to concepts of property and ownership. The Brazilian Constitution uses the term 'cultural patrimony' to describe tangible and intangible cultural manifestations which hold reference to the identity, the nation and the memory of different groups that form Brazilian society (Senado Federal, 1988, p 86). Although the idea of inheritance can be said to be implicit, the word is strongly linked to the concept of identity, which can be more easily associated with new and diverse forms of cultural expressions. The idea that this would result in more inclusive policies and practices, however, does not seem to be true.

In the Brazilian context, the traditional way of seeing heritage as a monument of the past, used to worship the past, has been criticised by Convenio Andres Bello (1999) who suggests that heritage should be appropriated by communities and turned into an active part of their daily lives. Heritage is seen as 'essential for social identity and collective purpose' (Lowenthal, 2000, p 18) and, according to the discourse from UNESCO and ICOMOS documents, to 'enrich people's lives, often providing a deep and inspirational sense of connection to community and landscape, to the past and to lived experiences' (ICOMOS Australia, 1999, p 216). However, heritage in this sense can also be a burden, something that has to be preserved in line with values or forms of social–cultural elitism from the past (Convenio Andres Bello, 1999). By contrast, Convenio Andres Bello suggests that heritage could be conceptualised differently: in terms of a creative regeneration of traditions, building up from the past. However, in order to be able to represent new values, conservation policy must be open to dialogue and regeneration.

In the UK, for instance, two perspectives seem to underlie policy and practice in heritage conservation (Clark, 2006). The first is that in order for young people to value traditional heritage there is a need to *teach* them the value of it. This perspective suggests a traditional top–down approach assuming that heritage is pre–defined, inherited and its value has to be learned by the group. However, it does not suggest or necessarily support the inclusion of what the group themselves value as heritage in policy and practice. The second still suggests the need to engage young people with the inherited heritage but in ways that they can express their interests and values, causing an impact on heritage conservation policy and practice. Following a bottom–up approach, this would include reviewing traditional methods of heritage interpretation and developing new ways of including the group in the process of heritage definition and conservation. The perspectives are not contradictory and should not be seen as mutually exclusive. Indeed, educational programmes focusing on traditional or inherited heritage can be compatible and complementary to the reinvention or creation of a 'new' heritage. An approach where professionals and young people interact and learn from each other about each other's values can surely facilitate the complementary character of both perspectives.

Percy-Smith's (2006) theoretical constructs of participatory action research, and the philosophy developed by the Brazilian educator Paulo Freire (1970) which argues that a dialogue can act as a catalyst for social change, support the assumption that adopting an interactive and dialogical approach to the participation of young people in heritage conservation would help to minimise conflicts generated by power relationships and maximise the group's empowerment and visibility. These two similar approaches serve as foundations for the collaborative nature of the approach adopted in the research as a potential model for developing more meaningful processes of participation and inclusion of young people's values in heritage conservation in Pelotas.

## Young people's values and heritage conservation policy and practice in Pelotas

Based on the considerations above, research on heritage conservation policy and practice concerning young people was conducted within the city of Pelotas in southern Brazil. Pelotas is a medium-size city with around 346,452 inhabitants, located in the southern-most state of Brazil, Rio Grande do Sul, and in 2003 was declared part of the Network of Historical Cities of the South. Within the Network, the city of Pelotas has the longest and strongest tradition in heritage conservation. Its conservation policy and practice has been serving as a model for other cities in the Rio Grande do Sul and lately, following national investments for the restoration of its architectural heritage, to other regions of Brazil.

## Methodology and analytical framework

The investigation of how inclusive policy is to what young people value as heritage required the development of an analytical framework. This followed the assumption that the more responsive policies are to the values of stakeholders, the more inclusive their character. The evaluation of the extent to which heritage conservation policy for Pelotas is responding to young people's heritage values was proposed through a model adapted from the 'triangle of heritage values' (Hewison and Holden, 2006, p 272). The model follows an approach that assesses policy responsiveness to 'cultural value' as based on society's values and as opposed to or complementing the 'economic value', the other main approach to heritage value. By identifying the cultural value of heritage, Hewison and Holden (2006) argue that it is easier for professionals and politicians to develop policies that can best represent those values, thus increasing their responsiveness and effectiveness. The model required three instances to discuss policy responsiveness to cultural values of heritage:

- 'Assigned' value: generated by the individual's experience of heritage (based on different types of values such as aesthetic, community or historical); the stakeholders in this case are young people;
- 'Instrumental' value: referring to 'practical benefits' of heritage – social or economical (such as urban regeneration or place making);
- 'Institutional' value: described as referring to the processes and techniques that organisations adopt to interact and engage with the public (by communicating heritage value, listening and learning about heritage value or mediating solutions between values).

The stakeholders in the case of instrumental and institutional value are politicians and policy-makers. The graphic concept of the model is a triangle in which all three corners have the same weight (see Figure 11.1).

This model provides a useful framework within which to evaluate the responsiveness of heritage policy and practice in Pelotas. This framework also helps to minimise historical criticisms of power imbalance between the general public and policy-makers, as different measures (assigned, instrumental and institutional) reinforce rather than contradict each other. The more positively one value impacts on the other, the less the historical arguments and power struggle between stakeholders will develop (Hewison and Holden, 2006, p 272).

**Figure 11.1:** Triangle of heritage values and stakeholders

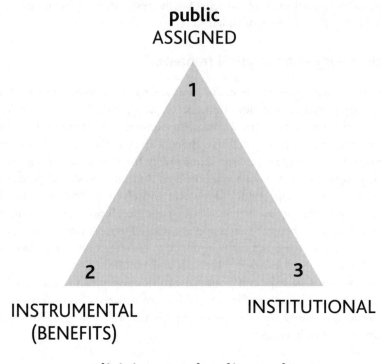

**public**
ASSIGNED

**1**

**2**                                          **3**

INSTRUMENTAL                    INSTITUTIONAL
(BENEFITS)

**politicians and policymakers**

*Source:* Adapted from Hewison and Holden (2006, p 272)

The study investigated each of the values or angles of the triangle through a series of questions:

- Assigned value: To what extent are young people's values defining heritage in current heritage conservation policy in Pelotas?
- Instrumental value: To what extent is current heritage conservation policy in Pelotas generating practical benefits for young people by including the group's heritage values in its practice?
- Institutional value: To what extent is current heritage conservation policy encouraging a meaningful process of participation of young people?

Three methodological stages, involving a variety of qualitative methods, were required to understand issues related to the inclusion of young people's values in heritage conservation policy in the context of Pelotas:

- Stage one investigated what young people value as heritage and underlying reasons for their constructs. (Methods used: wish tree, mental maps, open ended questionnaires, participatory arts workshops with young people in local schools.)

- Stage two considered the extent to which current heritage conservation policy in Pelotas is inclusive of young people's values. It investigated policy responsiveness to assigned value, the generation of instrumental value and the promotion of institutional value. (Methods used: analysis of documents, interviews and observation.)
- Stage three – within the discussion on institutional value, this stage considered the potential of dialogical and creative participatory approaches adopted for the investigation of stage one, in the format of 'participatory arts workshops', to increase policy responsiveness to young people's heritage values. (Methods used: analysis of documents, interviews and observation and structured discussions with adult participants in the arts workshops.)

## Discussion of findings

The investigation of assigned value – what young people value as their heritage in the context of Pelotas – identified four major categories within young people's *understandings* of heritage in the city. These were: nature, architecture, open spaces and cultural and social practices (the last subdivided into references to youth culture, cultural heritage, events and food). The word 'understanding' rather than 'definition' was chosen because the results indicated that when asked what they valued as heritage some of answers reflected what the participants had been *taught to be* heritage rather than their own conceptualisations of heritage.

The fieldwork findings, when explored using the theoretical and analytical frameworks, highlighted the limited and unbalanced response of heritage conservation policy in Pelotas to the heritage values of young people. Spider diagrams generated from the quantification of the themes used in policy documents (see Figure 11.2) helped to understand the levels of policy responsiveness to what young people valued as heritage in Pelotas (the assigned value) (see Figure 11.3).

Analysis of these diagrams reveals that while mentions from young people of architectural heritage find a strong response in local heritage conservation policy, other types of heritage more spontaneously identified by young people in Pelotas are barely considered in policy documents and by institutions responsible for preserving local heritage. According to the model of heritage values discussed in the analytical framework, this result suggests a very limited response to young people's assigned values.

**Figure 11.2:** Tabulation of policy documents

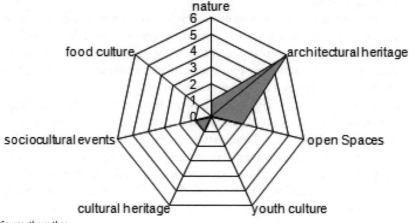

Source: the author

**Figure 11.3:** What is heritage for young people?

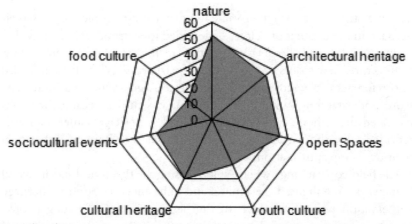

Source: the author

In a fieldwork interview (Azevedo, 2004), the Secretary of the Pelotas' Culture Secretariat indicated that one of the objectives of the Secretariat was to develop a cultural mapping methodology to identify types of heritage that are not only related to the architecture of the city. The interview revealed the Secretary's dissatisfaction with the fact that other cultural practices were not institutionally considered heritage. She attributed this to the fact that architects dominated the heritage world in the city and they were usually not open to a broader definition of heritage, based on the understanding of the general public. In an interview with the advisor for the MONUMENTA programme in Pelotas, a national programme to restore and to preserve urban historical and cultural sites under Federal protection, the difficulties in having segregated views of heritage were ratified. The advisor suggested that 'whenever heritage is in the sole hands of the planning department[2] it is at a disadvantage as it is based on a limited view of heritage, solely focused on architecture' (Azevedo, 2004).

In the cases where policy responded to the values of young people by generating direct benefits for the group (instrumental value), it was not considered to be intentional but as a consequence of generic programmes for the improvement of the city, mainly led by other government departments. An example of a direct action from the government's conservation department that creates value for young people is the restoration of the fountain at the city's central square (see Figure 11.4). Both the fountain and water in urban areas are elements that appeared very often in young people's responses to what they valued as heritage.

**Figure 11.4:** Restored fountain, an example of instrumental value

Young Person enjoying the experience provided by the restored fountain. Coronel Pedro Osório Square in Pelotas.
Source: the author

*Source:* the author

In general, assigned and instrumental values are mostly created by departments dealing with open spaces in the historic area and with the promotion of cultural practices and not by the department that deals with what is officially denominated heritage. The provision of social and cultural events in listed buildings is not always seen as a positive practice by those in charge of protecting the local heritage, as it is argued that these practices can cause more damage to heritage than promote its value (Azevedo, 2004).

Both local policies and practices of heritage conservation have mostly failed in delivering an inclusive process by responding to assigned, and generating institutional, value. They have also failed in understanding young people as part of 'the public' with rights equal to any adult in society to express and have their views taken into account in heritage matters, as no examples of meaningful participation of young people in heritage conservation in Pelotas were identified. Positive initiatives developed by the government's Culture Secretariat such as workshops with young people to identify local heritage were one-off events, and did not have a tangible impact on policy. These initiatives were not identified as being driven by a systematic approach to the inclusion of young people's values and therefore were not classified as generating institutional value. The observation of a meeting between the council and young people from a local school to discuss improvements for a playing area in a local square showed that young people are still not seen as capable of understanding the 'adult world' and providing 'useful' insights into the problems that are affecting their lives. Most speakers in the meeting were politicians describing the achievements of the government or questioning the government about actions that were being proposed about the flooding problem in the square. The redesign of the square was not discussed with the young people and there was only one quick mention of the intention of installing play equipment in the square. No work in the square has been done since this meeting in 2007. Findings such as this suggest that, in Pelotas, responses to assigned value are low, and that the implementation of meaningful participation is dependent on changes in adults' attitudes towards the participation of young people. On the basis of this research, wider doubts have been raised of the capacity of the government in Pelotas to deliver inclusive heritage conservation policies unless radical changes in adult attitudes occur.

The dialogical approach to participatory arts provided a useful method to generate proposals to foster social learning and affect adults' attitudes. The analysis of feedback on adult participation in the participatory arts workshop suggested that active engagement of researchers, teachers, conservation officers and students in solving the problem of defining heritage affected individuals' pre-established views on the subject. The observation of the dynamics in the workshops suggested that while adults' reflections on their own behaviour and assumptions can produce positive attitudes, in practice there is still a barrier to seeing young people as capable of producing informed views on heritage conservation. Together with the dialogical approach to participation, additional actions for enhancing young people's participation were identified as useful in achieving more meaningful participatory processes involving young people. These include capacity-building programmes for adults involved in the process, a commitment from the governments to principles of inclusion and respect for young people, and the development of legislation to act as an enforcement tool.

## Conclusion

For heritage conservation to be truly inclusive, at least in the context of Pelotas, processes and practices for the inclusion of young people (and other groups) need to be reconsidered. The stereotype of the architect who identifies what is heritage and fills in 'fiches of register' that attest historic and architectural value was found to be true in the study. Arguments can be built around the fact that most educational or awareness-raising programmes are targeted *at* young people and therefore fail to consider the values inherent in this group. This study has revealed that, especially in the case of Brazil, these have the objective of teaching young people the value of traditional forms of heritage. If heritage education has an important role in raising awareness to the value of traditional heritage, but programmes do not encourage the group to reflect critically upon the concept of heritage, then it is unlikely that it will be accepted or contested, or that new forms of heritage will emerge that better represent the cultural values of young people. Although not strongly identified as excluded in the same way as women, indigenous groups and ethnic minorities, young people are still largely excluded from policy-making in heritage conservation. Important aspects of the group's lives such as the development of a sense of belonging and the construction of individual and group identities through heritage become compromised by this situation of exclusion.

Providing visibility to young people in civic society is a key ingredient in changing adult attitudes towards the group. However, within the area of heritage conservation, this visibility must not be raised through positioning the group as in need of care and protection as required in other fields. Instead, it must shed light on the young people's competence to contribute to address issues that affect their lives. The position of vulnerability may encourage a situation where young people's values are filtered, interpreted and expressed through adults. The danger of this is that discrepancies such as the ones illustrated in Figures 11.2 and 11.3 can become even stronger. Rather than pushing young people towards the future, as the future generation, there is a need to increase the discussion of young people as one of those under-represented groups in heritage conservation.

In order to increase policy responsiveness to young people's values it is necessary to produce direct, practical benefits to young people. Decentralised heritage programmes, including actions for heritage education, were found to benefit young people as they increase access to traditional forms of heritage and awareness of more local representations of heritage. The research has also indicated the importance of planning and designing robust historic areas that support a variety of uses and aesthetic experiences. For example, places that support a variety of events such as occasional arts exhibitions, dance and hip hop were assessed positively by young people and the design for the support of these activities would generate instrumental value, or practical benefits. Robust spaces can also be positive in accommodating shifting generational values in the process of constructing local identities and developing new forms of heritage and meanings. An inclusive approach is also required for the planning and design of historic areas.

Finally, strong government participatory agendas and specific legislation requiring the participation of young people in political life do not suffice for implementing effective and meaningful participation and increasing institutional value. It is also not a guarantee that young people will be considered as stakeholders in heritage conservation. A shift in adult thinking and behaviour towards young people was found to be necessary to increase the inclusion of the latter group in heritage conservation. This is both in terms of defining the group as part of the 'present' generation with certain rights equal to any other individual and in term of understanding the group as capable of informing policy. Institutional expectations about the interaction between young people and heritage reflect either a fear that it will result in damage of the latter or a need to 'educate young minds' to understand what heritage is.

Although examples of more systematic and long-lasting methodologies for the implementation of meaningful participation of young people with heritage conservation were found to be in development in the UK (Shier, 2001; Local Heritage Initiative, 2006; Heritage Lottery Fund, 2007), none were found in the context of the case study in southern Brazil. While there are positive examples of young people directly participating in decision-making in issues related to heritage – for example the construction of a skate park in Pelotas through a demand on the participatory budget system (Bruce, 2004; Azevedo, 2004) – these lack continuity. The initial assumption that the involvement of young people with heritage was mostly done through 'one-off' projects was found to be true in the case of Pelotas. It highlights the need to develop more structural avenues for the participation of young people and for the consideration of a diversity of participatory forums.

**Notes**

[1] The United Nations Educational, Scientific and Cultural Organization (UNESCO) and the International Council on Monuments and Sites (ICOMOS) are the two main organisations working to establish international and local standards for heritage conservation theory and practice. UNESCO and ICOMOS documents typically take the form of agreements and conventions, which are legally binding, or recommendations

and declarations to be adopted by the Member States, and can be found on the organisations' websites.

[2] It is important to mention here that in Brazil architecture and urbanism (including urban and regional planning) are not studied and practised separately as they are in the UK. Most officers working for planning departments at local authorities are architects and urbanists, with rare exceptions.

## References

Agyeman, J. (1995) 'Environment, heritage and multiculturalism', *Interpretation*, vol 1, no 1, pp 5-6.

Azevedo, L.N. de (2000) *Patrimônio Arquitetônico x Qualidade Visual do Cenário Urbano: um caso para avaliação de preferências em Pelotas/RS*, PROPUR/ UFRGS, Porto Alegre: Universidade Federal do Rio Grande do Sul.

Azevedo, L.N. de. (2004) *Various research interviews in Pelotas, July 2004,* digital recording and transcription files in possession of the author.

Bruce, I. (ed) (2004) *The Porto Alegre alternative: direct democracy in action*, London: Pluto Press.

Clark, K. (2006) (ed) *Capturing public value of heritage: the proceedings of the London conference, 25-26 January 2006*, London: English Heritage.

Convenio Andres Bello (1999) *Somos patrimonio*, Bogota: Convenio Andres Bello.

Freire, P. (1970) *Pedagogy of the oppressed*, New York: Continuum.

Gardner, J.M. (2004) 'Heritage protection and social inclusion: a case study from the Bangladeshi community of east London', *International Journal of Heritage Studies*, vol 10, no 1, pp 75-92.

Heritage Lottery Fund and The National Youth Agency (2007) *Young people's heritage projects: a model of practice*, London and Leicester: Heritage Lottery Fund and The National Youth Agency.

Hewison, R. and Holden, J. (2006) 'Public value as a framework for analysing the value of heritage: the ideas', in K. Clark (ed) *Capturing public value of heritage: the proceedings of the London conference, 25-26 January 2006*, London: English Heritage, pp 14–18.

ICOMOS Australia (1999) *The Burra charter: the Australia ICOMOS charter for places of cultural significance*, Burra, Australia: ICOMOS.

Jokilehto, J. (1999) *A history of architectural conservation*, Oxford: Butterworth-Heinemann.

Jokilehto, J. (2002) *Recent international trends in safeguarding cultural heritage*, Seoul, Korea: Korean National Commission for UNESCO.

Local Heritage Initiative (2006) *Lessons learnt: a review of the local heritage initiative*, London: The Countryside Agency.

Lowenthal, D. (2000) 'Stewarding the past in a perplexing present', in E. Avrami, R. Manson and M. de la Torre (eds) *Values and heritage conservation*, Los Angeles: Getty Conservation Institute, pp 18-25.

Matthews, H. (2001) *Children and community regeneration: creating better neighbourhoods*, London: Save the Children.

MORI (2000) *Attitudes towards heritage*, London: English Heritage.

Pendlebury, J. and Townshend, T. (1997) *Public perceptions and historic areas: a research agenda*, electronic working paper no 30, School of Architecture, Planning and Landscape Global Urban Research Unit, University of Newcastle upon Tyne, www.ncl.ac.uk/guru/assets/documents/ewp30.pdf.

Percy-Smith, B. (2006) 'From consultation to social learning in community participation with young people', *Children, Youth and Environments*, vol 16, no 2, pp 153-79.

Roker, D. and Richardson, H. (2003) *Young people and heritage: a review of current literature*, London: Heritage Lottery Fund.

Senado Federal (1988) *Constituição Federal do Brasil de 1988*, Brasília: Republica Federativa do Brasil.

Turnpenny, M. (2004) 'Cultural heritage, an ill-defined concept? A call for joined-up policy', *International Journal of Heritage Studies*, vol 10, no 3, pp 295–307.

Shier, H. (2001) 'Pathways to participation: openings, opportunities and obligations', *Children and Society*, vol 15, pp 107-17.

UNESCO (1976) *Recommendation concerning the safeguarding and contemporary role of historic areas*, Warsaw, Nairobi: UNESCO.

Walter, E. (2005) (ed) *Cambridge advanced learner's dictionary* (2nd edn), Cambridge: Cambridge University Press.

# twelve

# Anchoring identity: the construction of responsibility for and by young offenders in the US

*Alexandra Cox*

## Introduction

This chapter poses some theoretical propositions and raises questions for empirical analysis about young people's perspectives on responsibility in the context of a criminal case. Legally coercive interventions which are administered to young offenders in the juvenile courts are said to be aimed at re-shaping, responsibilising and governing young people's selves (Muncie and Hughes, 2002; Muncie, 2006). This responsibilising demand is twofold: adolescents in the criminal justice system must be able both to express responsibility with respect to social citizenship but also to demonstrate appropriate development into adulthood. This chapter is concerned with some of the ways that court actors (a group of professional practitioners working with young people) and young people express and understand 'responsibility', and it attempts to situate the term in the context of its social practices and meanings. The chapter examines the role that 'responsibility' plays within the 'social topology' (Bourdieu, 1989) of the lives of impoverished young people charged with crimes. It also attempts to understand how the uses of 'responsibility' may reflect some 'commonsense beliefs' (Fraser and Gordon, 1994, p 310) about the term that escape critical scrutiny.

Young people exercise forms of responsibility and identity which are parallel – and often resistant – to the normative forms offered within the youth justice system as a way of getting 'out' of that system. They often seek ways to express growth and maturity which more meaningfully reflect some of the ways in which their life opportunities are bounded by poverty, their age, and the social and political landscapes which they find themselves bound by. This chapter focuses on young people's experiences in spaces (the courts and prisons) which are aimed at the regulation of criminal conduct and that are constructed and controlled by adults for young people (see also Barker et al, 2010).

## State interventions into the lives of young people

In the US, separate courts and prisons were established for young offenders in the late nineteenth and early twentieth centuries out of concern for the welfare of children, creating a strongly paternalist foundation for youth justice interventions (Platt, 1969/1977). The welfarist practices of the youth justice system are premised on notion that young people have limited autonomy to determine their 'lives and values without outside intervention' (Pupavac, 2001, p 101). Though it is debatable whether these interventions are aimed at 'protecting' young people, the shape they take derives from the idea that young people (and in particular, young offenders) have limited agency in determining their own lives. Young people charged with crimes are regarded as an agglomeration of risk factors, their bodies and minds exhaustively 'mapped' (Ruddick, 2007, p 516) in order to better target efforts at crime prevention.

In recent years, neoliberal penal practices in youth justice contexts in the US and England and Wales have emphasised individuals' 'responsibility' for their actions. Some have argued that there has been a shift in emphasis on responsibility from the state to individual and community in the domains of schooling, social welfare, and crime control.[1] Scholars have described this shift as a *responsibilisation* strategy (O'Malley, 1992; Rose, 2000). Muncie says that, 'at its most basic it draws attention to any crime control strategy that aims to make offenders face up to their own responsibilities or that encourages the private sector and communities to take a more active interest in reducing criminal opportunities' (2006, p 773). Garland (1996, p 353) argues that one of the underlying assumptions of a responsibilisation strategy is the notion that the state cannot be fully responsible for preventing and controlling crime, and that social order is best maintained through social processes.

Responsibilising policies include what has been termed the 'adulteration' of youth justice, in which young people are increasingly given more serious penalties for their crimes, as in Canada and some American states, which have altered their ages of criminal responsibility, and through the abolition of *doli incapax* in England and Wales in 1998 (Muncie, 2005, pp 38–9). Other neoliberal penal practices include assessments of an offender's risk of re-offending as a means of determining levels of sanctions and forms of interventions, an attendant focus on efficiency and a rise in managerialist penal practices, and an expansion of 'penal and exclusionary practices' (Muncie, 2005, pp 39–40), such as a reliance on CCTV and electronic monitoring, an uptick in the punishment of young people in school (Hirschfield, 2008; Barker et al, 2010), and the criminalisation of immigrants and sex offenders. It is common for judges and other court actors to create highly structured service plans for young people charged with crimes, and though young people may be given the option of doing their time in the community as opposed to in prison, they face serious consequences if they fail to meet a detailed set of rules. The juvenile court *legislates* a young person's process of self-determination, mandating programmes of self-improvement. Some scholars have observed that there is an elision between the agenda of care and that of control in the area of youth justice (Sharland, 2006; Phoenix, 2009).

The requirement for young people to take responsibility for their advancement or progress in treatment is common to programmes aimed at reducing offending (Fox, 1999; Banks, 2008; Crewe, 2009). The central premise behind these programmes is that the denial of responsibility represents an externalisation of blame, and thus the displacement of the processes of change to sources beyond one's control (Maruna and Mann, 2006). An implicit link is made between these 'excuses' and a continuing proclivity for offending (Maruna and Mann, 2006, p 156). Yet Maruna and Mann (2006), drawing upon extensive research on the processes of responsibility-taking in sex offender treatment, have argued that excuse-making is a normative reaction to shame, blame and stigma.

The question of criminal responsibility in the youth justice context is a thorny one. The age of criminal responsibility differs by jurisdiction, and legal scholars and philosophers have not reached consensus on the nature of young people's agency and responsibility for criminal offences (Schrag, 1977; Scarre, 1980; von Hirsch, 2005). Bandalli points out that 'in criminal law, the *moral agency* of the offender is reflected in the *mens rea* requirement, the mental element which, in explanations of the principles of criminal liability, normally accompanies the *actus reus*, the conduct element' (2000, p 87). She argues that the question of young people's limited liability and responsibility, which is related to their subordinate status in social citizenship, is often sidelined in the contemporary youth justice context, where, as noted above, young people have been overwhelmingly adultified (2000).[2]

## Adolescence and the individualising process

As indicated above, the call from judges, probation officers, and other youth justice system workers to young people to take responsibility for their actions is usually coupled with demands for these young people to engage in more active 'citizenship'. In the youth court context, 'successful' demonstration of such active citizenship includes the completion of school, transition out of the home, and acquisition of a job. These markers of success are considered to be part of the transition to successful adulthood. In fact, some developmental psychologists argue that those young people caught in the criminal justice system have experienced 'developmental challenges' (Chung et al, 2005, p 71) that have prevented them from making this successful transition. There is perhaps a kind of double weight on adolescents caught in the criminal justice system to take responsibility: they must be able to express both responsibility with respect to social citizenship but also demonstrate appropriate development into adulthood.

What, then, are seen as the markers of 'successful adulthood'? Perhaps emblematic of the hegemonic discourse about adolescent transitions, Chung et al (2005, p 77) argue that some of the core components of 'successful adulthood' include: 'mastery and competence, interpersonal relationships and social functioning, and self-definition and self-governance'. Young people, in other words, are expected to move from a state of dependence to *independence* and autonomy. This transition is also the route to social inclusion (Sharland, 2006, p 250). Yet Valentine argues that 'transitions from childhood to adulthood can be complex and fluid' and are mediated by race, class, gender and geography (2003, p 38; see also Hopkins and Pain, 2007). She argues that geographers should focus their research on some of the 'different life spaces' that these young people must transition through in order to move from 'dependent childhood to independent adulthood' (Valentine, 2003, p 48). This paper is concerned with young people's expressions of responsibility as they transition into adulthood while they inhabit the regulatory space of the courts.

Beck argues that young people are now expected to become active, engaged participants in the process of individualisation (1998). He claims that 'young people no longer *become* individualised. They individualise *themselves*. The "biographization" of youth means becoming active, struggling and designing one's own life' (1998, p 78). Integral to this new process of 'biographization' is the engagement with the 'insecurity and reflexivity' (Beck, 1992, p 98) that characterises contemporary life. A 'successful' transition in this context is one in which a young person plays an active role in the determination of their life outcomes. Adolescents are *expected* to be engaged in a deeply reflective project of the self as they move into adulthood, yet the very nature of adolescence as a transitional moment means that young people lack both the status and the opportunities for the full expression of selfhood, and ultimately, citizenship, as well as the capacity for 'social recognition' (Barry, 2006, p 6).

What, then, can be made of young people who fail to play such an 'active' role in this process, which is often those who end up in the youth justice system?[3] Some argue that young offenders have a disproportionate amount of 'risk factors' which have led them to engage in offending (Farrington, 2007). Young people's ability to exercise independent thinking, autonomy, self-reflection and so on is seen to have been hampered by their exposure to abuse or neglect, their parents' 'criminality', or the level of 'disorganisation' in their community. These young people have failed to participate in the 'compulsive and obligatory self-determination' (Bauman, 2000) that is considered to be necessary for them to be successful participants in social life. Efforts in the UK, such as New Labour's Social Exclusion Unit and other education initiatives aimed at strongly encouraging young people to become successful participants in the labour market, in part exist to facilitate this kind of self-determination process (Mizen, 2003).

Some scholars have argued that we should examine the socio-structural factors that may impact on an individual's ability to 'successfully' transition into adulthood. Thomson et al (2002, p 351) found that 'while most young people may speak the language of individual choice, control and agency, it is only for some that the rhetoric is accompanied by the requisite resources and opportunities' to 'successfully' transition into adulthood. Such has been demonstrated by the relative lack of success in the UK of New Labour's efforts at improving the lives of socially excluded youth (Mizen, 2003). Furlong and Cartmel (2007) argue that levels of social inequality still determine young people's life outcomes.

## A qualitative study of young people's engagement with youth justice interventions

The research described below includes data from a pilot study and a larger research project about the lives of young people charged with crimes in an Eastern American state called Olympia.[4] The research involved in-depth, semi-structured interviews with a group of young people between the ages of 14 and 21 who were charged with crimes (n = 45), as well as observational fieldwork in courts, community supervision sites, and secure residential treatment facilities. There were 12 young women and 33 young men. They were overwhelmingly from impoverished urban communities. This group is largely comprised of young people from ethnic minority groups, with an overwhelming majority of them identifying as African-American, which is reflective of the composition of Olympia's juvenile justice system.

## Contours of responsibility

The young people in this research confronted efforts aimed at engendering their 'personal responsibility' at multiple stages of their experience in the space of the youth justice system. They were exhorted to take responsibility for their actions *as well as* for their future productivity by police, judges, probation officers, social workers and attorneys. Fox (1999) describes the ways in which 'self-discipline is disciplined' in prison contexts; the same can said to be true of the spectrum of court-related interventions that young people face in Olympia. These forms of discipline are often experienced as onerous and tight:

"With me, it's that I'm already caught. They're just giving me enough rope to where they can pull me back at any time. You know, so it's like … I'm just a dog on their leash. If they want to take me out on walks they can, but they can bring me back in." (Nina)

While in residential facilities, young people were not only expected to take responsibility for their crimes, but they were also encouraged to take responsibility for their success in treatment: 'You come in here alone, you leave here alone' was an oft-repeated mantra that staff encouraged the young people to embrace. Staff members in residential facilities often conveyed the belief that a successful behavioural change programme was built on a kind of hyper-individualised, atomised sense of responsibility, one in which the individual is divorced from their context and where they should be simply and clear-mindedly focused on their personal goals. One staff member spoke about how the young people 'feed off the victim mentality that's been taught to them', and that this prevented them from changing fully. The goals of treatment, they argued, should include the reduction of 'thinking errors' and the neutralisation and control of anger, which reflected the content of the treatment curricula.

Many staff in therapeutic programmes conveyed the belief that young people should single-mindedly focus on the exercise of 'personal responsibility' for their actions. There was a sense among many staff that the young people came from criminogenic communities where they had not learned the meanings of personal responsibility, and where, according to one staff member, they dictated their own 'rules'. These staff would use the word 'structured' to describe the kind of programme that the young people needed to instill in them a sense of this responsibility. As one staff psychologist said, the community offers 'very little accountability' for young people, which they *need* to have instilled in them.[5] The cognitive change curriculum which was used in the facilities included exhortations like 'you are capable and worthy of positive changes in your life but you are the only one who can make them happen'. These discourses of responsibility can be compared to Brickman et al's (1982, p 371) 'moral' model of responsibility, which is when 'actors see themselves and are seen by others as lazy or as failing to make the critical effort that is the necessary and sufficient condition for their progress'. These discourses of 'bootstrap' development also reflect a broader discourse of personal responsibility codified in federal legislation passed in 1996 in the US (the Personal Responsibility and Work Opportunity Reconciliation Act) aimed at reducing welfare rolls and encouraging the psychological 'uplift' of impoverished people.

In many cases, the young people who were exposed to these interventions would embrace this discourse of personal responsibility. Elena spoke about how she had realised during her time in custody that doing her treatment was her own 'responsibility'. Newz said that while he was in the residential facility "I've been in control 100% of the time" and that "every decision I made was on my own". Oliver similarly spoke about his realisation that the only way he could do his time in residential custody was to "do me", and that it was best to ignore other people in that process. Other young people spoke about their 'responsibility' to exercise leadership and demonstrate the ways that they had taken responsibility for their discipline and self-control within treatment. Yet, as will be argued below, this was a rather ambivalent relationship, which obscured some of the alternative perspectives on responsibility that the young people also embraced.

## Expressions of responsibility

Such and Walker (2004, pp 231-2) argue that responsibility is a 'key variable in the definition of modern childhood and generational difference', because children are constructed as free from the responsibilities of the adult world. Yet the individualisation processes present in late modernity emphasise participation and accountability. This tension is embodied in the *UN Convention on the Rights of the Child*, which simultaneously describes the needs of children to be protected as well as their rights to be participants (United Nations, 1989).

Scholars who have researched young people's conceptions of selfhood have found that young people, despite their lower status in the moral community, do engage in constructing moral, responsible selfhood. Thomson and Holland (2002, p 104) have found that young people are 'deeply engaged in the emotional and ethical labour involved in constructing their identities and their lives'. The young people in my research overwhelmingly expressed a faithfulness to personal integrity, and a strong sense of bearing responsibility for the elaboration and development of themselves, rather than a personal transformation that was effectuated by others:

> "When you're like a teenager, you can kind of like dissect yourself, and like throw away what you don't want, and keep what you wanna keep, add what you want to add, or whatever, and it's like the only time you can really do that, and from there, you'll be kind of focused ... as a teenager that's your time to, you know, like, get rid of what you don't want, those views that your parents taught you, whatever the case may be, and you say that, 'you know, I don't agree with that'. ... but you're still young enough to say, you know, this is my opinion, so this is where I'm going to stand on it, and this is how I'm going to *show* that this is where I stand on it ..." (Nina)

Nina conveys the sense that the process of becoming responsible occurs through introspection, insight, and the growth process that happens parallel to, but not as a result of, the court interventions she faced. Although she does not directly use the word 'responsible', she is describing some of the ways in which she can be productive in her life, and start 'taking responsibility' for herself. Many young people similarly described the process of growing up as one in which they could take more responsibility for their actions and their potential. This was highly correlated for some of the young men with 'becoming a man', which for them was associated with the gendered act of being a provider. Nina strives for her expressions of growth and responsibility to be recognised, and, to a certain extent, to be held to account.

Sennett (1998) argues that an individual's social legitimacy in a capitalist economy derives from what that person produces; they are not *seen* until they are economically productive. The young people in this research, as indicated above, all came from impoverished backgrounds. For them, becoming 'responsible' involved rather complex ideas about accumulating capital: several young people used the term 'survive' to describe their objective in achieving responsibility (see also Mizen, 2003). Their goal was not to become rich, but to be able to arrive at a sustainable balancing point. In this context, 'survival' contrasts with 'self-sufficiency', a term that has popular currency in neoliberal welfare and penal practices. It links in this instance to place. Survival has as much to do with one's own place in life as it does with where one is actually from: their neighbourhoods were places to 'survive' – and for a number of the participants, to escape.

A number of the young men expressed a desire to join the army, even during the time of America's engagement in protracted wars in Iraq and Afghanistan. So perhaps rather than just 'finding a job' – the language of the court – young people's desire to survive involves a much deeper engagement with responsibility than simply that of accepting one's blameworthiness and engaging with the state's idea of responsible citizenship:

Q: Are there any things you worry about as you grow older?

A: I worry about … just surviving. I worry about surviving. 'Cause where I'm at … where I live at.

Q: What do you mean by 'surviving'?

A: Being able to, you know, take care of myself. Being able to do the things that I need to do. It's not so much of the things I want, you understand, because there's a lot of people that wants things that's not able to get it, but able to have the things that I need, you know, being able if I need health insurance or something, I can go and do it, you know, I don't have to be on public assistance or anything, I'm able to say I pay taxes. (Nelson)

Nelson describes a desire to 'take care of himself' that relates to his self-sufficiency from the standpoint of a citizen: he wants to be able to pay taxes, and thus to *participate* as a citizen, and, implicitly, gain those rights that come with being a taxpayer. However, he says that where he lives – in this case one of the most impoverished neighbourhoods in his city – may play a role in preventing him from surviving. Nelson does not relinquish responsibility for his social inclusion, but in a rather nuanced way expresses a sense of anxiety about what role the social structure plays in his life. He acknowledges the reality of his ability to exercise agency and responsibility in the context of differential life chances – something that scholars have recognised (Evans and Rudd, 1998; Valentine, 2003).

Luis, who spent almost three years in custody in residential facilities, came home and then was arrested again and charged as an adult. He said that while he was in the residential facility, he had learned that "they teach you a few things that you can run with" but "it's just my decisions" that continue to keep him in trouble. After he was released from the residential facility, he started selling drugs in order to support his family. He said he was desperate to do anything to "keep me off the corner", whether it was changing diapers or construction work. He said "I'm like a dog that's been playing in the dark all day", and it was enormously difficult to leverage that decision-making power when he was in that condition. Thus, there is some tension in Luis' notion of control: he recognises that his experience in the institutions hampered his abilities to exercise decisions about his life because he was made to act like an animal, without the faculties and senses of a human. Wacquant (2007, p 67) has described the ways that 'advanced marginality tends to concentrate in isolated and bounded territories increasingly perceived by both outsiders and insiders as social purgatories, leprous badlands at the heart of the postindustrial metropolis where only the refuse of society would accept to dwell'. Wacquant's comments point also to the potentially internalised sense of stigmatisation that people like Nelson and Luis feel in their associations with the marginal space they come from, as well as their sense about mobility through and out of those spaces.

## (In)visible responsibility?

The young participants overwhelmingly expressed a desire for legal actors to, in the words of one young man, "know who I really am" (Malcolm). They desired to be understood, respected, and treated with dignity, and they stated that their experience was overwhelmingly the opposite of that. For more than half of the young people, simply being *seen* or *heard,* despite being *addressed* often by the courts and in custody, was a struggle. For example, when speaking about what court actors might think of him, David said that "they judge you by what's on paper, they don't judge you on how they see you". He expressed a desire for his judge to be able to see a video recording of him on his street, interacting with people in his neighbourhood – a candid glimpse into how he *really* was, rather than how he was represented by the crime on his rap sheet. Malcolm conveyed a sense of dejection as he described how his judge saw him: "Bad. Bad person". Each of these young people expressed some sense that their core selves were missing from the courtroom process. These young people's selves are arguably divided by the call to responsibility that is entailed in this process: the person being held accountable may actually be a mirage, a 'self' that is a vision of the officials of the courts themselves.

Often, young people felt a strong desire to exercise responsibility in spaces which were outside of the reach of the courts. At least 12 of the young people (and in particular, the young men) spoke about the 'responsibility' that they felt toward their younger siblings and family members as providers, mentors, and as role models. Strikingly, they often spoke about this ability in the context of confinement, where their capacity to exercise this form of responsibility was deeply restricted. Panama, a 19-year-old who had spent over five years in custody for a serious felony offence and was soon to be released, said that he wanted to teach his younger siblings about how to be a 'good citizen'. Newz, convicted of a serious sex offence for which he faced lifetime sex offender registration and potentially serious and significant barriers to successful reintegration, spoke about his desire to demonstrate his personal strengths to his siblings. He had achieved the highest-level stage in the incentives and earned privileges system in his facility, and was seen as a 'model' resident, a status in which he took great pride. His sense that he could act as a role model to his younger siblings was related to his sense that it was possible to overcome a "bad situation", but also not to be "bad like me". He said, "I'm going to show them that once you're down, you can get back up". Equally important to the young people in confinement was their ability to demonstrate their responsibility to younger residents, which generated a sense of pride and hope in them.

It is possible that the young people's desires to exercise responsibility for others, both within the institutions and without, relates to their interest in taking 'control' in contexts where they potentially lack such control over their own lives and outcomes. They are constantly expected to 'model' adult behaviour, yet have the ability to model such behaviour for others very infrequently. They want to find a way to 'give back' in the face of their limited ability to do so. They are arguably seeking out opportunities for generativity, or the ability to 'care for others and to feel needed through productive and intergenerational outlets' (Barry, 2006, p 190). David's desire for his judge to see a videotape of his actions on the street speaks to this desire to be respected and seen in the parallel world he inhabits outside of the reach of the courts (see also Gaskell, 2008). This is a geographical tension that exists between the way that he sees his everyday life and experience in his neighbourhood as 'good', in contrast to what he believes the judge's perception is of his neighbourhood, which is signified as 'bad' in the popular press and public imagination. Brown (this volume, Chapter Six) also considers this conflation of aspiration and place.

For the young people, growing up, and gaining insights and perspective, was a process which almost always occurred *parallel* to the interventions of the criminal case. Tony, who had a sentence of 15 years to life, asked "what is the state doing to help you be successful?". He received his sentence when he was 15, and at the age of 19 said that he had matured significantly since his arrest and was able to exercise substantial responsibility within the facility and among his peers, but, he asked, "how can you show this change?".

The thoughts of the young people correspond with research on individual perceptions of procedural fairness, which has found that the extent to which people are treated with respect and dignity, or 'ethicality', impacts their attributions of fairness to the legal process (Paternoster et al, 1997). Sennett (2003) argues that respect is related to the recognition of an individual's autonomy – and perhaps their right to self-determination. It may also be related to responsibility – that is, the responsibility of state actors to take their role obligations seriously.

## Concluding comments

For young people, the expression of responsibility is tied to relationships and obligations – to families, to peers, and even to broader social structures. Scholars have demonstrated that responsibility is associated with accountability and caring for others; these things may be linked to one's ability to desist from crime (Maruna, 2006). It might be important to examine how young people understand responsibility as it connects to relationships – particularly as these relationships are mediated by race, ethnicity, class and gender, as well as one's position in social space.

Young people's perceptions of responsibility may have consequences for probation and social work practice as well as secure residential treatment. If we could gain a greater understanding about how young people negotiate responsibility in their complex social terrain, we may be able to break through the complex entanglement of care and control that has come to characterise the helping professions directed at young offender. Sharland (2006, p 256), a scholar in the field of social work, has noted that young people's well-being and risk-taking is 'associated with their material, cultural and relational contexts, the resources and role models available, and the extent to which they feel connected, supported, recognized'. In other words, young people's 'success' may depend on their ability to be embedded in a context that is filled with responsibilities and relationships which are reciprocal, supportive, and contain a dimension of accountability.

This chapter is concerned with some of the ways that young people's opportunities for growth are tightly controlled in contemporary youth justice systems. It has been argued that young people's meaningful growth and development can only occur in a context in which an understanding of their expressions of 'responsibility' extends beyond compliance with programme requirements.

## Notes

[1] Brown (this volume, Chapter Six) considers the restructuring of education and welfare services under New Labour and their focus on engendering responsibility and aspiration by the general public. See also Pykett (this volume, Chapter Two) for a discussion of 'Citizenship Education', aimed at engendering young people's sense of responsibility as a possibly positive strategy in helping young people to understand 'how they as citizens are made governable'. The courses thus may potentially create spaces of resistance to responsibilising projects.

[2] However, the United States Supreme Court has consistently found that young people are categorically less culpable than adults. They have also affirmed and reaffirmed that the Constitution and fundamental rights apply to the young.

[3] Active engagement with youth justice interventions is actually more often a kind of passive adherence to a clear sentencing agenda or plan. Halsey (2007, pp 176-7) has argued that young people in this context are often treated as vessels to be 'filled to the brim with techniques and strategies for desistance'.

[4] The name of the state has been changed, as have the names of the participants in this research.

[5] Over the course of this research, significant reforms were taking place in Olympia in which staff were stripped of their ability to use physical restraints, and more therapeutic interventions were introduced. One staff member described these changes as an attempt to "take away responsibility" from the young people.

# References

Bandalli, S. (2000) 'Children, responsibility and the new youth justice', in B. Goldson (ed) *The new youth justice,* Dorset: Russell House Publishing, pp 81-95.

Banks, C. (2008) *Alaska native juveniles in detention: a qualitative study of treatment and resistance,* Lewiston, NY: The Edwin Mellen Press.

Barker, J., Alldred, P., Watts, M. and Dodman, H. (2010) 'Pupils or prisoners? Institutional geographies and internal exclusion in UK secondary schools', *Area,* vol 42, no 3, pp 378-86.

Barry, M. (2006) *Youth offending in transition: the search for social recognition,* Abingdon: Routledge.

Bauman, Z. (2000) *Liquid modernity,* Cambridge: Polity Press.

Beck, U. (1992) *Risk society: towards a new modernity,* London: Sage Publications.

Beck, U. (1998) *Democracy without enemies,* Cambridge: Polity Press.

Bourdieu, P. (1989) 'Social space and symbolic power', *Sociological Theory,* vol 7, no 1, pp 14-25.

Brickman, P., Rabinowitz, V.C., Karuza, J., Coates, D., Cohn, E. and Kidder, L. (1982) 'Models of helping and coping', *American Psychologist,* vol 37, no 4, pp 368-84.

Chung, H.L., Little, M. and Steinberg, L. (2005) 'The transition to adulthood for adolescents in the juvenile justice system: a developmental perspective', in D.W. Osgood, E.M. Foster, C. Flanagan, and G.R. Ruth (eds) *On your own without a net: the transition to adulthood for vulnerable populations,* Chicago: University of Chicago Press, pp 68–91.

Crewe, B. (2009) *The prisoner society: power, adaptation, and social life in an English prison,* Oxford: Oxford University Press.

Evans, K. and Rudd, P. (1998) *Structure and agency in young adult transitions,* Social Research Association Conference, San Diego, CA.

Farrington, D.P. (2007) 'Childhood risk factors and risk focused prevention', in M. Maguire, R. Morgan and R. Reiner (eds) *Oxford handbook of criminology,* 4th edn, Oxford: Oxford University Press, pp 602-40.

Fox, K.J. (1999) 'Changing violent minds: discursive correction and resistance in the cognitive treatment of violent offenders in prison', *Social Problems,* vol 46, no 1, pp 88-103.

Fraser, N. and Gordon, L. (1994) 'A genealogy of dependency: tracing a keyword of the US welfare state', *Signs,* vol 19, no 2, pp 309-36.

Furlong, A. and Cartmel, F. (2007) *Young people and social change: new perspectives,* Maidenhead: Open University Press.

Garland, D. (1996) 'The limits of the sovereign state', *The British Journal of Criminology,* vol 36, no 4, pp 445-71.

Gaskell, C. (2008) '"But they just don't respect us": young people's experiences of (dis)respected citizenship and the New Labour Respect Agenda', *Children's Geographies,* vol 6, no 3, pp 223-38.

Halsey, M.J. (2007) 'Negotiating conditional release: juvenile narratives of repeat incarceration', *Punishment and Society,* vol 8, no 2, pp 147-81.

Hirschfield, P.J. (2008) 'Preparing for prison? The criminalization of school discipline in the USA', *Theoretical Criminology,* vol 12, no 1, pp 79-101.

Hopkins, P. and Pain, R. (2007) 'Geographies of age: thinking relationally', *Area,* vol 39, no 3, pp 287-94.

Maruna, S. (2006) '"Saying sorry" or "making things right": from passive to active responsibility in work with young offenders', in M. Tansey (ed) *Re-integration of offenders,* Dublin: ACJRD, pp 30-5.

Maruna, S. and Mann, R. (2006) 'A fundamental attribution error? Rethinking cognitive distortions', *Legal and Criminological Psychology,* vol 11, pp 155-77.

Mizen, P. (2003) 'The best days of your life? Youth, policy and Blair's New Labour', *Critical Social Policy,* vol 23, no 4, pp 453-76.

Muncie, J. (2005) 'The globalization of crime control: the case of youth and juvenile justice. Neo-liberalism, policy convergence and international conventions', *Theoretical Criminology,* vol 9, no 1, pp 35-64.

Muncie, J. (2006) 'Governing young people: coherence and contradiction in contemporary youth justice', *Critical Social Policy,* vol 26, no 4, pp 770-93.

Muncie, J. and Hughes, G. (2002) 'Modes of youth governance: political rationalities, criminalization and resistance', in J. Muncie, G. Hughes and E. Mclaughlin (eds) *Youth justice: critical readings,* London: Sage, pp 1-18.

O'Malley, P. (1992) 'Risk, power and crime prevention', *Economy and Society,* vol 21, no 3, pp 252-75.

Paternoster, R., Brame, R., Bachman, R. and Sherman, L.W. (1997) 'Do fair procedures matter? The effect of procedural justice on spouse assault', *Law and Society Review,* vol 31, no 1, pp 163-204.

Phoenix, J. (2009) 'Beyond risk assessment: the return of repressive welfarism?', in F. McNeill and M. Barry (eds) *Youth offending and youth justice,* London: Jessica Kingsley Publishers.

Platt, A. (1969/1977) *The child savers: the invention of delinquency,* Chicago: University of Chicago Press.

Pupavac, V. (2001) 'Misanthropy without borders: the international chldren's rights regime', *Disasters,* vol 25, no 2, pp 95-112.

Rose, N. (2000) 'Government and control', *British Journal of Criminology,* vol 40, pp 321-39.

Ruddick, S. (2007) 'At the horizons of the subject: neo-liberalism, neo-conservatism and the rights of the child. Part one: from "knowing" fetus to "confused" child', *Gender, Place & Culture,* vol 14, no 5, pp 513-27.

Scarre, G. (1980) 'Children and paternalism', *Philosophy,* vol 55, no 117-24.

Schrag, F. (1977) 'The child in the moral order', *Philosophy,* vol 52, no 200, pp 167-77.

Sennett, R. (1998) *The corrosion of character: the personal consequences of work in the new capitalism,* New York: W.W. Norton.

Sennett, R. (2003) *Respect: the formation of character in an age of inequality,* London: Penguin.

Sharland, E. (2006) 'Young people, risk taking and risk making: some thoughts for social work', *British Journal of Social Work,* vol 36, pp 247-65.

Such, E. and Walker, R. (2004) 'Being responsible and responsible beings: children's understanding of responsibility', *Children & Society,* vol 18, pp 231-42.

Thomson, R. and Holland, J. (2002) 'Young people, social change and the negotiation of moral authority', *Children & Society,* vol 16, pp 103-15.

Thomson, R., Bell, R., Holland, J., Henderson, S., McGrellis, S. and Sharpe, S. (2002) 'Critical moments: choice, chance and opportunity in young people's narratives of transition', *Sociology,* vol 36, no 2, pp 335-54.

United Nations (1989) *Convention on the rights of the child,* New York: United Nations.

Valentine, G. (2003) 'Boundary crossings: transitions from childhood to adulthood', *Children's Geographies,* vol 1, no 1, pp 37-52.

von Hirsch, A. (2005) 'Proportionate sentences for juvenile offenders', in A. Von Hirsch and A. Ashworth (eds) *Proportionate sentencing: exploring the principles,* Oxford: Oxford University Press, pp 35-49.

Wacquant, L. (2007) 'Territorial stigmatization in the age of advanced marginality', *Thesis Eleven,* vol 91, pp 66-77.

## thirteen

# Parenting policy and the geographies of friendship: encounters in an English Sure Start Children's Centre

*Eleanor Jupp*

## Introduction

"What is a Children's Centre and why would I come here to play with the children when I can do that at home?" (Interview, Sue, volunteer co-ordinator, Eastfields Sure Start Children's Centre)

This chapter is based on research undertaken at one Sure Start Children's Centre in Oxford, UK,[1] and the question above was posed rhetorically during an interview with a worker (although formally a user), as she talked about the difficulties of encouraging 'local' parents to access the centre. Her question, was also, in some ways, my own research question, in that I was broadly interested in understanding the meanings and uses of Children's Centres as a particular kind of *space*. As explored below, Children's Centres are neighbourhood-based spaces aimed at children under five and their families which have been developed over the past decade in the UK, initially via a programme called 'Sure Start' (DCSF, 2010). Because of the ways in which they have operated (with an emphasis on community involvement and flexibility) and the range of services brought together (education, childcare, health, family support) these centres can be understood as a new manifestation of the welfare state at a neighbourhood level (Whalley, 2006; on scale, see Barker, this volume, Chapter Ten). In undertaking the research I was interested both in the centre's relationship to 'home' or private lives, and to policy programmes and directives within a public sphere. As my interviewee's question suggests, Children's Centres may seem to occupy a kind of uncertain space between public and private, of a kind that Buckingham et al (2006) describe as 'liminal'. A term from anthropology (Turner, 1975), liminality denotes a space of transition between spheres or states, and Buckingham et al (2006) see such liminality as positive in enabling users to connect with new contexts beyond their home lives. However, in starting to undertake research into Children's Centres, I also began to develop a more specific concern, which the asking of the question above points to: it was clear that the geographical issue of *access* to the centre was a major preoccupation for many of the staff. In particular there were questions about whether enough 'local' parents were using the space, understood to mean the disadvantaged or working–class parents that reflected the socio-demographics of the neighbourhood in which the centre was situated. Such concerns are also echoed in national policy evaluation and media debate about Sure Start (Belsky et al, 2007; Anning and Ball, 2008; Clegg, 2010; Cornish, 2010) as well as the subsequent programme of Children's Centres. At the time of writing there is renewed discussion among politicians about whether Children's Centres should become more 'targeted' (Cameron, 2010a) at the poorest parents.

This chapter argues that Children's Centres have sought to insert themselves into the 'everyday' lives of parents with young children in particular ways. This also means that use of the centres becomes bound up with different kinds of relationships and spaces locally. I argue in particular that for parents who regularly used the centre, it was experienced as a place of *friendship* above all. These friendships were in turn part of wider 'caringscapes' (Bowlby et al, 2010) via which parents looked after their children, which might include playgroups, visits to other houses and other times, spaces and practice of care. This notion of 'caringscapes' is further explored in the next section. In the rest of this chapter some background on the policy context of Sure Start and Children's Centres is provided, some commentaries on local geographies of 'parenting' are given, and material from fieldwork in Eastfields is presented. In so doing a sense of the particular spatialities of a Children's Centre is sketched out, and issues of inclusion and exclusion are explored via a wider set of concerns around power and friendship.

## Spaces of 'parenting' in policy and research

### Parenting in policy

'Parenting' is clearly a highly contested terrain, and the social and cultural ambivalences surrounding it have been augmented under recent UK policy regimes which have constructed 'parenting' as a specific field of policy intervention (Gambles, 2010). Indeed this has combined with a media fascination for the performance of 'defective' parenting (Jensen, 2010) to construct a climate in which public debate concerns itself with topics such as feeding, sleeping, discipline and so on as never before. For policy-makers, the parenting 'agenda' seems to offer the opportunity for cost-effective 'early intervention' in the lives of those who might potentially rely heavily on the welfare state throughout the life course. As Gill and Jensen (2008) and others have pointed out, concern about 'poor parenting' has often stood in for 'poverty', and indeed the whole discourse can be seen a replacing a broader political focus on socio-economic inequality (Gillies, 2007).

Such a concern with parenting and pre-school children can be seen as lying behind the Sure Start programme (Weinberger et al, 2005; Belsky et al, 2007), which was launched in 1998 and brought together different service providers (especially health, education, family support and childcare) to focus on pre-school children. Via the provision of local centres and programmes, it aimed to tackle 'problems' around parenting and the lives of young children (for example, relating to breastfeeding and childhood nutrition, preparedness for future education and more), which Lister (2005) describes as investing in 'citizen-workers in becoming'. It was held up as 'the cornerstone of the Government's drive to tackle child poverty and social exclusion' (DCSF, 2010) and was often promoted as a 'flagship' policy of New Labour. The first Sure Start Centres were located in defined areas of need, normally areas of cities defined as containing concentrations of deprivation or disadvantage. The local programmes and centres were given flexibility in their operation and varied considerably, but they tended to have the provision of 'drop-in-play-space' as central, often designed to function as a 'gateway' for other services being offered, which might include childcare within a crèche setting, midwife and health visitor services, language and play therapy, training and advice on employment for parents and more.

The programme was also designed to involve parents in the running of local programmes and centres, and to build community engagement and 'responsibilisation' among them (Bagley and Ackerley, 2006). In this approach, and in the focus on intervening in parenting practices and behaviours at an individual level (Clarke, 2005), the centres could be seen as seeking to insert themselves into the 'everyday' and domestic lives of parents with young children in particular ways. Indeed, although many Sure Start programmes were closely linked to schools and healthcare services (for example physically sharing sites) there has been an emphasis on new forms of professional practice (Gustafsson and Driver, 2005). For example, a number of staff interviewed during the research reported that they worked hard to show parents that they were not part of the school which was located next door.

Sure Start as a time-limited programme has now been overlain by a national programme of Sure Start Children's Centres (DfES, 2005), which continue to be judged by a range of such targets (Ofsted, 2008), focusing particularly on disadvantaged families, although they are now present in all neighbourhoods in some form, not just the poorest. As already noted, there is renewed debate at present about how far they should be targeted only at the most deprived families and whether they have been over-used by the 'sharp-elbowed middle classes' (Cameron, 2010b). There is also debate about how a more targeted service might be achieved, against the background of huge cuts to welfare services and the removal of protected funding for the centres against other 'early years' activities.

In critically evaluating the programme within the context of the 'parenting' agenda, it can be argued that the story of Sure Start and Children's Centres *in practice* is not a necessarily straightforward one of a government attempt to control or intervene in 'poor parenting' as a set of behaviours in targeted ways. Also behind the initiative was a somewhat more radical agenda about providing local support and an infrastructure of care and solidarity for all parents with young families. Indeed, neighbourhood and community activists have a tradition of providing such spaces and care for families and young children (see Jupp, 2006), who are in need of practical and emotional support as well as a caring context beyond the confines of domestic life in which to bring up their children. Lister (2006), who sets out a largely critical commentary about Sure Start in relation to its policy focus on children's futures, also concedes that in practice the centres have had the potential to impact positively on children's lives 'in the here and now'.

Indeed as will become clear in relation to this case study, many Children's Centre workers come from community development backgrounds, and some Children's Centres have been developed out of existing voluntary and community sector activity. In Oxford, where the research was based, there was a particular history of 'family centres' (Warren-Adamson, 2006), a term which has a variety of meanings, but in the case of Oxford seems to refer to centres run mainly by voluntary sector organisations, offering broad-based support for local families. As the chapter goes on to discuss, the centre where the research was undertaken had previously been such a family centre, and some of the same staff were employed in it. Therefore there were a range of rationalities and dynamics at play, not only within policy discourses and programmes, but also among staff and in the spaces of the Children's Centre itself, as indeed is a feature of much social policy interventions initiated under the previous Labour administration (Newman and Clarke, 2009). These dynamics shaped a potentially productive but also somewhat uneasy space, in which, to return to the question with which the chapter opened, there was some uncertainty about what the purpose of the centre was, and who might use it.

## Geographies of parenting

From a different analytical perspective, 'parenting' has been an important area of research within social and cultural geography, for some years, in relation to how performances of parenting might impact on children's identities and agency (Valentine, 1997; Holloway and Valentine, 2000), but also crucially in relation to issues of childcare (for example, England, 1996; Smith and Barker, 2001; Pratt, 2003; Jarvis, 2009). A particular concern, of relevance here, has been conceptualising the nature and influence of *place* on patterns of childcare and networks and practices of parenting. A number of commentators explore how locality, class, gender, employment status and childcare choices intersect around what Holloway (1998) calls 'local childcare cultures'. Barker (2011, p 5) suggests that 'local moral landscapes of care create local moral orders, ideologies and practices of care'. However, McDowell et al (2005) suggest that seeing such parenting cultures as 'locally' defined is over-deterministic, at least in relation to their case studies of highly socially divided London neighbourhoods where a wide range of individual approaches to issues of childcare were identified. Nonetheless, they agree that 'women's experiences and meanings of motherhood are mediated through the networks and cultures in which they are embedded' (p 235).

Bowlby et al (2010) suggest the term 'caringscapes' as a way of framing the informal geographies of care for young children, which include times as well as spaces and practices of care. They describe these caringscapes in terms of a 'terrain' that may both open-up or shut-down opportunities, become routinised or restricted over time, but also offer carers some degree of choice over how they navigate it. An important aspect of caringscapes will be *friendships*, and following Spencer and Pahl (2006) they identify different kinds of friendships which play different roles within practices of care, in a context where familial and friendship bonds or roles may be becoming more blurred. 'Friendship' is also beginning to receive more attention within social and cultural geography, for example, Dyson (2010) draws attention to the potentially ambivalent role of friendships (between children in India in her case) as both a source of solidarity and support among individuals, but also a means by which inequality and forms of exclusion get reinforced.

However, there has been a lack of attention within recent geographical literature to times and spaces of care involved with parenting *policy* in the UK, and Children's Centres in particular. One exception is work by Horton and Kraftl (2009a; 2009b) which points to a need to think about the 'emotional geographies' (2009b) of such centres in more complex ways and to see beyond them as spaces for the implementation of particular policy imperatives. In analysing Children's Centres as spaces it may therefore be instructive to consider other commentaries on 'semi-institutional spaces' (see Parr, 2000) or liminal spaces which seek to relate to private or domestic lives in particular ways. As will become clear, this notion of homely space is also relevant to my case study centre where the idea of 'home' was invoked in many discussions and descriptions. Milligan (2003) also talks about the ways in which meanings of home and institution are reconfigured in new practices of offering social care in home settings. These examples suggest new 'modalities of the domestic' (Das et al, 2008) which may move beyond actual home spaces. Furthermore, in considering the above examples, it is clear that analysis of such spaces calls for an approach which focuses on embodied practices, affect and emotions as well as talk and the discursive registers of policy discourses.

## Encounters in the uneasy spaces of parenting policy

### Introducing Eastfields

The research on which this chapter draws took place between 2009 and 2010 and focused on professionals' and parents' experiences of using the centre at Eastfields. Eastfields is on the outskirts of Oxford and is an area of housing developed as council housing, but which now has more mixed tenure, including new private developments undertaken by a housing association. It is ethnically diverse in relation to the rest of the city and is identified as one its most deprived neighbourhoods. The centre there has had various incarnations under different policy frameworks, but underwent substantial investment when it became a Sure Start Centre. The spaces of the centre overall are light and modern, at the hub of which is a cafe providing lunches, with other spaces and rooms, including the drop-in Play Room, leading off it. The Play Room itself seemed to be very appealing to children, with a large outdoor garden leading off it, as well as indoor tunnels and climbing frames and all kinds of toys and activities for children. In the centre of the room was a table mostly used for 'craft' activities. The 'drop-in play sessions' are times when the Play Room was simply open to anyone with a child under five. There were usually around three staff present in the room although parents stayed with their children at the sessions and were expected to be looking after them.

As well as drop-in play sessions, the centre offered training and support to parents of various degrees of formality, including training around skills for employment, on 'parenting' itself, and provided support to various specific groups of parents, for example teenage parents, an African women's group and an Arabic women's group (discussed further below). However, my research focused on the drop-in play sessions in the Play Room, partly because of access for the research, but also because it was here that some of the issues of inclusion and dynamics around public and private lives seemed most apparent.

In-depth interviews were undertaken with six key professionals who worked at the centre in a variety of roles, mostly focused on outreach and different kinds of work with families. After this a series of visits were made to the Play Room, which was open four mornings per week. Following two 'scoping' visits, ten interviews were undertaken with parents, as well as observations of interactions between parents and between staff and parents. The interviews with parents were inevitably less structured than those with staff as they took place while looking after children and often while other parents were present. It should be noted that the focus of the research is therefore on parents and parenting rather than children; however, the presence of young children was clearly an important aspect of the space. The next section discusses the idea of the centre as a place in which policy imperatives were enacted, and how this impacted on interactions between staff and users.

### Enacting policy?

From the perspective of staff, the interviews confirmed that they saw the space as framing much 'more than' (Horton and Kraftl, 2009b) the enactment of policy imperatives or programmes. Notions of 'homeliness' and of familial relationships were regularly invoked in my discussions with them, and this was often set up in opposition to being like an 'institution'. For example, one senior children's worker, Catherine, said: "We just want to be like a friendly supportive family really". On the other hand, it was recognised that 'familial' relationships were not entirely appropriate either. An outreach worker, Sonia, said:

> "They see us like extended family – although if there's an issue that you've got to deal with you'd have to challenge them because you are still a professional."

The ambivalence of these relationships was also linked to the changing policy context, and indeed the physical form of the centre itself. As already noted, it had started life as a 'family centre' and then become a 'Sure Start' Centre before its current guise as a 'Sure Start Children's Centre'. Another outreach worker interviewed, Rose, had worked at the family centre and had stayed working there in its various phases. She reported that:

> "In the old days people, we didn't have any money so people would come in and get help and then would want to give something back. So people would come and cook at the start, it was just a Baby Belling stove ... and I hated the big new building [the Sure Start Centre] at first after our lovely, homely, scruffy set-up."

So a sense of an informal space was often held up as an ideal by some of the workers, as it seemed to suggest its successful insertion into the everyday lives of families within the neighbourhood. This quote also suggests the sense of it as a space over which local people felt a sense of 'ownership' or responsibility, which is what Sure Start Centres have also attempted to develop (Pemberton and Mason, 2008). Nonetheless Rose felt that this dynamic had been lost in a move to a more 'institutional' space:

"People who come in now, they don't want to do a lot. I can understand that, and I'd like it be a place where parents can have a rest, and we do try to give time out as much as possible ... But also we do want to challenge people, and that helps people move on, give them confidence. There are some very talented parents here."

This new need to 'challenge' people (rather than simply letting them 'have a rest' from parenting) could be seen as tied-up to working to particular targets and interventions, for example supporting parents into the job market, and encouraging certain parenting practices. How these interventions should be operationalised was somewhat uncertain though, and the research uncovered debates among practitioners about, for example, how to encourage healthy eating. Overall there was a kind of hesitancy and awkwardness around many of the interventions which the staff were tasked with making, and they clearly felt more comfortable describing their roles in terms of being 'friendly' and 'supportive'. In many ways this goes against some of the more sweeping social policy narratives about the 'governmentalisation' of parents via this agenda (Lister, 2005; 2006).

This ambiguity of the staff's roles, as well as the purpose of the space overall, was also expressed in discussions with centre users. Nonetheless, users interviewed did generally speak very positively about the centre as a 'supportive' space and a place to get away from the difficulties of home life with small children. As one user commented: "staying at home is a nightmare". A number of interviewees spoke warmly about the advice and help they had received from staff. Another parent said "people here help each other". Observations indicated that interactions between staff and users the Play Room were friendly, but not necessarily very prolonged, perhaps having a word on arrival and then chatting a little about their children as they took part in some of the activities on offer. Once their children 'settled' into some activities, parents tended to sit on the sofas or chairs around the room, whereas staff often hovered around one or other of the activities on offer, such as the painting or sticking on the central craft table, although on occasion staff were observed sitting on the sofas with parents. One parent commented that she usually had a bit of "banter" with the staff but that they weren't "in your face".

There was a strong sense that parents did not want staff to be intervening in certain ways with their parenting. While they seemed happy to receive straightforward 'help' from professionals, it was the potential atmosphere of what Jarvis (2009) calls 'moral surveillance' that they felt uncomfortable with. No parents reported that they felt judged or uncomfortable with staff; however, a number mentioned that coming to the centre for the first time was 'a big step':

"Even though I only lived over the road, for me to come to the centre it was like it was a million miles away and I had to get three buses."

Also parents reported that they had felt more 'uncomfortable' under previous guises as a family centre and then Sure Start centre. Sue, the parent mentioned at the chapter's opening, explained that:

"In the old days the place had a stigma to it ... people thought that other people would know about their problems if they came here."

Similarly, Rose said that some parents often sat in the cafe with their children running around, but would not take the next step and go into the Play Room, because of not feeling 'confident' enough. This seems to have been partly about the interactions with staff but another interviewee, Janet, told me that the Play Room had, 'in the past', been perceived as a place for 'posh people', and this begins to touch on dynamics of interactions among parents as well as with staff, discussed further below. Nonetheless, from the sample of parents interviewed, the notion of feeling potentially 'uncomfortable' around staff was present among interviewees from a range of backgrounds.

As should be clear from the quotes above, staff did feel aware of these concerns and spoke often about trying to make the space feel welcoming and accessible. In relation to the Play Room itself, they had recently changed the way the space was used so that activities were less structured, and it felt less 'schooly'. Catherine told me that this was because some of their potential users might have had negative experiences of school, and that they wanted to make the centre feel more like 'home'.

### The centre as a site of friendships

Given this potentially uncomfortable sense of the interactions that might take place at a Children's Centre, it is perhaps surprising that regular users nonetheless spoke very warmly about the centre and its impact. As already noted, users spoke positively about the facilities and saw it as a place that the children enjoyed as well as they themselves. However, it was notable that regular users of the Play Room tended to come to meet a group of 'friends', and that these were a distinct group among the other parents or carers who might be present. One mother, Annie, who seemed to be a key member of one of these friendship groups said:

"We text in the morning and arrange to meet ... so there's a difference between people you are friendly with here and friends that you meet here."

If parents were by themselves in the Play Room they often said that they were 'waiting for a friend', and it seemed to be unusual for parents to visit by themselves; those that did, did not seem to stay around for very long, or did not return the following week. Indeed, because I tended to visit the Play Room on the same days of the week, the same groups of parents were often observed, as they timed their visit as part of weekly patterns of visits to the Centre, and perhaps to other playgroups and to meetings in houses and parks. As already mentioned, Bowlby et al (2010) describe patterns of times and spaces of informal care in terms of 'caringscapes' and it was clear that these had important *collective* dimensions in this context. The groups who met at the centre therefore shared experiences which went beyond the everyday interactions at the centre. For example, parents were seen to bring along birthday presents to celebrate a child's birthday, and discussions were heard about partners and other family members that suggested that their friends knew them too.

These friendship groups among parents consisted of individuals who identified with each other in quite specific ways, delineating inclusions as well as exclusions to their groups. Annie, the mother who spoke about texting also reported that her group of friends (around five or six individuals) were all 'professional', although they were not working at present. In response to a question about whether they accessed other services at the centre, she said:

> "We're not the target group ... We just do the middle-class thing of accessing the best bits and not bothering with the rest ... We're middle class but then we're also all skint because we're not working."

By 'target group', Annie was referring to the working-class or 'disadvantaged' families who might be seen as the object of the centre's concerns, and this seemed to be important in defining their relationship with the space.

Another group encountered was a group of Arabic-speaking women from various different ethnic backgrounds. An Iraqi woman, Amira, appeared to be one of the key figures within this group, and she was clearly a catalyst for socialising among many of the users. For example, she was observed approaching a Somali woman who had not been to the centre before and encouraging her to join in a discussion. The first time I met her she was 'threading' (or shaping) a friend's eyebrows, and this had clearly been pre-arranged by them. Amira also ran a separate formalised Arabic women's group, which met at the centre on a different day and in a different space. She had also used the centre for taking English classes and gaining other skills which she hoped would enable her to get a job when her children were older. In this way, her 'caringscape' also included times and spaces which were linked to spheres of education and employment. Another, older, Asian woman, who came to the Play Room with her grandson, stated that she and a group of friends also used the centre for language classes.

These friendships were a source of considerable support for the women interviewed, enabling them to escape from domestic spaces where they often reported feeling bored, isolated, overwhelmed or depressed. However, as McDowell et al (2005) and others have pointed out, such friendship circles are linked to class positions as well as other aspects of identity, understandings of parenting and mothering, and as such reinforce certain norms and practices as well as potentially exclude others. Given that they clearly played a mediating role in relation to using the Play Room at the centre, for those who were not part of such a group, and did not possess the specific attributes which might delineate membership, this could result in being effectively excluded from the space. Such feelings of exclusion might potentially have been overcome by the practices of the staff, yet the uncertainty and ambiguity of their role meant that many parents did not necessarily wish to interact with them too intimately either. Overall, it seemed that without such a friendship group users did not generally feel 'comfortable', and certainly unlikely to access the centre for the first time. As Sue said, "if you don't know someone who comes here, you've got no way of knowing what it's like".

## Conclusions

As noted at the start, there has been media and policy discussion about issues of access to Children's Centres, with discussion of the 'sharp-elbowed middle classes' effectively 'colonising' spaces and excluding others (Cameron, 2010b). In the face of overall cuts to welfare spending, attempts are being made to re-focus spending on the most 'disadvantaged' families, although it is also being argued that this would 'stigmatise' them as spaces and make poorer families even less likely to access them (Cornish, 2010).

This chapter has set out to explore issues of access and inclusion within a Children's Centre from a more nuanced perspective. Although, as should be clear, some evidence of middle-class dominance of the space was found at the centre this could be seen as part of a wider set of dynamics around the space, and two issues in particular can be highlighted. Firstly, the Centre's remit to intervene in 'parenting' created a somewhat uneasy space, in which parents might feel subject to forms of 'moral surveillance' (Jarvis, 2009), and in which staff might feel conflicted about their role and practices. This uneasiness was expressed by parents from a range of backgrounds, although it is also likely that certain parents might feel more 'confident' than others within such a space.

Secondly, the research found that inclusion within a friendship group could effectively mediate access to the centre, enabling parents to feel 'comfortable' and attend regularly. Although middle-class groups might be assumed to feel more 'comfortable' than others, from observations it can be suggested that these groups might have a range of class, ethnic or other dimensions (for example, language). However, they were quite finely delineated and once established could effectively exclude others from use of the space. Furthermore, the friendship groups did not simply revolve around use of the Children's Centre, but rather encompassed wider 'caringscapes' (Bowlby et al, 2010) of times and spaces of care within and across the locality and beyond. Indeed some parents travelled several miles to the centre because they had become connected with a friendship group who met there. As other research has shown (for example, Holloway, 1998; McDowell et al, 2005) it seems that practices of parenting can be particularly bound-up with such informal networks or finely delineated 'parenting' geographies. This suggests that in order to understand (and improve) access to spaces of Children's Centres, an understanding of such geographies should be developed. It also suggests that the policy framework of 'parenting' is a problematic one, and more straightforward notions of welfare and support for families might frame a more inviting space. Indeed the extent to which parenting practices and behaviours have been changed through the Sure Start programme remains open to question (Belsky et al, 2007). Such problematics are likely to be common to other spaces in which government seeks to intervene in everyday and intimate aspects of life, and therefore to draw on the rationalities of domestic or community spaces (Jupp, 2006).

Overall, the research also points to the need to continue to explore the nature of 'caringscapes' in shaping the spatial, material and emotional contexts of care for young children, and the relationship between these and particular localities. While the idea of 'the community' or 'the neighbourhood' as the context for parenting is clearly based on simplistic notions of place (Aitken, 2000), place clearly *does* matter in these issues, although, as the quote from Sue above demonstrated, a local centre can still feel 'a million miles way'. Nonetheless, during the research it appeared that there was still a value in a neighbourhood space which was potentially used by different groups of parents and young children, however diverse or fragmented their groups and parenting approaches. When parents arrived early before their friends got there, or sat down to talk to a staff member for longer, helped their children to paint or negotiate the tunnel, small-scale new connections or identifications might take place (Jupp, 2008). While the space might never feel like a 'home from home' for all local parents, all of the time, it did hold potential to provide moments of solidarity and support within the seemingly unending work of looking after small children. In recognising the value of such moments, new kinds of values might also be placed on Sure Start Children's Centres at a moment of funding cuts.

## Note

[1] The pseudonym 'Eastfields' is used for the centre and its neighbourhood. Participants' names are also pseudonyms.

## References

Aitken, S. (2000) 'Mothers, communities and the scale of difference', *Social and Cultural Geography*, vol 1, no 1, pp 65-82.

Anning, A. and Ball, M. (eds) (2008) *Improving services for young children: from Sure Start to Children's Centres,* London: Sage.

Bagley, C. and Ackerley, C. (2006) '"I am much more than just a mum", social capital, empowerment and Sure Start', *Journal of Education Policy*, vol 21, no 6, pp 717-34.

Barker, J. (2011) '"Manic mums" and "distant dads"? Gendered geographies of care and the journey to school', *Health and Place*, vol 17, no 2, pp 413-21.

Belsky, J., Barnes, J. and Melhuish, E. (2007) *The national evaluation of Sure Start: does area-based early intervention work?,* Bristol: Policy Press.

Bowlby, S., McKie, L., Gregory, S. and Macpherson, I. (2010) *Interdependency and care over the lifecourse*, Oxford: Routledge.

Buckingham, S., Marandet, E., Smith, F., Wainwright, E. and Diosi, M. (2006) 'The liminality of training spaces: places of private/public transitions', *Geoforum*, vol 37, pp 895-905.

Cameron, D. (2010a) *The big society*, speech given on 19 July 2010, http://www.number10.gov.uk/news/big-society-speech/.

Cameron, D. (2010b) *PM direct on Manchester*, speech given on 10 August 2010, http://www.number10.gov.uk/news/pm-direct-in-manchester-2/.

Clegg, N. (2010) *Supporting families and children*, speech given on 17 June 2010, http://www.libdems.org.uk/latest_news_detail.aspx?title=Nick_Clegg's_speech_on_supporting_families_and_children&pPK=6d739b75-08a1-4262-9309-39b0fc8fc45c.

Clarke, K. (2005) 'Childhood, parenting and early intervention: a critical examination of Sure Start national programme', *Critical Social Policy*, 26, 4, 699-721.

Cornish, J. (2010) 'Too posh for children's centres?', *Children and Young People Now*, http://www.cypnow.co.uk/news/1009537/Early-Years-posh-childrens-centres.

Das, V., Ellen, J.M. and Leonard, L. (2008) 'On the modalities of the domestic', *Home Cultures*, vol 5, no 3, pp 349-72.

DCSF (Department for Children, Schools and Families) (2010) *Every child matters: about Sure Start Children's Centres*, London: DCSF.

DfES (Department for Education and Skills) (2005) *Children's Centres: phase two guidance*, London: HMSO.

Dyson, J. (2010) 'Friendship in practice: girls' work in the Indian Himalayas', *American Ethnologist*, vol 37, no 3, pp 482-98.

England, K. (1996) *Who will mind the baby? Geographies of child-care and working mothers*, London and New York: Routledge.

Gambles, R. (2010) 'Going public? Articulations of the personal and political on Mumsnet.com', in N. Mahony, J. Newman and C. Barnett (eds) *Rethinking the public*, Bristol: Policy Press, pp 75-90.

Gill, R. and Jensen, T. (2008) *Public intimacies and the intimate public: the personal, political and mediated intimacy*, paper presented at ESRC seminar series Emergent Publics, Milton Keynes, March.

Gillies, V. (2007) *Marginalised mothers: exploring working-class experiences of parenting*, Oxford: Routledge.

Gustafsson, U. and Driver, S. (2005) 'Parents, power and public participation: sure start, an experiment in New Labour governance', *Social Policy and Administration*, vol 39, no 5, pp 528-43.

Holloway, S. (1998) 'Local childcare cultures: moral geographies of mothering and the social organisation of pre-school education', *Gender, Place and Culture*, vol 5, no 1, pp 29-53.

Holloway, S and Valentine, G. (2000) *Children's geographies: playing, living, learning*, Oxford: Routledge.

Horton, J. and Kraftl, P. (2009a) 'Small acts, kind words and "not too much fuss": implicit activisms', *Emotions, Space and Society*, vol 2, no 1, pp 14-23.

Horton, J. and Kraftl, P. (2009b) 'What (else) matters? Policy contexts, emotional geographies', *Environment and Planning A*, vol 41, pp 2984-3002.

Jarvis, H. (2009) *Cities and gender*, Oxford: Routledge.

Jensen, T. (2010) '"What kind of mum are you at the moment?" Supernanny and the psychologising of classed embodiment', *Subjectivity*, vol 3, pp 170-92.

Jupp, E. (2006) *Making public space: community groups and local participation in Stoke-on-Trent*, unpublished PhD thesis, Open University, Milton Keynes.

Jupp, E. (2008) 'The feeling of participation: everyday spaces and urban change', *Geoforum*, vol 39, no 1, pp 331-43.

Lister, R. (2005) 'Investing in the citizen-workers of the future', in H. Hendrick (ed), *Child welfare and social policy: an essential reader*, Bristol: The Policy Press, pp 449-61.

Lister, R. (2006) 'Children (but not women) first: New Labour, child welfare and gender', *Critical Social Policy*, vol 26, no 2, pp 315-35.

McDowell, L., Ray, K., Perrons, D., Fagan, C. and Ward, K. (2005) 'Women's paid work and moral economies of care', *Social and Cultural Geography*, vol 6, pp 219-35.

Milligan, C. (2003) 'Location or Dis-Location: from community to long term care - the caring experience', *Journal of Social and Cultural Geography*, vol 4, no 4, pp 455-70.

Newman, J. and Clarke, J. (2009), *Publics, politics and power: remaking the public in public services,* London: Sage.

Ofsted (2008) *How well are they doing? The impact of children's centres and extended schools,* London: OFSTED.

Parr, H. (2000) 'Interpreting the hidden social geographies of mental health', *Health and Place,* vol 6, no 3, pp 225-37.

Pemberton, S. and Mason, J. (2008) 'Co-production and sure start children's centres: reflecting upon users' perspectives and implications for service delivery, planning and evaluation', *Social Policy and Society,* vol 8, no 1, pp 13-24.

Pratt, G. (2003) 'Valuing childcare: troubles in suburbia', *Antipode,* vol 35, pp 581-602.

Smith, F. and Barker, J. (2001) 'Out of school, in school: a social geography of out of school care', in S. Holloway and G. Valentine (eds) *Children's geographies: playing, living, learning,* London: Routledge, pp 245-56.

Spencer, L. and Pahl, R. (2006) *Rethinking friendship: hidden solidarities today,* Princeton: Princeton University Press.

Turner, V. (1975) *Drama, fields and metaphors: symbolic action in human society,* Ithaca, NY: Cornell University Press.

Valentine, G. (1997) '"Oh yes you can", "Oh no you can't": children and parents' understandings of kids' competence to negotiate public space safely', *Urban Geography,* vol 17, pp 205-20.

Warren-Adamson, C. (2006) 'Research review: family centres. A review of the literature', *Child and Family Social Work,* vol 11, pp 171-82.

Weinberger, J., Pickstone, C. and Hannon, P. (2005) *Learning from Sure Start: working with young children and their families,* Buckingham: Open University Press.

Whalley, M. (2006) *Children's centres: the new frontier for the welfare state and the education system,* paper presented to the international 'early interventions for families and small children at risk' conference, Oslo, Norway, www.nationalcollege.org.uk/index/docinfo.htm?id=17124.

fourteen

# Youth homelessness policy in Wales: improving housing rights and addressing geographical wrongs

*Peter K. Mackie*

## Introduction

Over the past decade youth homelessness has received increasing political priority in the UK (Quilgars et al, 2008) and across much of the developed world (Chamberlain and MacKenzie, 2004; Minnery and Greenhalgh, 2007; USICH, 2010). The extent of prioritisation varies between countries; with arguably the most significant changes having taken place in Scotland, where the entire homelessness system has been redesigned (Scottish Executive, 2005; Anderson 2007). In the rest of the UK changes have been significant but less extensive. For example, the statutory safety net has been widened, rather than fundamentally redesigned and, like most developed world countries, homelessness prevention interventions have been prioritised. In 2009, the Welsh Assembly Government, inspired by changes in Scotland, set out a clear commitment to review impacts of the current homelessness system in order to inform an improved statutory framework that ensures everyone has access to the help that they need (WAG, 2009). A decade of policy change under devolved government in Wales provides the context for this chapter, which aims to identify the impacts of homelessness policies on young people in Wales. While the chapter will centre on Wales, there is growing consensus across the developed world that youth homelessness policies must focus on the prevention of homelessness, while also dealing with the immediate needs of homeless people. Therefore the discussion will also have implications for youth homelessness policies elsewhere. Also, while this chapter will have clear political relevance, any study in this field must take into account recent critiques which claim homelessness research is theoretically weak and highly politicised, not least because most research funding is dominated by government and those wishing to criticise its policies (Clapham, 2002).

There is clearly scope for geographers to contribute to a more conceptually rigorous understanding of youth homelessness; concepts such as space, place, networks and mobility have rarely been considered. Studies that do consider these geographical concepts do not usually attend to the experiences of young people and tend to focus on street homelessness (Amster, 2003; Johnsen et al, 2005; DeVerteuil et al, 2009; Klodawsky and Blomley, 2009), which constitutes a small proportion of a much wider homeless population. It is well recognised that definitions of homelessness differ between countries (Edgar et al, 2002; Minnery and Greenhalgh, 2007) and this can make it difficult to undertake comparative research and to transfer lessons from one country to another. However, there is increasing consensus that in addition to street homelessness, broader conceptualisations include; houselessness (with a place to sleep but temporary in a shelter), living in insecure housing (threatened with eviction or domestic violence), or in inadequate housing (extreme overcrowding) (FEANTSA, 2011). In the past decade geographers have begun to engage with broader definitions of homelessness and to consider the hidden places and mobilities of homeless people, particularly in a rural context (Cloke et al, 2000; 2003), although these studies often fail to link conceptually rigorous understandings with policy implications. Thus, this chapter will explore the impacts of homelessness legislation in Wales on the social and physical spaces occupied by homeless young people. Informed by an understanding of key geographical concepts of place, networks and mobility – as well as sociological understandings of power and agency – it will consider the experiences of all homeless young people, not only those who occupy the streets. The critique will draw upon the author's own experiences of undertaking interviews with homeless young people during several research studies over the past four years.

Existing homelessness legislation is relatively complex, hence the chapter will begin with a brief introduction to the legislation in Wales. The chapter then describes how four youth sub-groups are socially constructed by the implementation of legislation and for each of these groups the socio-spatial implications of current legislation are identified. Reflecting on the experiences of young people in these sub-groups, the penultimate section illustrates the apparent limitations of existing policies. Finally, the author concludes by arguing that these limitations should be translated into key principles to underpin a more effective system of housing rights which in turn will address the geographical wrongs of the current system in Wales, with implications for homelessness prevention in other developed world countries as well.

## Homelessness: definition and legislation in Wales

Homelessness is a socially constructed phenomenon (Hutson and Liddiard, 1994; Pleace, 1998): in different places and times, the term means very different things to societies and to individuals (Minnery and Greenhalgh,

2007; Shinn, 2007). Despite the dominant public perception that homelessness refers to the occupation of the street by people who lack any alternative accommodation (Hutson and Liddiard, 1994; May et al, 2005), UK policies adopt much broader understandings of homelessness; in Wales the homelessness sector uses the 1996 Housing Act, which states that a person is homeless if there is no accommodation that they are entitled to occupy or they have accommodation but it is not reasonable for them to continue to occupy this. Clearly the definition of homelessness in Wales extends beyond the occupation of the street and is not restricted to those without accommodation. Strategies to address the social problem also differ considerably between and even within countries (Shinn, 2007): in Wales legislation forms the basis of the approach, giving homeless people a right to accommodation which can be defended through the courts. However, the system is complex and in Wales only extends to those considered to be deserving and in greatest need.

The first piece of homelessness legislation to be introduced in Wales, which also applied to England, Scotland and Northern Ireland, was the 1977 Housing (Homeless Persons) Act. This legislation was introduced as a response to concerns that homelessness was not only affecting young single adults but families as well. Consequently, the legislation introduced a duty on local authorities to provide accommodation for a small group of homeless people, namely families with children and people aged 60 years and over. Currently in Wales, under the 2002 Homelessness Act, all households which are officially recognised as homeless are entitled to advice and support from their local authority. In this policy context, a household might be one person living alone, or a group of people living at the same address who share a living room. Local authorities do not have a duty to accommodate all homeless households; in order to be allocated accommodation households must meet three criteria. Firstly, the local authority will determine if the household is in priority need (for instance, a pregnant woman or a person with dependent children). Clearly, the 1996 Housing Act includes many more groups than the original 1997 Housing (Homeless Persons) Act. Furthermore, in 2001 it was determined that these criteria still excluded too many vulnerable people, consequently the 2001 Priority Need (Homeless) Wales Order was introduced, broadening the categories of people to be considered in priority need in Wales.

Secondly, households must meet an examination of the reason for their homelessness: are they 'intentionally' homeless? According to the 1996 Housing Act, a household is intentionally homeless if they are perceived to have brought homelessness on themselves through a deliberate action or omission. For example, a household might be found intentionally homeless if they lost their tenancy because of rent arrears or antisocial behaviour. Where a household is found to be intentionally homeless, the local authority must provide accommodation for a reasonable amount of time to give the household an opportunity to find accommodation themselves. Generally, this equates to temporary accommodation provision for 28 days. Finally, the local authority will examine the household connection to the area. In very broad terms, a household is considered to hold a local connection if they have lived or worked in the area, they have family in the area, or for another special reason (for instance, they may be receiving care locally). If the household does not have a local connection and they hold a connection to another local authority, they will be referred to the area where they hold such a connection.

## Socio-spatial implications of homelessness legislation for young people

Homelessness legislation in Wales consists of many judgements and assumptions about deserving and undeserving homeless people, many of which are *place*-based. Therefore, it is inherent that the implementation of this legislation will create social divisions along a line of perceived deservedness. Moreover, some processes within the legislation, such as the allocation of housing or assessment of local connection, are likely to have implications for the spaces occupied by homeless people. Little is known about the potential impacts on people's mobility, their social networks, access to services, and sense of place; all of which can have significant implications for the individual. In order to identify key lessons for homelessness policy in Wales, the UK and beyond, this section will begin to address this knowledge gap, with particular reference to young people; a group clearly divided by homelessness legislation in Wales, which identifies 16–17 year olds as being in priority need but rejects the needs of those 18 years and older. Homelessness legislation appears to create four sub-groups of young people. With reference to each of these sub-groups, the author will next consider young people's accommodation pathways and develop a critique of the social and spatial implications of current legislation.

### Young people owed a full duty: accommodated but disconnected

Homeless young people who are most likely to be allocated accommodation are those aged 16–17, care leavers aged up to 21 years, or mothers (WAG, 2010). These groups of young people are identified as being in priority need and in the period April 2009 to March 2010 they constituted 2,451 homeless acceptances, more than half of all acceptances (WAG, 2010). Whist there is some heterogeneity of experiences, the majority of young people in this sub-group will follow a fairly similar, linear, housing pathway once a homelessness decision has been made; most will spend a period of time in temporary accommodation before moving on to supported, often shared, accommodation and then on to independent living, mostly in the social rented sector. The extract below, taken from a recent study of youth homelessness in one Welsh local authority, clearly illustrates this trend:

> Most young people who leave the family home and become homeless, will initially find themselves sofa surfing. Only a very small number of young people will go straight into a hostel or a B&B. Secondly, the vast majority of young people will take a very linear route towards finding independent accommodation: most will exit sofa surfing into temporary hostel accommodation, before entering Hales House [supported accommodation] and finally moving into independent accommodation. (Campbell and Mackie, 2010, p 28)

Studies have shown that young people owed a full duty often face limited choice and a lack of control (Ford et al, 2002; Thomas et al, 2002). Like all young people under the age of 35, they are likely to face Shared Room Rate (SRR) welfare restrictions, which limit them to benefits equivalent to the cost of a shared room. This means they can only afford very cheap accommodation or they must share. These restrictions are determined by the UK Government and this particular policy makes clear assumptions about the type of accommodation young people should be occupying. The policy has received considerable critique elsewhere as it distinguishes young people as different – something other than adult (SCSH, 2002; Harvey and Houston, 2005).

The lack of choice afforded to young people in this sub-group has socio-spatial implications. As a result of SRR restrictions, the predominant use of social housing and a general lack of housing in this tenure in desirable areas, young people tend to be accommodated in the poorer areas of Wales where they do not necessarily wish to live. In an in-depth study of youth homelessness in one Welsh local authority, Mackie (2007) found a high proportion of homeless young people were eventually accommodated away from family and friends, without easy access to essential services, and in areas where there were high levels of antisocial and criminal behaviour. Such policies disturb the social networks that homeless people themselves have reported to be extremely important (Ennett et al, 1999; Rice et al, 2007; Johnsen et al, 2008) and, more specifically, they can create barriers to important family support (Tyler, 2007). Irrespective of the potential dislocation of homeless young people from social networks, Brueckner et al (2011) claim that experiences of control and stability, associated with having permanent accommodation, lead some young people to see themselves in the same light as those in the mainstream; hence they no longer feel out of place. However, Brueckner et al (2011) also found that certain barriers reposition young people living in local authority provided-accommodation as outsiders, including interruptions by youth workers, and poor treatment by neighbours because of the high through-flow and ownership of the property.

### Young people owed a full duty but with no local connection: accommodated but displaced

Young people in this sub-group share the same characteristics as those in the previous sub-group, with one significant difference: they have no identifiable connection to the local authority where they presented as homeless. It is widely recognised that homeless people are a particularly mobile population (May, 2003), often moving to access services (Cloke et al, 2000) or to escape the stigma of having become homeless (Evans, 1999; Cloke et al, 2000). It is because of this mobility, and the perceived need to ration resources, that homelessness legislation in Wales incorporates a 'local connection' requirement. The number of young people who are found to have no local connection and are expected to access accommodation elsewhere is fairly small but their experiences raise three key issues. Firstly, local authority boundaries are politically determined and are designed to serve administrative purposes; such intangible boundaries do not necessarily reflect the spatial boundaries of a young person's everyday routine and their attachment to place. For example, a homeless young person living in the south of Borough A may feel greater attachment to a town in the north of Borough B, where they shop and spend leisure time, than to the next nearest town in the north of Borough A.

The second issue is the narrative created by a policy which excludes 'outsiders'. Cloke et al (2003) have described how local connection policy in rural areas depicts homeless people from neighbouring or even distant areas as outsiders for whom there is no moral obligation to intervene. At a time when homeless individuals are likely to be experiencing significant trauma (Goodman et al, 1991; Whitbeck et al, 2000), this policy is also perceived to reinforce self perceptions of being something other than normal. In a study conducted by the author in one Welsh local authority, a young homeless man claimed:

> "When I went to housing advice I was in and out within 10 minutes with no result ... Housing advice [services] need [to show] a bit of humanity for people who have no local connection. If you haven't got a local connection it's very hard to get accommodation ... There needs to be more focus on equality; you shouldn't get poor treatment just because you don't have local connections or family ties." (Mackie, 2007, p 39)

Finally, with the exception of people fleeing domestic violence, local connection policy ignores the reasons why a person is making an application in a different area. May (2000) found that homeless people often move to an area for similar reasons to the rest of the population, such as job hunting. It might be argued that a policy which ignores motivations for migration, restricting the ability of homeless people to seek and access employment, and where similar policies do not exist for the rest of the population, compounds the disadvantage experienced by homeless people.

### Priority need but intentionally homeless: socially constructed scroungers

Homelessness legislation in Wales creates a sub-group of young people who are identified as homeless, recognised as being in priority need but deemed to be intentionally homeless. Shelter Cymru (2007) explains that intentionality was a late introduction into the 1977 Housing (Homeless Persons) Act. Although it was not in the original Bill it was introduced to deter 'rent-dodgers', 'scroungers', 'queue jumpers' and the 'deliberate home-leaver'. The legislation essentially restricts anyone who is found to be intentionally homeless to a period of temporary accommodation for a reasonable amount of time, in order to give the household an opportunity to find accommodation themselves. Like other sub-groups, experiences of young people found to be intentionally homeless are heterogeneous but the majority do follow a typical housing pathway. But unlike the first two sub-groups of young people there will be no ongoing duty to provide support and accommodation. In many cases the intentionality legislation is misinterpreted and young people found to be intentionally homeless will not even receive 28 days in temporary accommodation:

> "When I was kicked out of the hostel I went to homelessness [advice services]. They said I was intentionally homeless so they couldn't or wouldn't help. It wasn't nice." (Cambpell and Mackie, 2010, p 43)

This small sub-group of young people are subject to particular social constructions which impact negatively on their housing pathways. The 1996 Housing Act sets out that a person becomes homeless intentionally if he deliberately does or fails to do anything in consequence of which he loses accommodation that was available to him and reasonable for him to occupy and continue occupying. This creates a unique geography for this sub-group as responses to individual actions will vary depending on the perceptions and attitudes of a range of key actors, including landlords, neighbours, the wider community, voluntary sector agencies and local authority staff. For example, the author's research in one local authority in Wales found that a young person, with very limited resources, was threatened with eviction for not putting up curtains in his ground floor property. Reportedly this breached his tenancy agreement and had he not responded positively he would have been evicted and found intentionally homeless. Another landlord might have had very different tenancy terms that did not penalise the young person for such an omission. The multiplicity of possible variations in individual and organisational practices and policies are further complicated by the wider discourses that inform them. The socio-geographical implications of intentionality legislation are clearly complex and it is argued that such legislation disproportionately affects young people. Shelter Cymru (2007, p 10) claims that 'very often the situation relates to factors or behaviour that one could associate with a young person for example, lack of responsibility and arguments or conflict within families'.

## Not in priority need: located on the fringes of society and place

The final sub-group of young people to emerge is those who are homeless but not in priority need; a group that constitutes a considerable proportion of all homeless young people. The predominant housing pathway of young people in this sub-group is a prolonged period of sofa surfing, rough sleeping and sleeping in night shelters, with potential moves into relatively poor quality accommodation in the private rented sector. These young people are generally entitled to and receive very limited support and they eventually find themselves in very similar housing circumstances to those in the intentionally homeless sub-group. Concerns about the lack of provision for homeless young people not in priority need are apparent in the following quotation from a local authority housing officer:

> "I suppose my main concern is the gap in service between 18 and 24 year olds. That's one of the biggest things that needs to be addressed. As much as you can improve the service for the 16 and 17 year olds there is a good effective service there at the moment for them. There's no accommodation, support and effective advice you can give an 18–24 year old who you haven't got a duty to accommodate, and I think there's a massive gap there." (Campbell and Mackie, 2010, p 41)

It is widely recognised that these young people often face multiple socioeconomic challenges such as a lack of employment, relationship difficulties, childhood adversity and experiences of criminal behaviour (Pleace, 1998), which leads the author to question the criteria that determine 'priority need'. Most young people not perceived to be in priority need are 18 years of age and older and have not been in care. The use of age to at least partly determine who is in priority need, irrespective of the multiple needs of the individual, ignores discourses about the social construction of childhood (Holloway and Valentine, 2000) which critique the arbitrary use of age as an indicator of transition into adulthood when a person is perceived to become less vulnerable.

Young people not in priority need are located on the fringes of society and place. They are recognised as homeless by legislation but there is no duty to provide accommodation or support, and yet the housing market does not serve their purposes well either. In their occupation of place, some will spend time on the streets at night and during the day, often marginalised to places out of view of the public gaze. Their location on the fringe of society and place pushes many homeless young people not in priority need to seek support from informal social networks. Like other homeless people, associations with previous social networks often lead to negative behaviour that has further detrimental impacts on their housing pathways.

## Limitations of homelessness legislation in Wales

The preceding discussion highlights that homelessness legislation in Wales has significant impacts on the spaces young people occupy within society and in place. By reflecting on the experiences of young people in the four emergent sub-groups, this penultimate section will deliver an overarching critique, identifying key limitations in current homelessness legislation. Such deliberations are particularly timely in light of the commitment in Wales to explore an alternative approach, which must be underpinned by a better understanding of the impacts of the current system (WAG, 2009).

Young people's experiences of homelessness in Wales reveal three key limitations of the current approach: a lack of choice and control; limited priority given to housing and support needs; and inequality. Lack of choice and lack of control feature in the experiences of young people in all sub-groups. The housing pathways of most homeless young people are constrained to either social or privately rented accommodation, often in undesirable locations. As a result of limited choice, for example in the location of their accommodation, homeless young people face disconnection from familiar spaces and sometimes from supportive family networks. Moreover, being accommodated in some locations causes young people to be seen as outsiders, part of a through-flow of homeless young people who cannot belong to the area.

Limited priority is given to the housing and support needs of homeless young people. This statement requires qualification: a lot of agencies do prioritise the needs of those they support, but the overarching system which determines who is entitled to support does not focus on individual needs. For example, a homeless young person's housing and wider support needs might be most effectively met in an area where that person has no local connection.

In this case, priority is given to the administration and management of resources rather than the needs of the individual. Consequently, young people can find themselves dislocated from familiar places and their disadvantage is potentially compounded by their distance from the labour market. Perhaps the most significant example of a limited focus on individual needs is the current priority need classification. Discussions in the previous section revealed the way in which arbitrary age divisions are used to depict vulnerability and to determine priority need groups. The justification for the existing priority need groups appears to be linked as much to ease of administration as it is to the needs of homeless individuals.

The current homelessness system is unequal in its treatment of homeless young people. Current categories of priority need groups again provide the most pertinent illustration; two young people might share similar experiences and support needs but they are treated very differently because of a small difference in age. Unequal treatment results in an unequal geography of homeless young people, as previously discussed. Inequality is also evident in the intentionality clause, which is applied in different ways in different places and times.

## Conclusion: towards more effective homelessness systems

Geographical concepts such as space, place, networks and mobility have rarely been considered in studies of homelessness policy, despite their potential to help critique policy effectiveness. In response, and with a focus on young people, this chapter describes how homelessness legislation in Wales, and its implementation, results in the emergence of four socially-constructed youth sub-groups. The experiences of each sub-group reveal the consequences of legislation for the spaces and places they occupy and the impacts on their mobility and social networks. In relation to homeless young people's occupation of space and place, it is clear that an over reliance on a limited social rented sector frequently confines homeless young people to undesirable locations, characterised by antisocial behaviour and crime, and located at significant distances from services and employment. Such implications compound the disadvantage experienced by homeless young people who already face difficulties accessing employment. Additionally, the temporary nature of many of the young people's housing experiences prevents them from developing a sense of belonging to the communities in which they are located.

Homelessness legislation in Wales assumes that homeless people are mobile and may seek to access support and accommodation outside of the area where they became homeless. The legislation consequently seeks to restrict this mobility by limiting local authority support to those people with a local connection. It is also apparent that day-to-day mobility is sometimes reduced by allocating accommodation in areas significant distances from personal networks, which are consequently disrupted because of the cost of travel. While beneficial personal networks, including supportive family networks, may be disrupted, the allocation of housing in unfamiliar and potentially distant locations can have positive implications by removing young people from detrimental networks that they have established elsewhere.

Young people's homeless experiences in Wales provide a clear insight into the key limitations of homelessness legislation, and it is argued that by addressing these limitations it is possible to deliver a more effective system of housing rights which in turn will address the geographical wrongs of the current system. Three principles emerge as essential elements of a more effective system: choice, a focus on individual needs, and equality. An improved system should firstly enable homeless young people to make choices and exert agency in their housing pathways. While it is not within the scope of this chapter to set out in detail how additional choice might be achieved, one change would be to make greater use of a wider variety of tenures when allocating housing to homeless young people (although this in turn may require greater regulation of the private rented sector). Improved mobility within tenures would also enable young people to shape their housing pathways. A further intervention to improve choice would be to end the Shared Room Rate restriction, which currently limits the housing benefit of young people and therefore confines them to poorer, less desirable accommodation. Refocusing homelessness services on choice would reduce the likelihood of young people being disconnected from important social networks and wider opportunities such as employment, while also enabling them to escape negative social networks. Notably, Wales is not alone, in that discourses of choice rarely feature in homelessness policy and practice in other countries of the developed world. For example, the recently introduced US Federal Strategic Plan to prevent and end homelessness aims to increase access to stable and affordable accommodation, but there is little evidence of choice in the types of neighbourhoods people will be able to access (USICH, 2010). The policy of improving choice clearly has implications beyond Wales.

The second principle underpinning the proposed system is to focus on the individual needs of homeless young people. All homeless young people should have an opportunity to discuss their housing and related support needs and appropriate action should be taken to meet these needs, rather than expecting young people to conform to prescriptive and linear forms of support. This approach would have terminal consequences for existing intentionality and local connection clauses in Wales, which both focus on the management of resources rather than individual need. Again, this approach will ensure young people are not dislocated from important social networks and employment. Moreover, they will not be subject to inconsistent and socially constructed decisions associated with intentionality. Refocusing support on the needs of the individual offers an approach which is significantly different not only to the model currently used in Wales but also to the prescriptive status quo that exists in most homelessness policies operating in the developed world. However, pilot projects in England have begun to explore personalised support interventions and a recent evaluation has demonstrated their effectiveness (Hough and Rice, 2010), which might provide the evidence to support a change of approach in other countries.

The final principle that should underpin an alternative system is equality: all homeless people should be entitled to accommodation and related support. An approach based on the premise that everyone has a right to housing would require the abolition of the priority need clause and would significantly increase the number of homeless people eligible for support. Achieving this considerable change would require more flexible use of existing housing stock, similar to that outlined in the proposal relating to increased choice. Moving towards a system based on equality would potentially alter the geography of homelessness in Wales: those who are currently located on the fringes of society and space because they are excluded in the current legislation would be relocated within mainstream society and spaces. As in Wales, most homelessness policies in developed world countries currently focus on meeting the needs of particular groups, at the cost of others. For example, the previously mentioned US Federal Strategic Plan to prevent and end homelessness focuses on families with children, unaccompanied youth, individual adults and veterans, with no mention of other vulnerable groups such as former prisoners (USICH, 2010). The approach in Scotland provides the only exception, where priority need groups are being abolished and homeless people will face equal access to support (Scottish Executive, 2005; Anderson, 2007). Future evaluation of the Scottish system, based upon equal rights to housing, may provide the basis for subsequent changes to policies in other developed world contexts; a change clearly supported by the discussion in this chapter.

The Welsh Assembly Government has recently committed to review the homelessness safety net by first exploring the impacts of the current system. This chapter contributes to this important agenda by adopting a rare socio-geographical perspective and it is hoped that the principles which emerge are encapsulated in any future legislative and policy revisions. Beyond Wales, countries are facing economic challenges which will have varying consequences for programmes that seek to address homelessness. There are likely to be considerable changes to homelessness policy and practices across the developed world, as they seek to deliver better outcomes at less cost, and the principles outlined in this chapter will offer some guidance to policy makers as they debate innovative and cost-effective approaches.

## References

Amster, R. (2003) 'Patterns of exclusion: sanitizing space, criminalizing homelessness', *Social Justice,* vol 30, pp 195-221.

Anderson, I. (2007) 'Sustainable solutions to homelessness: the Scottish case', *European Journal of Homelessness*, vol 1, pp 163-83.

Brueckner, M., Green, M. and Saggers, S. (2011) 'The trappings of home: young homeless people's transitions towards independent living', *Housing Studies,* vol 26, pp 1-16.

Campbell, J. and Mackie, P. (2010) *Improving the system of services for vulnerable young people: research into an approach to the housing, social care and support needs of young homeless people and young people leaving care in Torfaen*, Cardiff: Shelter Cymru.

Chamberlain, C. and MacKenzie, D. (2004) *Youth homelessness: four policy proposals, final report*, Melbourne: Australian Housing and Urban Research Institute.

Clapham, D. (2002) 'Housing pathways: a postmodern analytical framework', *Housing, Theory and Society,* vol 19, no 2, pp 57-68.

Cloke, P., Milbourne, P. and Widdowfield, R. (2000) 'The hidden and emerging spaces of rural homelessness', *Environment and Planning A*, vol 32, pp 77-90.

Cloke, P., Milbourne, P. and Widdowfield, R. (2003) 'The complex mobilities of homeless people in rural England', *Geoforum,* vol 34, pp 21-35.

DeVerteuil, G., May, J. and von Mahs, J. (2009) 'Complexity not collapse: recasting the geographies of homelessness in a "punitive" age', *Progress in Human Geography*, vol 33, no 5, pp 646-66.

Edgar, B., Doherty, J. and Meert, H. (2002) *European observatory on homelessness: review of statistics on homelessness in Europe*, Brussels: FEANTSA.

Ennett, S.T., Bailey, S.L. and Belle Federman, E. (1999) 'Social network characteristics associated with risky behaviors among homeless and runaway youth', *Journal of Health and Social Behavior*, vol 40, pp 63-78.

Evans, A. (1999) *They don't think I exist: the hidden nature of rural homelessness*, London: Crisis.

FEANTSA (Fédération Européenne d'Associations Nationales Travaillant avec les Sans-Abri) (2011) *ETHOS: European typology of homelessness and housing exclusion*, Brussels: FEANTSA, www.feantsa.org/files/freshstart/Toolkits/Ethos/Leaflet/EN.pdf.

Ford, J., Rugg, J. and Burrows, R. (2002) 'Conceptualising the contemporary role of housing in the transition to adult life in England', *Urban Studies*, vol 39, no 13, pp 2455-67.

Goodman, L., Saxe, L. and Harvey, M. (1991) 'Homelessness as psychological trauma', *American Psychologist*, vol 46, pp 1219-25.

Harvey, J. and Houston, D. (2005) *Research into the single room rent regulations*, Leeds: DWP.

Hough, J. and Rice, B. (2010) *Providing personalised support to rough sleepers: an evaluation of the city of London pilot*, York: Joseph Rowntree Foundation.

Holloway, S.L. and Valentine, G. (2000) 'Children's geographies and the new social studies of childhood', in S.L. Holloway and G. Valentine (eds) *Children's geographies: playing, living, learning,* London: Routledge, pp 1-26.

Hutson, S. and Liddiard, M. (1994) *Youth homelessness: the construction of a social issue,* London: Macmillan.

Johnsen, S., Cloke, P. and May, J. (2005) 'Transitory spaces of care: serving homeless people on the street', *Health and Place,* vol 11, pp 323-36.

Johnsen, S., May, J. and Cloke, P. (2008) 'Imag(in)ing "homeless places": using auto-photography to (re)examine the geographies of homelessness', *Area,* vol 40, no 2, pp 194-207.

Klodawsky, F. and Blomley, N. (2009) 'Introduction: rights, space and homelessness', *Urban Geography,* vol 30, no 6, pp 573-76.

Mackie, P.K. (2007) *Equality and access: research into the housing needs of young people in Rhondda Cynon Taf,* Cardiff: Shelter Cymru.

May, J. (2000) 'Of nomads and vagrants: single homelessness and narratives of home as place', *Environment and Planning D: Society and Space,* vol 18, pp 737-59.

May, J. (2003) 'Local connection criteria and single homeless people's geographical mobility: evidence from Brighton and Hove', *Housing Studies,* vol 18, no 1, pp 29-46.

May, J., Cloke, P. and Johnsen, S. (2005) 'Re-phasing neoliberalism: New Labour and Britain's crisis of street homelessness', *Antipode,* vol 37, no 4, pp 703-30.

Minnery, J. and Greenhalgh, E. (2007) 'Approaches to homelessness policy in Europe, the United States and Australia', *Journal of Social Issues,* vol 63, pp 643-57.

Pleace, N. (1998) 'Single homelessness as social exclusion: the unique and the extreme', *Social Policy and Administration,* vol 32, pp 46-59.

Quilgars, D., Johnsen, S. and Pleace, N. (2008) *Youth homelessness in the UK: a decade of progress?,* York: Joseph Rowntree Foundation.

Rice, E.M., Norweeta, G. and Rotheram-Borus, M.J. (2007) 'Pro-social and problematic social network influences on HIV/AIDS risk behaviours among newly homeless youth in Los Angeles', *AIDS Care,* vol 19, pp 697-704.

Scottish Council for Single Homeless (2002) *Single room rent and the private rented sector,* Edinburgh: SCSH.

Scottish Executive (2005) *Helping homeless people: homelessness statement on abolition of priority need by 2012,* Edinburgh: Scottish Executive.

Shelter Cymru (2007) *Clear intentions,* Cardiff: Shelter Cymru.

Shinn, M. (2007) 'International homelessness: policy, socio-cultural, and individual perspectives', *Journal of Social Issues,* vol 63, no 3, pp 657-77.

Thomas, R., Bell, R., Holland, J., Henderson, S., McGrellis S. and Sharpe, S. (2002) 'Critical moments: choice, chance and opportunity in young people's narratives of transition', *Sociology,* vol 36, pp 335-54.

Tyler, K.A. (2007) 'Social network characteristics and risky sexual and drug related behaviors among homeless young adults', *Social Science Research,* vol 37, pp 673-85.

USICH (United States Interagency Council on Homelessness) (2010) *Opening doors: federal strategic plan to prevent and end homelessness,* Washington, DC: United States Interagency Council on Homelessness.

WAG (Welsh Assembly Government) (2009) *Ten year homelessness plan for Wales: 2009-2019,* Cardiff: WAG.

WAG (Welsh Assembly Government) (2010) *Homelessness first release additional tables,* Cardiff: WAG.

Whitbeck, L.B., Hoyt, D.R. and Bao, W. (2000) 'Depressive symptoms and co-occurring depressive symptoms, substance abuse, and conduct problems among runaway and homeless adolescents', *Child Development,* vol 71, pp 721-32.

# fifteen

# Childhood in South Africa in the time of HIV/AIDS: reconsidering policy and practice

*Amy Norman*

## Introduction

In the wake of the HIV/AIDS epidemic in sub-Saharan Africa, a 'crisis of childhood' has been presented, the result of a complex interplay between globalised notions of childhood, the international media, development policy, and donor agendas. Today, there are an estimated 12 million 'orphans'[1] due to AIDS, and two million children have been infected with HIV (UNAIDS, 2008). In South Africa, the most highly affected country in the world, 3.7 million children, or 20 per cent of all children have been classified as orphans (Meintjes and Hall, 2009). These burgeoning statistics have created a sense of urgency within policy and programming circles. Indeed, the onset of the epidemic has fostered an environment where definitions have been deemed necessary for 'operationalisation' and 'intervention,' with dominant discourses repeatedly deployed in efforts to mobilise funding and support. As a result, children in sub-Saharan Africa have become the 'AIDS generation,' the targets of various prevention campaigns, donor-funded charity and 'child-oriented' programmes.

However, due to the nature of this development-related focus, conceptualisations of childhood have been marred by 'crisis' discourse. Children have been constructed as 'a generation at risk', and a 'generation deprived of their childhoods', with an unrelenting focus on deviant childhoods such as 'orphans' and 'child-headed households' (Foster et al, 2005; Barnett and Whiteside, 2006). The discourse has been dominated by a linear trajectory: children increasingly take on 'adult' household and caring responsibilities, leading to the deprivation of educational opportunities (see Children's Geographers such as Robson et al, 2006 and Evans and Becker, 2009, whose work critiques binary notions of vulnerability and care). In such scenarios, children face increasing destitution and stigmatisation as households fall deeper into poverty, ultimately leading to family dissolution, with orphaned children left to fend for themselves on the street (for example,

247

Booysen and Arntz, 2002). Due to this trajectory, 'AIDS orphans' are seen to present a significant cost to the future of society, not only in terms of the provision of foster care, education and other needs, but also in terms of the potential for increased juvenile crime, the result of orphans' inability to partake constructively in the economic and social life of society (Desmond and Gow, 2002). Such anxiety is part of an increasingly global 'generalising tendency to futurity' (Horton and Kraftl, 2006, p 83) in policy engagements with children and young people, where children occupy a paradoxical position, existing simultaneously as children in the here and now, and adults of the future (for an in-depth case study of such processes in the UK, see Evans and Honeyford, this volume, Chapter Four).

This chapter critically reflects upon these discourses in the time of HIV/AIDS, and in particular, conceptualisations of children's geographies of care and everyday family life, interrogating taken-for-granted assumptions and definitions that have underpinned policy rationales and programmes in South Africa. Drawing on a PhD study of childhood in KwaZulu-Natal, a province that exhibits an endemic HIV epidemic, it is argued that policy and practice should be recognised. The study took an alternate approach by exploring childhood holistically, with a methodology that did not separate 'orphans' and 'other vulnerable children' from *other* and *all* children in the study communities. Further, childhood was explored generationally, by including both adults and children as research participants (Vanderbeck, 2007). Sixty-four children and 65 adults were included in the study across 28 families and three communities in both urban and rural KwaZulu-Natal.

Alongside other authors in this book, there is an emphasis in this chapter on the notion that 'childhood' cannot be regarded as an unproblematic description of the early part of the life course. 'Childhood' as much as 'adulthood' is fragmented by diversity: children are not just children; they are boys and girls, members of different social classes and ethnic groups, living in different geographical landscapes (James et al, 1998). The research therefore aimed to move beyond the commonality of 'age' in childhood, toward an acknowledgement of *place* and *time,* approaching childhood generationally, and utilising continuity and change as analytic tools (Alanen, 2001). Within discussions of 'children in the time of HIV/AIDS' there has remained a general failure of critical reflexivity in approaches to researching 'the problem': by beginning analyses with a focus on 'crisis', researchers have marginalised 'everyday' childhood experiences, and in particular, historical and cultural contexts. This chapter begins by analysing the dominant discourses of childhood in the era of HIV/AIDS, before building the connections between such 'crisis' discourses and the policy and programming landscape. A case study in the South African context is presented, then policy and practice reconsidered.

## Discourse in the era of HIV/AIDS

Conceptualisations of childhood are ultimately constituted through discourse. The placement of children on the HIV/AIDS agenda has been underpinned by a historical movement of globalised public concern for children. Over the last two decades, in large part a result of the United Nations Convention on the Rights of the Child (UNCRC), 'injustices' to children have been characterised by international concern, rather than being purely a matter for national or local politics (Aitken, 2001). As with other international 'childhood crises' (child labour, street children, child prostitution) it is adults in the West (governments, the media, academics) who have been bestowed the role of first defining and locating child vulnerabilities, and then leading the agenda to reinstate such 'lost' childhoods through various policies, programmes and charity work.

In the context of the HIV/AIDS epidemic in Africa, the globally circulated spectre of the 'AIDS orphan' has been dominated by perceptions of 'children left behind', abandoned, innately vulnerable, and in need of care (Guest, 2003; Black, 2008). Such constructions are rooted in attachment theory, a highly influential theory of care which posits that healthy child development depends on the existence of an attachment relationship between child and mother, or permanent mother-substitute (Ainsworth, 1989; Bowlby, 1952). Theorists suggest that children who lack secure attachment are vulnerable to psychological challenges and impaired cognitive development. The responsibility for providing a suitable upbringing is thus placed unequivocally on parents who relate to a particular child, emphasising both moral and economic responsibility (Panter-Brick, 2000). Such scenarios of caregiving dynamics ignore a fundamental aspect of care in many societies in the developing world, where customary law dictates that children are the responsibility of the extended rather than nuclear family, and the role of relatives other than parents in childcare is vital (for example, Adato et al, 2005).

However, due to such prevailing vulnerability and protection discourses, the potential for the weakened capacity of adults due to HIV and AIDS is presented as 'threatening' to children and their very wellbeing. Policy makers have thus constructed a 'crisis of care' based on the assumption that parental care is the standard model. Without parents, assertions are made that children will be deprived of 'love, attention and affection' and the 'interpersonal and environmental stimulation' necessary for child development (UNAIDS et al, 2004, p 9). As in a number of constructions of children in the Global South, the child is disconnected from context, alone and with no available support mechanisms (Ruddick, 2003). In the discourse of HIV/AIDS, the extended family is either absent, or in crisis, as it 'overstretches', 'erodes', with a complete breakdown imminent (for example, Guest, 2003; UNAIDS et al, 2004). In the dominant scenarios presented, household dissolution is inevitable, cataclysmic, and wholly negative (Hosegood, 2008).

In historicising the discursive landscape of 'children affected by HIV/ AIDS', what becomes immediately apparent is the recurring nature of public concern. In contemporary discourses of childhood, 'crisis' is a recurring theme, located at various times and places, and not solely confined to the Global South. In such discourses, anxieties about young people are centred on the premise that the political and social condition of whole societies can be gauged by the status of 'their children' (Boyden, 1997). 'Crises of childhood' arise out of a complex entanglement of social and political concerns about the nature of what childhood should be; during particular historical-geographical 'events', childhood can be 'corrupted', 'at risk', or entirely 'lost' (Scraton, 1997; Pivnick and Villegas, 2000; Foster et al, 2005; Killian, 2005; Kraftl, 2010[2]).

In the context of HIV/AIDS in South Africa, this is not the first time Black South African children have been targeted and labelled as 'vulnerable' and in 'crisis'. During the apartheid regime, academics and activists expressed considerable concern for children who were growing up in a repressive and violent society (for example, Burman and Reynolds, 1986; Swartz and Levitt, 1989; Thomas, 1990). During the 1980s, concerns were raised for children 'robbed of their childhoods' and their universal 'right to be children'. Such constructions were based on notions of childhood as a time for 'children to be children', which entailed aspects of play and schooling, and not having to make 'adult'-like decisions, such as those related to safety, health or work. Furthermore, a 'crisis of care' also existed within the discourse, with children the ultimate victims (Jones, 1993; Ramphele, 1993). Historically, the country's system of migrant labour was seen as responsible for fragmenting, 'ravaging' and ultimately 'decimating' the African extended family (Burman and Reynolds, 1986; Burman and Preston-Whyte, 1992; Jones, 1993). Overarching narratives such as 'the extended family of yesteryear no longer exists to absorb the stresses …' (Loening, 1981, p 3) could today be reinterpreted and repeated in the context if HIV/AIDS. Within historical discourses of 'crisis', children were at risk of losing their very childhoods, both because of the context of violence, but also because the critical capacity of adults to care for children had been undermined.

## From crisis to action: the policy and programming landscape

From the outset of the epidemic the policy landscape has evolved, partly as a result of the 'children in crisis' discourse that continues to operate at global, national and local scales. Across sub-Saharan Africa, there has been a resounding focus on creating 'workable' and 'measurable' indicators of child vulnerability (Birdthistle, 2004; Williamson et al, 2004; Skweyiya, 2006). Such indicators have led to a narrow focus on specific categories of children – in particular, orphaned children, those who are HIV positive, and child-headed households, who are often described as 'particularly desperate' (Booysen and Arntz, 2002, p 172). The formulation of policy based on 'crisis'-driven discourse and particularised childhoods has led to a number of issues within the policy and programming landscape.

First, despite prominent usage of the term 'AIDS orphan' in the history of response, there remains much confusion over its meaning. The definition utilised within the field, for example, would confound many: children who have lost either one or both biological parents (UNAIDS et al, 2004). Within the academic community, a recent review of the term found that over 70 per cent of studies do not differentiate or clearly define the term, and in only 3.4 per cent of cases was the term used to describe children who had lost both parents (Sherr et al, 2008). Within the international media, the term 'AIDS orphan' has led activists and citizens to the assumption that there has been no one left to care for such children, a direct affront to those in the social network who are providing care and support to the child (Meintjes and Giese, 2006). Indeed, contrary to everyday understandings, more than 80 per cent of children defined as orphans have a surviving parent, with the vast majority being cared for by that parent (UNAIDS et al, 2004; Richter and Desmond, 2008).

Furthermore, as with 'AIDS orphans', there is a general misconception about the prevalence and nature of child-headed households. Despite recent critiques about the very definition of 'child-headed households' (MacLellan, 2005; Payne, 2009), invariably such households are highlighted as 'an easily observable indicator of children who are not receiving traditional extended family care' (Foster, 2004, n p), with the plight of these child-headed households 'particularly desperate ... in many cases these orphans are isolated completely from their extended family' (Booysen and Arntz, 2002, p 172). While such households face unique challenges, only very small numbers of orphaned children find themselves living without any resident adult caregiver (Meintjes and Giese, 2006; Floyd et al, 2007). Further, while these households may emerge following the death of adult members of a household, they tend to be temporary, fluid and transitional with adults moving in to care for children, or children moving to join other households (Hosegood and Timaeus, 2005; Chizororo, 2008).

In recent years, attempts to broaden the understanding of how children are impacted by HIV/AIDS (and to move beyond the concept of the 'AIDS orphan') have led to the creation, and now prominent use of the term 'orphans and vulnerable children' (OVC) by UNICEF and other international agencies. The creation of this term reflected a desire to widen policy and programming 'targets' to include not only orphaned children but also 'other vulnerable children'. Thus, the definition of OVCs has come to include the following sub-groups of children: children who are HIV-positive or living with AIDS; children who have lost one or both parents to HIV/AIDS; children who are living in households with adult caregivers, or other siblings who are chronically ill, possibly due to HIV/AIDS; children in poor households who are not orphaned but experience an adult death; and children who are living with their parents in fostering households which may have recently taken in an orphaned child (Gillespie et al, 2005).

Although the OVC concept has been useful in terms of alleviating stigma, the term remains problematic. In attempting to become all-encompassing, the term has arguably lost meaning in contexts where the vast majority of children would be considered OVCs. Indeed, the underlying purpose of the term remains transfixed on 'operationalisation' rather than genuine understanding of childhood vulnerability. Moreover, the continued hegemony of campaigns such as those aimed at alleviating 'orphan vulnerability', has displaced attention from the broader arena of economic inequalities (Desmond, 2009). Chazan (2008) has termed this process 'AIDS exceptionalism', where a focus on HIV/AIDS occurs over and above issues such as poverty, violence or food insecurity. For children living in regions and communities with high HIV prevalence rates, 'impacts' have been completely decontextualised from the wider landscape of childhood: the epidemic has been 'exceptionalised' as the greatest threat, and children have been socio-isolated from family structures and social support systems. In reality, in contexts where many children are marginalised due to poverty, the circumstances of poor, non-orphaned children may not be that different from those of children who have lost one or both parents to HIV/AIDS (Meintjes et al, 2004; Richter and Desmond, 2008; Sherr et al, 2008).

Furthermore, a disproportionate focus on particularised childhoods and AIDS exceptionalism holds consequences for the support of vulnerable families generally, as such efforts are marginalised within donor agendas (Floyd et al, 2007; Richter and Norman, 2010). In a recent review of community-based interventions, Schenk (2009) found that even well-designed programmes which target particular children such as orphans may have inadvertent detrimental effects because they potentially create instances of the so-called 'lucky orphan syndrome', where orphans are resented because they are seen to be receiving benefits. Such programmes tend to provide material assistance such as the provision of school vouchers, after-school feeding schemes and food parcels to particular children who are 'HIV/AIDS-affected'.

A related, and particularly disconcerting issue is the link between 'crisis' discourse and a focus on particularised childhoods, and the growth and support of residential care facilities in response to the 'crisis of care'. The dominant assumption that large numbers of children are without care has fuelled the funding and establishment of residential care homes. Between 1999 and 2003, a study of six southern African countries found that there was a 35 per cent increase in residential care institutions (Foster, 2004), despite a large number of institutions operating unregistered. Such homes face potential unsustainability, as well as management and operational issues (Abdulla et al, 2007). In terms of a large-scale response to the 'crisis of care', residential care has a number of disadvantages. It has been shown to be at least 10 times and up to 100 times more costly than family care (Desmond and Gow, 2002). Further, there is consistent evidence that for children who are institutionalised at a young age, a variety of emotional, social, behavioural and educational problems develop and persist over time (Berrick et al, 1997; Rutter, 2002). In this study, the majority of participants felt that families should be supported, rather than orphanages:

> "I don't think orphanages are the best situations. I believe in family preservation … if the child goes to an orphanage they lose their sense of way in life. … People expect these caregivers to do great wonders for these orphans and to me that's not fair." (Sbongiseni, male, 35)

Residential care should only be seen as a viable option when families and communities – supported by government and civil society – are unable to protect children from vulnerability.

In part, the misleading nature of 'crisis' discourse has been the result of the exclusion or marginalisation of those actually 'affected' by the epidemic. In one South African study where communities *were* included, the term 'vulnerable' was used to identify those who were particularly poor, and in many cases not 'affected' by HIV/AIDS at all (Henderson, 2006). In the generational study of childhood reported here, 'vulnerability' was defined in diverse ways: children who were abused, who were chronically poor, or who were disrespectful to their parents (an adult opinion repeated by some children as well). Furthermore, a large number of adults and children did not feel they could define the term at all:

> Interviewer: Who are the most vulnerable children in the community?
>
> Bulelani: How?
>
> Interpreter: Those mostly vulnerable …
>
> Bulelani: Vulnerable how?

Interpreter: If the President were to ask you if you knew any vulnerable children, who would they be?

Bulelani: You mean children who are not living well or treated well?

Interpreter: Yeah, something like that …

Bulelani: I don't know, we don't have any around here.

(Bulelani, male, 41)

Across the three study communities, the term did not hold meaning in the vast majority of people's lives.

The interconnection between 'crisis' discourse, AIDS exceptionalism and dominant models of international development practice has created a situation whereby policies to alleviate child vulnerability have remained ineffective, and where knowledge of children's everyday lives in the context of HIV/AIDS has been marginalised. The following story from this study demonstrates some of the tensions surrounding discourse, policy and practice in the time of HIV/AIDS and particularly within children's geographies of care.

## Reconsidering policy in practice

The Khumalo family was originally introduced to us as a 'child-headed household', and presumed to be highly vulnerable. Wendy and Wonderboy, both 16, 'headed' the household, taking care of their two siblings, both ten. The four children used to live with their aunt until last year, when they moved to another township. The house they now live in was originally the Khumalo family home, where the children grew up with their grandmother, uncles, aunt and various cousins, until all three of their uncles and their grandmother passed away between 1999 and 2000. All of these family members passed away at home, with the children aware, and present for some of their last moments. After these losses, the children moved in with their aunt. Their mother continued to work as a domestic worker in neighbouring towns as she had always done, and the children were cared for by their aunt and supported financially by their mother. However, after five years of this situation, the aunt decided she wanted to sell the family house, but the children's mother refused. In the end, the aunt agreed not to sell on the condition that the children reside there, and no longer live with her. And so, in 2005, the children moved to their old family house on their own, while their mother continued to live at her place of work.

On the surface, this was a highly vulnerable 'child–headed household', and likely 'affected by HIV/AIDS' through the loss of their uncles to debilitating illness in previous years. In the everyday sense, the household was run by Wendy, and received external support from a local NGO in the way of monthly food parcels based on this fact. However, the dynamics were far more complex, and the Khumalos could not easily be defined as a 'child–headed household'. For the vast majority of time, the four children lived on their own. However, their mother made monthly visits, paid their school fees, and made large grocery purchases when she was home. The children also accessed water from their neighbour's taps, and benefited from free electricity through illegally spliced wiring. However, not just in terms of these direct, consistent sources of support were the children managing to survive: the dynamics of this household seemed to change constantly, as was the case each time we visited the family (five times). In the first instance, the children seemed to live completely on their own. In all subsequent visits, we found elder family members present, primarily cousins, and on one occasion an uncle who seemed to be 'parenting' Wendy about a boy she was dating.

The Khumalos were the only family we could locate who fit the description of 'child–headed household' in any of the study communities. The NGO which had been supporting them believed that both of their parents had passed away, when in fact their mother, along with both fathers (the two sets of twins had different fathers), were alive, but inactive.[3] We also believed, even after an initial interview with the children, that they lived on their own, and were only visited by their mother. However, it seemed that other family members stayed at the house when they needed to, or were looking for work nearby, and took the opportunity to, in some senses, care for the children. The Khumalos also present an interesting case study for the ways in which 'OVC' discourse can lead to misinterpretations at the community level, as well as the ways in which families manipulate NGO support in an environment where simply being poor is not enough to ensure external support.

In a time when access to support is based on the utilisation of terms and categories of vulnerability, it is unsurprising that families such as the Khumalos have discovered ways of 'getting around' rigid programme definitions. Indeed, it is not only families, but practitioners themselves who allow for flexibility 'on the ground' to support vulnerable children and families. In Van der Ruit's (2009) study of AIDS orphan policy and practice, the author notes apparent contradictions between directions advocated by humanitarian and government agencies, and agencies working on the ground. For example, while agencies critiqued the use of terms such as 'AIDS orphans' and 'child–headed households' within discussions, they admitted freely that the use of such emotive terms in project proposals or marketing materials helped in securing international assistance. As a way to get around these issues, some youth and child care workers accepted very poor children as well as orphans, despite apparent contradictions in programme provisions.

## Moving beyond the rhetoric

In the context of HIV/AIDS, it is evident that rigid understandings of 'orphans' and OVCs simply do not work in practice. Policy-makers and donors should be more flexible about definitions, and enable organisations at the grassroots to provide relevant assistance to all vulnerable children. In so doing, academics and policy-makers need to be aware of the multiple layers of structural, social, economic and psychological disadvantage that not only affect orphaned children, but also families and communities as a whole (Bray, 2003).

In terms of the 'crisis of care' currently presented within the discourse, children must be supported where they currently reside – with their extended families. In numerous studies of HIV/AIDS-affected households, nearly every factor identified as critical to fostering vulnerability in childhood had a financial aspect (for example, Adato et al, 2005; Chazan, 2008; Schenk et al, 2008). The capacities and strengths of the informal, traditional family system can and do support a large number of orphans, despite the threat imposed by the HIV/AIDS epidemic. The 'family' has not been decimated, but has remained resilient despite recurring stresses. Indeed, this research supports the work of others that suggests that traditional arrangements of care are flexible and resilient and offer a range of possibilities for care (Adato et al, 2005; Adebe and Aase, 2007; Richter and Desmond, 2008). The results of this study demonstrate a significant and continuing resiliency within the South African extended family. As with previous generations, families in this study continued to cope, children continued to be cared for within their families (and often by biological parents), and there was no evidence of 'a crisis of care' in the time of HIV/AIDS.

One of the most significant findings of this research was the emerging role of the state in alleviating poverty and supporting family-based care for children. Government grants have been shown to be highly redistributive, with those households who access grants significantly better off than comparable households (for example Adato et al, 2005; Nattrass, 2006; Aguero et al, 2007). Indeed, making social grants available to all South Africans has been one of the most significant government initiatives in the post-apartheid era. However, the administrative and bureaucratic logistics remain major obstacles for many eligible South Africans. Major barriers include the complexity of the application process, difficulty in obtaining necessary documentation and logistical support, as well as associated transport costs. Since the Taylor Report in 2002, a number of researchers in South Africa have called on the government to implement a Basic Income Grant (BIG), or what is also known as a 'citizens income' (Taylor Committee, 2002; Makino, 2004; Nattrass, 2006). In contrast to conventional social assistance subject to means tests, the BIG is paid to everyone irrespective of income (Makino, 2004). Previous research and financial simulations have shown that even a modest BIG for all South Africans could contribute substantially to reducing poverty and inequality in South Africa, and would be relatively easily subsidised by those who are better off through the tax system (Nattrass, 2006). Although controversial in South Africa at the moment, the tide seems to be turning in favour of cash transfers on social protection agendas generally and within the context of HIV/AIDS (UNAIDS, 2008), so it may be that in the future such support is granted, which would nullify at some level, the operational concerns with targeting 'AIDS-affected households' and 'orphans'.

Ultimately, what is needed is large-scale support to communities, the reduction of generalised poverty, and improved access to services. Targeting is the optimal approach when only a few individuals or groups need help; this is not the situation in many southern African countries. It is clear that *all* children living in poverty-stricken, HIV/AIDS-affected communities are vulnerable. Indeed, 'child-centred' development practice must not be 'child-only': social and economic justice for poor children must be tackled in the context of families and communities.

## Conclusion

In the context of child advocacy and policy-making, discourses centred upon 'crisis' are by their very nature powerful and deliberate, deployed with the intent of evoking emotion, as well as action. For children in the time of HIV/AIDS, globalised 'crisis' discourses have led to particular forms of action within the policy and programming landscape.

The HIV/AIDS epidemic is clearly having an impact on children and childhood, and to argue an opposing view would be irresponsible. However, it is unhelpful to portray children as helpless victims: the 'ultimate HIV/AIDS victim' label denies children both agency and competency, and ignores the reality of the situation by assuming that the epidemic is the greatest threat to children. Despite the inability of researchers to gain consensus and untangle 'orphanhood' from other factors related to poverty, gender and the particular national and community context, the desire to measure such outcomes remains, and policy-makers and advocates repeatedly use negative outcomes to promote particular views of childhood experiences. While the global apparatus of the AIDS community continues to utilise 'crisis' discourse, with a desire to 'measure' outcomes and indicators, children and families on the ground are experiencing their own realities which do not necessarily conform. It is critical to listen to their stories, to reconceptualise the way we approach childhood in the time of HIV/AIDS, and to shift focus to supporting the broader, social structures that support children.

## Notes

[1] UNAIDS and UNICEF define an orphan as any child under the age of 18 who has lost *either* one or both parents. In this chapter, and in line with international conventions and policy documents, a child is defined as under the age of 18.

[2] Kraftl's (2010) work highlights the temporal nature of childhood 'in crisis' by arguing that childhood is thrown into stark relief at particular historical-geographical moments: each event marks a time and place where childhood *matters*.

[3] Although the children presumed their fathers were alive, they had very little communication over the course of their lives, had received no support from them, and were not sure of their whereabouts.

## References

Abdulla, G., Nott, V. and Hoddinott, G. (2007) *No place like home: a research study of the operations, management and care offered by registered and unregistered facilities for orphaned and vulnerable children,* Durban: Built Environment Support Group.

Adato, M., Kadiyala, S., Roopnaraine, T., Biermayr-Jenzano, P. and Norman, A. (2005) *Children in the shadow of AIDS: studies of vulnerable children and orphans in three provinces in South Africa,* Washington, DC: International Food Policy Research Institute.

Adebe, T. and Aase, A. (2007) 'Children, AIDS and the politics of orphan care in Ethiopia: the extended family revisited', *Social Science and Medicine,* vol 64, pp 2058-69.

Aguero, J., Carter, M.R. and May, J. (2007) 'Poverty and inequality in the first decade of democracy: evidence from KwaZulu-Natal', *Journal of African Economies,* vol 16, pp 782-812.

Ainsworth, M. (1989) 'Attachments beyond infancy', *American Psychologist,* vol 44, pp 709-16.

Aitken, S. (2001) 'Global crises of childhood: rights, justice and the unchildlike child', *Area,* vol 33, pp 119-27.

Alanen, L. (2001) 'Explorations in generational analysis', in Alanen, L. and Mayall, B. 2001. *Conceptualizing child-adult relations*, London: Routledge, pp 11–22.

Barnett, T. and Whiteside, A. (2006) *AIDS in the twenty-first century: disease and globalization* (2nd edn), London: Palgrave Macmillan.

Berrick, J., Barth, R., Needall, B. and Jonson-Reid, M. (1997) 'Group care and young children', *The Social Service Review*, vol 71, pp 257–73.

Birdthistle, I. (2004) *Understanding the needs of orphans and other children affected by HIV and AIDS in Africa: state of the science*, Washington, DC: USAID Working Draft.

Black, D. (2008) 'Rescuing AIDS Orphans', *The Toronto Star*, 25 May 2008.

Booysen, F. and Arntz, T. (2002) 'Children of the storm: HIV/AIDS and children in South Africa', *Social Dynamics*, vol 28, pp 170–92.

Bowlby, J. (1952) *Maternal care and mental health: a report prepared on behalf of the World Health Organization as a contribution to the United Nations programme for the welfare of homeless children*, Geneva: World Health Organization.

Boyden, J. (1997) 'Childhood and the policy makers: a comparative perspective on the globalisation of childhood', in A. James and A. Prout (eds) *Constructing and reconstructing childhood* (2nd edn), London: Falmer Press, pp 190–229.

Bray, R. (2003) *Predicting the social consequences of orphanhood in South Africa*, Cape Town: Centre for Social Science Research, University of Cape Town.

Burman, S. and Preston-Whyte, E. (1992) (eds) *Questionable issue: illegitimacy in South Africa,* Cape Town: Oxford University Press.

Burman, S. and Reynolds, P. (1986) *Growing up in a divided society*, Evanston, IL: Northwestern University Press.

Chazan, M. (2008) 'Seven "deadly" assumptions: unravelling the implications of HIV/AIDS among grandmothers in South Africa and beyond', *Ageing & Society*, vol 28, pp 935–58.

Chizororo, M. (2008) *The formation, constitution and social dynamics of orphaned child-headed households in rural Zimbabwe in the era of HIV/AIDS pandemic*, unpublished PhD thesis, Department of Geography, University of St Andrews.

Desmond, C. (2009) 'Consequences of HIV for children: avoidable or inevitable?', *AIDS Care*, vol 21, pp 98–104.

Desmond, C. and Gow, C.J. (eds) (2002) *Impacts and interventions: the HIV/AIDS epidemic and the children of South Africa*, Pietermaritzburg: University of Natal Press.

Evans, R. and Becker, S. (2009) *Children caring for parents with HIV and AIDS*, Bristol: The Policy Press.

Floyd, S., Crampin, A.C., Glynn, J.R., Madise, N., Mwenebabu, M., Mnkhondia, A., Ngwira, B., Zaba, B. and Fine, P.E.M. (2007) 'The social and economic impact of parental HIV on children in northern Malawi: retrospective population-based cohort study', *AIDS Care,* vol 19, pp 781-90.

Foster, G. (2004) 'Safety nets for children affected by HIV/AIDS in southern Africa', in R. Pharoah (ed) *A generation at risk? HIV/AIDS, vulnerable children and security in southern Africa,* Monograph No 109, Institute for Security Studies, n p.

Foster, G., Levine, C. and Williamson, J. (eds) (2005) *A generation at risk: the global impact of HIV/AIDS on orphans and vulnerable children,* Cambridge: Cambridge University Press.

Gillespie, S., Norman, A. and Finley, B. (2005) 'Child vulnerability and HIV/AIDS in sub-Saharan Africa: what we know and what can be done', *IFPRI,* pp 1-34.

Guest, E. (2003) *Children of AIDS: Africa's orphan crisis,* London: Pluto Press.

Henderson, P. (2006) 'South African AIDS orphans: examining assumptions around vulnerability from the perspective of rural children and youth', *Childhood,* vol 13, pp 303-27.

Horton, J. and Kraftl, P. (2006) 'What else? Some more ways of thinking about and doing children's geographies', *Children's Geographies,* vol 4, pp 69-95.

Hosegood, V. (2008) Demographic evidence of family and household changes in response to the effects of HIV/AIDS in southern Africa: implication for efforts to strengthen families, *Joint Learning Initiative on Children and HIV/AIDS,* www.jlica.org/resources/publications.php.

Hosegood, V. and Timaeus, I.M. (2005) 'The impact of adult mortality on the living arrangements of older people in rural South Africa', *Ageing & Society,* vol 25, pp 431-44.

James, A., Jenks, C. and Prout, A. (1998) *Theorizing childhood,* Cambridge: Polity Press.

Jones, S. (1993) *Assaulting childhood: children's experiences of migrancy and hostel life in South Africa,* Johannesburg: Wits University Press.

Killian, B. (2005) 'Risk and resilience', in R. Pharoah (ed) *A generation at risk? HIV/AIDS, vulnerable children and security in Southern Africa,* Monograph No 109, Institute for Security Studies, n p.

Kraftl, P. (2010) 'Events of hope and events of crisis: young people and hope in the UK', in J. Leaman and M. Woersching (eds) *Youth in contemporary Europe,* London: Routledge, pp 103-18.

Loening, W.E.K. (1981) 'Child abuse among the Zulus: a people in cultural transition', *Child Abuse and Neglect,* vol 5, no 3, pp 3-7.

MacLellan, M. (2005) *Child headed households: dilemmas of definition and livelihood rights,* Paper presented at the 4th World Congress on Family Law and Children's Rights, Cape Town, March 2005.

Makino, K. (2004) *Social security policy reform in post-apartheid South Africa: a focus on the basic income grant,* Centre for Civil Society Research Report No. 11, Durban: Centre for Civil Society.

Meintjes, H. and Giese, S. (2006) 'Spinning the epidemic: the making of mythologies of orphanhood in the context of AIDS', *Childhood,* vol 13, pp 407-30.

Meintjes, H. and Hall, K. (2009) 'Demography of South Africa's children', in S. Pendlebury, L. Lake and C. Smith (eds) *South African Child Gauge 2008/2009,* Cape Town: Children's Institute, University of Cape Town, pp 71-8.

Meintjes, H., Budlender, D., Giese, S. and Johnson, L. (2004) 'Social security for children in the context of AIDS: questioning the state's response', *AIDS Bulletin,* vol 13, no 2, pp 11-17.

Nattrass, N. (2006) 'Trading off income and health? AIDS and the disability grant in South Africa', *Journal of Social Policy,* vol 35, pp 3-19.

Panter-Brick, C. (ed) (2000) *Biosocial perspectives on children,* Cambridge: Cambridge University Press.

Payne, R. (2009) *Confronting the realities of child-headed households in Zambia: re-considering policy and practice,* Paper presented at the 3rd European Conference on African Studies, Leipzig, 4–7 June 2009.

Pivnick, A. and Villegas, N. (2000) 'Resilience and risk: childhood and uncertainty in the AIDS epidemic', *Culture, Medicine and Psychiatry,* vol 24, pp 101-36.

Ramphele, M. (1993) *A bed called home: life in the migrant labour hostels of Cape Town,* Cape Town: David Philip.

Richter, L. and Desmond, C. (2008) 'Targeting AIDS orphans and child-headed households? A perspective from national surveys in South Africa, 1995–2005', *AIDS Care,* vol 20, pp 1019-28.

Richter, L. and Norman, A. (2010) 'AIDS orphan tourism: A threat to young children in residential care', *Vulnerable Children and Youth Studies,* vol 5, pp 217-29.

Robson, E., Ansell, N., Huber, U.S., Gould, W.T.S. and van Blerk, L. (2006) 'Young caregivers in the context of the HIV/AIDS pandemic in sub-Saharan Africa', *Population, Space and Place,* vol 12, pp 93-111.

Ruddick, S. (2003) 'The politics of aging: globalization and the restructuring of youth and childhood, *Antipode,* vol 35, pp 334-62.

Rutter, M. (2002) 'Children in substitute care: some conceptual considerations and research implications', *Children and Youth Services Review,* vol 22, pp 685-703.

Schenk, K.D. (2009) 'Community interventions providing care and support to orphans and vulnerable children: a review of evaluation evidence', *AIDS Care*, vol 21, no 7, pp. 918-42.

Schenk, K., Ndhlovu, L., Tembo, S., Nsune, A., Nkhata, C., Walusiku, B. and Watts, C. (2008) 'Supporting orphans and vulnerable children affected by AIDS: using community-generated definitions to explore patterns of children's vulnerability in Zambia', *AIDS Care*, vol 20, no 8, pp 894-903.

Scraton, P. (1997) *'Childhood' in 'crisis'?*, London: UCL Press.

Sherr, L., Varrall, R., Mueller, J., Richter, L., Wakhweya, A., Adato, M., Belsey, M., Chandan, U., Drimie, S., Haour-Knipe, M., Hosegood, V., Kimou, J., Madhavan, S., Mathambo, V. and Desmond, C. (2008) 'A systematic review on the meaning of the concept 'AIDS orphan': confusion over definitions and implications for care', *AIDS Care,* vol 20, pp 527-36.

Skweyiya, Z. (2006) *Opening address by the Minister of Social Development to the conference on orphans and other children made vulnerable by HIV and AIDS*, Gallagher Estate, Midrand, South Africa, 12 July 2006.

Swartz, L. and Levitt, A. (1989) 'Political repression and children in South Africa: the social construction of damaging effects', *Social Science and Medicine*, vol 28, pp 741-50.

Taylor Committee (2002) *Transforming the present: protecting the future. Report of the committee of inquiry into a comprehensive system of social security for South Africa*, RP/53/2002, Pretoria: Government Printer.

Thomas, A. (1990) 'Children in detention in South Africa: the response of a child care organisation', *Southern African Journal of Child and Adolescent Psychiatry*, vol 2, pp 1-6.

UNAIDS (2008) *Report on the global HIV/AIDS epidemic 2008*, Geneva: Joint United Nations Programme on HIV/AIDS (UNAIDS).

UNAIDS/UNICEF/USAID (2004) *Children on the brink 2004: a joint report of new orphan estimates and a framework for action,* New York: UNAIDS/UNICEF/USAID.

Vanderbeck, R.M. (2007) 'Intergenerational geographies: age relations, segregation, and re-engagements', *Geography Compass*, vol 1-2, pp 200-11.

Van der Ruit, C. (2009) *Institutionalizing AIDS orphan policy in South Africa: securing socioeconomic rights under a neoliberal regime*, Paper presented at the annual meeting of the American Sociological Association, Hilton San Francisco, San Francisco, CA, 7 August 2009.

Williamson, J., Cox, A. and Johnston, B. (2004) *Conducting a situation analysis of orphans and vulnerable children affected by HIV/AIDS,* Washington, DC: USAID, Bureau for Africa, Office of Sustainable Development.

# Part IV
## Concluding reflections

## sixteen

# Concluding reflections: what next and where next for critical geographies of youth policy and practice?

*Peter Kraftl, John Horton and Faith Tucker*

## What next? Where next?

The chapters in this collection demonstrate the various ways in which spatial forms, processes, metaphors and practices are often fundamental to youth policy and practice. Individually and collectively, the chapters highlight how space and place matter to the formulation, application and experience of youth policies, and contemporary policy discourses more generally. As outlined in the editorial introduction, the chapters have in common a sense of criticality. Some are critical of the problematic ways in which young people are 'placed' by policies for education, health, transport and housing, and of the ongoing difficulties in allowing children rights within diverse geographical contexts. Others are critical in a more affirmative sense – of the ways in which young people can be afforded space for creative or resistant thinking, for forging affiliations with adults, or for informing national policy-making.

Other chapters are critical of the role of both spatial discourses *in* policy-making and the limitations that geographical analyses may contain for rigorous, and 'traditionally' critical (in the radical/Marxist vein) analyses of policy and practice. Clearly, geographical analyses only take us so far. While the authors in this book were asked to highlight the importance of 'geography', virtually all of them have addressed the truism that analyses of youth policy must also be interdisciplinary. In particular, they must be interdisciplinary in the deployment of key analytical motifs – like society, power, time, responsibility, association – *alongside* notions like space and place. As Latour (2005) highlights in his introduction to actor-network theory, concepts like 'society' (in his analysis) and space are not immutable, pre-given and natural; and neither do they operate in a vacuum. Rather, they are constructed and operationalised and *done*. They are *put to practice*, and only gain shape, form and the power to create effects through particular processes, situations and contingencies, at a particular time and place, by particular social actors, in particular combinations with other (equally mutable) concepts.

As the contributions to this book have shown, it is in the *doing* of youth policy that we can begin to see the workings of policy discourses and the importance of space and place therein. As noted in the editorial introduction, human geographers have increasingly moved from conceptions of space as a pre-given container for social action to notions of space that are always-under-construction. Space is lively, and ongoing. Spaces can be changed, used and abused. Spatial metaphors and practices are used to create effects and represent power – from the 'localism' of much policy work with children, to the reliance upon boundaries and built spaces in institutions, to critiques of institutional spaces in youth work and informal education.

Rather than repeat any of the conclusions of individual chapters – and the discussion of the book's key themes in our introduction – we want in this brief, concluding chapter to reflect upon the question of 'what and where next' for critical geographies of youth policies and practice. These reflections are based upon implicit themes (and gaps) that emerge from the chapters in this volume and are necessarily partial. But they give an indication of the continued role that thinking geographically – about space, place, flow and relations – might have for academics, policy-makers and practitioners who want to think about youth policy in new ways.

First, it will be clear from a glance at the contents page to this volume that many of the case studies come from Anglocentric contexts (although there are several exceptions). It will come of no surprise, therefore, that we would advocate similar, critical-geographical analyses of youth policy and practice in other contexts. While youth policy may be more or less well-developed in different regions or nations (and their under-development may not always be a bad thing), it is important to understand more about the putting-to-practice of youth policies in different contexts. This will lead not only to the ability to make more-informed studies of comparative youth policy but also, specifically, to comparative studies that explore the variety of ways in which key spatial motifs (like scale) are put to work. This is an easy point to make, however. Thus, it is important *not* to privilege what could become a simple, additive task of empirical investigation in different contexts. Rather, as Ansell et al (this volume) highlight, a pressing task is to explore how scales of youth policy-making intersect: how certain ideals (like participation, responsibility or neuroscience) travel or may travel in the future; how Anglocentric assumptions (about child-rearing practices or learning) over-ride local concerns in dictating how children and adults 'should' relate; how and why youth policies are *put to practice* by complex and contested affiliations of governmental, voluntary, NGO and community participants; and how, among all of these intra- and international flows, children's experiences of places (near and far) are constituted.

Second, a number of chapters in this book are hopeful and future-orientated. A critical geography does not have to be negative – indeed, we insist that the task of being critical is as much a positive and creative one. Thus, chapters by Pykett and Barker identify positive outcomes from youth policies which have otherwise been repeatedly problematised (in the forms of citizenship education and participation in transport planning, respectively). Other chapters provoke debate about alternative political and professional practices that may overcome some of the spatial limitations of contemporary policy context and discourses: for instance in Brown and Mackie's discussion of (respectively) widening participation and homelessness policies. In addition, these chapters and virtually all of the others in this volume (perhaps notably by Davies, Cartwright, Norman, and Evans and Honeyford) articulate more hopeful and, sometimes, radically alternative ways of thinking about the future. To be more precise, they try to begin to recast the long-term association between young people and the future. They move beyond well-worn critiques of this association, and an equally well-worn (and in other ways limited) conception of children 'as present social actors'.

Rather, several chapters suggest ways of opening out *futures that involve young people*: through informal learning and youth work not tied to institutions; through association with resistant practices and (adult) advocates, perhaps in work with creative widening participation practitioners; through findings *spaces* and opportunities within existing policy frameworks to find moments of joyfulness or compassion (such as in Jupp's work on Children's Centres). Note in particular that these futures must 'involve' young people – they should neither be imagined without them nor imagined solely by young people (in the majority of cases) – and nor should they be about participation 'in' some pre-given discussion. Rather – in whatever form might be appropriate in whatever context – they might be created by (temporary) affiliations – *involvements* – of children and adults of different ages, backgrounds and skills in the production of what Connolly (2008) terms 'interim visions' or Gibson-Graham (2006) terms 'alternative economic practices'. Replace the term 'economic' with 'youth' – or avoid the term altogether and use the term 'youth-friendly community'; either way, alternative youth-friendly community practices require intergenerational dialogue, learning and investment and will likely create alternative youth-friendly youth *spaces* in the process. The chapters in this book do little more than to suggest that these kinds of practices and space exist, or might or should exist (to do more would have been to exceed the remit of this book). But, taking a lead from Gibson-Graham's (2006) charting of diverse economic practices around the world (also Holt, 2004; Brown, 2009), future work might begin what Davies (this volume, Chapter Five) considers the explicitly *moral* task of at least addressing the question: what might a better (or 'good') world look like for young people and how can they have a stake in producing that world?

Third, and finally, the chapters in this book offer a number of theoretical perspectives that we (and their authors) hope will be useful to academics, policy-makers and practitioners working both in similar and different geographical contexts. Some of these have been formulated within the (highly porous) boundaries of disciplinary human geography – especially theories of scale, futurity and the production of space. Others draw significantly on cross-disciplinary work – theories of mobilities, power/discourse, social capital, affect/emotion and responsibility. In this regard we want to make a couple of (potentially controversial) points.

The first is that in organising this book – and glancing at the chapters by each author – the foundational principles of the New Social Studies of Childhood (NSSC) (for example, James and James, 2004), upon which work in subdisciplinary 'Children's Geographies' is based, have become so assumed that they go largely unspoken. There is little discussion of the 'social construction of childhood' and relatively few chapters are arguments for better or more 'participation'. This raises the question – and this is the provocation – of what significance the approaches developed by the NSSC now have to critical work on the spaces and places of youth policy (and, by implication, on work by Children's Geographers). For commentators like Conroy (2010) the significance of NSSC is becoming ever-more diminished. He finds examples of historical family practices in Asia that suggest that childhood is a more 'natural' stage in the lifecourse than many NSSC researchers would allow; he also argues that the 'social construction of childhood' and 'participation' theses are responsible for as many negative impacts on children as they are positive – not least in questioning the ability of parents to raise their children as they see fit when they may indeed be best-placed to make such judgements. Conroy's is clearly a position that requires more discussion than space allows here. Nevertheless, a perhaps more modest critique is that, while informed by the conceptual bases of the NSSC, new theoretical approaches to the geographies of childhood and youth are being developed that promise to operate at some distance from that work. That may be because of an increasing insistence to focus on the future (see above). That may be because of influences from youth work and informal educators who are less interested in children *as children* and more *as human beings* (in other words, less with the question of a child as a social actor and more as a collaborator in something 'good'). Or that may be because 'advances' in educational neuroscience, for instance, require new (spatial) vocabularies that have yet to be fully developed and cannot rely on the NSSC paradigm for the right terms. Without wishing to set

NSSC up as a 'straw man' for critique, it would, admittedly, be unfair to characterise it as either a singular approach or as acting at the very heart of social-scientific research on childhood since the 1990s (one has only to think of the influence of sub-cultures work on many youth scholars since the 1970s). However, there remains an open question about the place of the NSSC in critical research on youth policy as conceptual debates move on.

The second point we want to make is that critical geographical scholarship should – as we argued at some length in our introduction – be a *public* endeavour. Already, then, as editors, as contributors, as readers, we should be turning the lens on ourselves and on our potential readers, to ask: in what ways might the words in this book be 'put-to-practice' in the doing of youth policy and practice in different geographical contexts? Of course, once again, the answer will vary with each context. But we should seek to question how to use this book – and critical geographical scholarship on youth – as a point of departure, of dialogue, and of debate; perhaps about the kinds of alternative futures in which young people might be involved, perhaps about the rights and responsibilities they should (or should not) have (Vanderbeck, 2008). Could this book provide the beginnings of conversations 'across the divide' – between involvements of academics, policy-makers, activists and community groups who find some measure of resonance with a particular idea – or is that just a pipe dream? We should also turn the lens elsewhere, of course: a text like this has limited 'reach' – and some alternative tactics for engaging in critical public geographies are outlined in the introduction to this volume, and warrant further thought for future, critical geographies of childhood and youth. At the very least, it would be exciting to see further, critical work on childhood and youth that considers the many possible ways in which theoretical rigour and public 'relevance' may be combined.

## References

Brown, G. (2009) 'Thinking beyond homonormativity: performative explorations of diverse gay economies', *Environment & Planning A*, vol 41, pp 1496-510.

Connolly, W. (2008) *Capitalism and Christianity, American style*, Durham: Duke University Press.

Conroy, J. (2010) 'The state, parenting, and the populist energies of anxiety', *Educational Theory*, vol 60, pp 325-40.

Gibson-Graham, J.K. (2006) *A postcapitalist politics*, Minneapolis: University of Minnesota Press.

Holt, J. (2004 [1976]) *Instead of education: ways to help people do things better*, Boulder, CO: Sentient.

James, A. and James, A. (2004) *Constructing childhood: theory, policy and practice*, Basingstoke: Palgrave Macmillan.

Latour, B. (2005) *Reassembling the social: an introduction to actor-network theory*, Oxford: Oxford University Press.

Vanderbeck, R. (2008) 'Reaching critical mass? Theory, politics, and the culture of debate in children's geographies', *Area*, vol 40, pp 393–400.

# Index

The letter n following a page number indicates an endnote.